THE MILWAUKEE ROAD
REVISITED

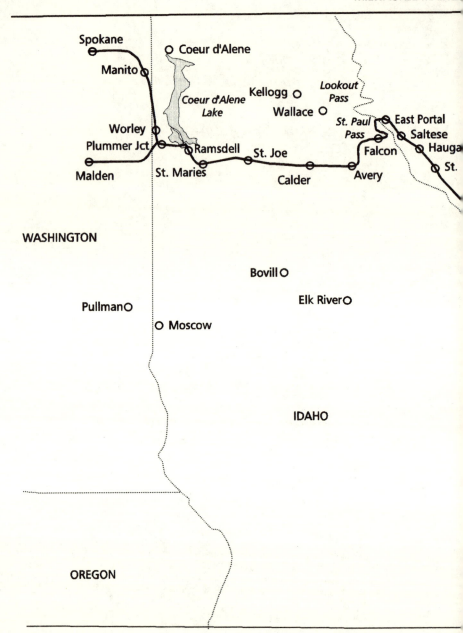

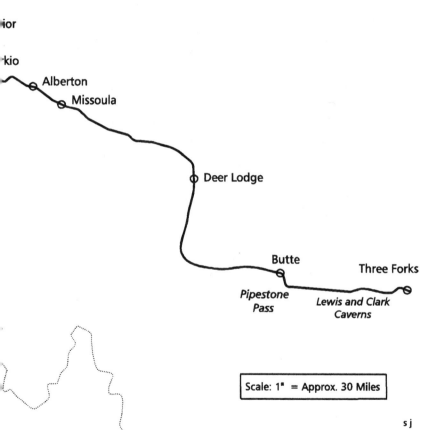

MONTANA

ior

kio

Alberton

Missoula

Deer Lodge

Butte

Three Forks

*Pipestone
Pass*

*Lewis and Clark
Caverns*

Scale: 1" = Approx. 30 Miles

s j

Frank Fiebelkorn (1880–1969)
My stepfather started to work for the Milwaukee in Wisconsin at the
age of 20. In 1907 he came west to Idaho with that railroad during
construction and worked in Washington, Idaho, and Montana until
he retired in 1953, completing 53 years of railroading.
Photo by S. Johnson

THE MILWAUKEE ROAD REVISITED

STANLEY W. JOHNSON

University of Idaho Press
Moscow, Idaho
1997

Copyright © 1997 Stanley W. Johnson
Published by the University of Idaho Press
Moscow, Idaho 83844-1107
Printed in the United States of America

Typography by WolfPack

01 00 99 98 97 5 4 3 2 1

Library of Congress Cataloging-in-Publication Data

Johnson, Stanley W., 1928–
    The Milwaukee Road Revisited / Stanley W. Johnson
       p.   cm.
    Includes index.
    ISBN 0–89301–198–3 (alk. paper)
      1. Chicago, Milwuakee, St. Paul, and Pacific Railroad.
    2. Railroads—Northwest, Pacific.   I. Title.
    TF25.C5J64   1997
    385'.0973—dc20   96–31786
                             CIP

To

Amy,

Christopher,

Dennis,

Timothy,

Wendy,

and their Grandfather Frank

CONTENTS

ACKNOWLEDGMENTS

So many lent assistance to the preparation of this work that it is difficult to know where to start in acknowledging their help. A list of those who contributed meaningfully would include town clerks; librarians; retired railroad employees and their families; U.S. Forest Service personnel; a precious handful of still-living pioneers; city and county engineers; railroad memorabilia collectors and buffs; photographers; local citizens in many different localities, strangers only until I asked for their help; newspaper staffs; academic and amateur historians; and a number of people I met and frequently questioned as I walked, and from whom I very often received helpful answers. To each of these, most of whom I do not even know by name, I wish to express my appreciation and to say thank you as sincerely as I can.

There are a few I must mention by name because they offered extraordinary understanding and support for my project, frequent assistance, a wealth of information, and that which I needed most—personal encouragement. A special thanks to David Asleson, Wade Bilbrey, Darrel Dewald, Frank Kobe, and Cort Sims. Their love for the Milwaukee Road and the geographical area through which it ran was contagious. My late friend, Sam Kimura, skillfully and patiently mentored and developed whatever photographic skills I may possess.

I initially started this book as a personal legacy for my children. They subsequently surprised me by encouraging me to do more. My older sisters were equally appreciative of my efforts and urged me to continue. My wife has always been my strongest supporter and firmest, though gentle, critic. She initially read this material because of her interest in my past, and then read and reread it countless times out of love and concern. I thank her for both the love and the hard work.

Finally, I wish to express a very warm and personal thank you to Jaime Schmidt. She read the rough draft at a time when I was still uncertain about whether to publish it. Her immediate warm and positive response was so strong that it could not be ignored. I knew then that if the shared memories of my stepfather and the railroad he loved could move my family and someone like Jaime, whom I had only just met, I was willing to commit to the effort necessary to share it with others.

As you read the following pages, I ask only that you take away with you memories of the scenes described in the way I have sought to present them—a gift of past treasures to be shared so they will be neither forgotten nor lost.

I thank the staff at the University of Idaho Press for giving me the opportunity to share my memories.

Stanley Johnson
Silverdale, Washington
February 1996

INTRODUCTION

☞ What I have written here is not solely about trains: It is about people—those who worked on or nearby the railroad, my family, and me, although it is not intended in any way to be an autobiography. I grew up in a home that was more than casually touched by the railroad. My stepfather, who married my mother when I was three, was a man whose life was focused on railroads, specifically the Milwaukee Road. Though a stepfather, he was the only father I knew and I loved him very much. He greatly influenced my life, and because of him I have always felt a bond to railroaders and the railroad.

Dad worked for the Milwaukee Road for fifty-three years. He came west with it from Wisconsin when the Milwaukee constructed its transcontinental route across the Bitterroots: his seniority as a passenger conductor dated back to August 1908. He witnessed the railroad being built in Washington, Idaho, and Montana and remained with it until he retired in 1953. I am grateful to have ridden with him during my childhood and adolescence.

My stepfather played an active and important role in my development, far greater than one might have expected of a man having married my mother when he was over forty, with no experience rearing children. My stepfather's values, though drawn from a different family background than my mother's, were in complete harmony with those of the other side of the family. But, probably because he was the only significant male role model of my youth, I usually think of him rather than my mother when I contemplate my value and belief systems.

I sometimes called my stepfather Dad, but as I grew older I often called him Frank with his full consent and approval. His railroad friends called him Feebee, a derivation of his old German family name, Fiebelkorn. My children called him Grandpa Frank. I tendered him my respect when I gave one of my sons the middle name of Frank. My oldest son named his only son after him directly.

Frank was kind, gentle, and considerate to all. He kept much to himself, only occasionally revealing his inner thoughts and feelings. But through his actions he shared many important ideas and concepts with me. He revered honesty and rated a sense of personal responsibility and dependability as two of life's most important values. He was universally liked and respected by his railroad peers.

He achieved and maintained a personal sense of dignity. One day during the depression years, as our family walked out the front door of the Union Station in Spokane, Washington, we were approached by a destitute man selling apples. Frank gave the man a nickel and took an apple.

"We don't have all that many nickels to spare," my mother remonstrated truthfully as we walked on down the street.

"I know," Frank responded, "but perhaps he didn't have any nickels at all."

"Then why didn't you give him the nickel and not take the apple?" Mother asked.

"Because then I would have been taking more than an apple, I would have been taking his dignity," he replied, and Mother agreed.

I've never forgotten that lesson even though he has been gone for over twenty-five years. I still think of him often and try to find him in myself. I know I am not as kind or gentle or considerate as he was, but I highly value honesty and reliability and dependability, and I have tried to use them as guidelines for my own life. I don't think my development would have disappointed him—he gave too much credence to the importance of individuality for that to be so. I do wish, however, that I were a more direct reflection of him, for that would have better honored him as he deserved.

Many years after he was gone, and several years after I had retired, I drove and walked the abandoned Milwaukee Trackbed Route through the mountains of Idaho and Montana during five summers. On each of these trips I sought to include family in my recollections of my stepfather and the railroad that meant so much to him, but I soon realized that others could only vicariously share an approximation of what I was seeing and feeling.

The scene has eroded too far for even my family to recognize. The depots have succumbed to the ravages of time and have been carried away or left to decay in piles of unidentifiable rubble. Dust-streaked railroad cars, the long, black, gear-grinding electric locomotives, and even the tracks are gone. The sounds of moving railroad cars and the voices of the working crews are silent. Most important of all, Frank is not there either, to anyone but me.

I treasure my memories of the railroad, but it is not just the sound of a lonely whistle echoing down a mountain valley whose call I heed. I answer as well to the fading voice of other valued things these trains remind me of, in a land I love. And so, I invite you to come with me as I travel these venues once more, carried along on my trains of thought, hoping to preserve my memories by making them part of yours.

1

A RAILROAD WITHOUT RAILS

Although I had been forewarned, the long-anticipated initial return to the scenes of my childhood train trips was shocking. It didn't seem possible that in the relatively few years since the railroad's demise so many changes could have occurred.

I knew from previous visits to my hometown of Spokane that the old Union Station with its magnificent brick facade had been razed in 1973, but having been a city dweller most of my life I was familiar with urban growth and so-called development. Nevertheless, the disappearance of that fine old building had not caused me to consider similar vast and sweeping changes that might be occurring along the railroad right-of-way.

Perhaps this was because I still retained such clear memories of climbing the long, scary iron staircase bolted to the cavernous walls of the baggage room of the Union Station to emerge on the platform of Dad's train, of following him aboard, and of seeing the station platform drop behind as we left for Idaho and Montana on one of his runs. These remained with me and caused me to recall other places that were as alive as ever in my mind. I could visualize the lower-profiled and friendly small-town depots, peacefully resting, unthreatened and unassailed in the protective isolation of the wooded hillsides. It was as if it could still be as it was when Dad and I routinely traded bustling gray backyards and dirty industrial storage lots for the tranquil verdant valleys and cascade-laced mountainsides experienced on his run, happy to leave the noisy for the quiet, the dirty for the clean, the cold indifference of strangers for the warm acceptance of old friends along the trackside.

But it wasn't that way at all. Not only was the Union Station gone but also most of the village depots and country trackside platforms as well. They had suffered and died together with the Union Station. Those that hadn't been crushed and swept away by the bulldozer had collapsed upon themselves, victims of decay, neglect, and inattention. I remembered the crisp white and black of wartime Milwaukee stations with their clean-swept platforms and passenger cars whose windows and sides were

Time and vandals have taken their toll of the old Cle Elum, Washington, depot and substation. Note the chain-link fence erected to protect the substation. Photo by S. Johnson, Milwaukee, Wisc., Public Library Collection

washed by car-men even during brief stops. Now I found dirt, decay, and rubbish, and what hurt most of all, a generally widespread disinterest in the preservation of any of these things that were precious to me.

One of the first places we visited was Cle Elum, Washington. The proud brick substation was still standing, and its present owner was striving to prevent its destruction at the hands of vandals by enclosing it with an eight-foot chain-link fence. Despite this, hardly any of the hundreds of panes in its stately windows were unbroken, and pieces of brick had been knocked or shot off.

Dismayed, I walked to the middle of what had once been the Milwaukee right-of-way through Cle Elum. If I had returned ten years earlier, the high heavy-duty rails of the mainline track would have stretched on both sides of where I was standing, reaching to the eastern and western horizons. But now they were gone. My feet, clad in lightweight walking shoes, were uncomfortable from the pressure of the sharp-edged ballast that remained.

I looked westward toward the Cascades, then to the east, and finally, once more, at the distressed substation and the old station—all that was left of one of the Milwaukee Road's finest small-town depots. The beautiful sloping roof with wide eaves and gingerbread supports that once had sheltered waiting passengers was torn and ragged on one end, with numerous missing shingles, making it look hapless and ashamed. Windows were boarded up with scraps of old lumber. Where the wide station platform had formerly linked the tracks with the depot for expectant passengers there were now piles and heaps of junk—empty and dented barrels, a wrecked delivery truck, discarded tires and empty beer cans, broken glass, scraps of cardboard boxes, and a decrepit old van. Between the depot and the substation was a field of weeds that only partially hid still more trash.

Behind me, across an overgrown flat that had once been a working railroad yard of almost a dozen tracks, a renovated railroad bunkhouse, now a bed-and-breakfast, sat in contrast. My wife and I had stayed there the previous night. Its walls were covered with pictures of the Milwaukee Road, and it was nostalgic to search for familiar scenes. A partially restored automatic block signal tower stood in the front yard, moved there from its original home along the right-of-way where it had once greeted and waved along proud streamliners and hardworking freight trains.

The evening before, pleasant memories had been awakened by our stopping there. Almost a half-century earlier I had experienced the railroad firsthand as a young boy standing at the side of his father, who proudly wore the uniform of a passenger train conductor with the bright red logo lapel buttons, crimson-tilted rectangles that read "The Milwaukee Road."

The glow from those recollections faded in the reality of daylight as I surveyed the scene before me. It hurt too much to remember what once had been, and I felt like weeping. I found it even more difficult to explain the warm and beautiful childhood experiences to my wife, who, having been raised in upstate New York, had never even heard of the Milwaukee Railroad before marrying me.

"I guess people are right when they say, 'You can't go back,'" I said, turning to leave.

"But you can . . . in a way," she insisted in her typically upbeat manner.

"What is there to go back to? Almost everything is gone. What remains looks terrible," I argued.

"You can visit all those places you've told me about and relive your own private memories, which no one throwing stones at windows or dumping trash in a yard can ever erase."

I stopped walking and turned to look again at the scene I had found so distasteful. Looking more carefully, I could see a hint of beauty still present in the graceful lines of the long-suffering depot and the orderly march of stately rows of bricks across the facade of the substation. The buildings, reserved septuagenarians standing together as though hand-in-hand, seemed to return my gaze—the faces of two old friends who needed help but whose dignity would never give them leave to ask. Now I could see the visible traces of the beauty and energy of their youth, visible despite the travail they had experienced. It was like leafing through childhood photographs and seeing two distinguished but aged relatives. Though the details of their faces might have changed, hidden by the obscuring wrinkles of age, the elegant lines remained.

"Perhaps you're right. Maybe I could photograph some of the old scenes as they look now and work out a way to tell about the past from today's scenes."

"It's worth a try," she replied earnestly. "At the very least, you'd enjoy the photography and see lots of pretty country. It would give me a chance to learn about this railroad that's so important to you."

I turned to look at her and realized she was right. What I had lost was irretrievable, but it was not totally irreplaceable.

"All right," I agreed, still struggling with my disappointment. "I'll give it a try." And so, what was to grow into a personal odyssey was born.

We decided to start where the Milwaukee right-of-way parallels I-90 in western Washington State on the mountainside above as it climbs to Snoqualmie Pass. But before we could make firm plans we subscribed to *Lines West Lines*, a quarterly magazine about the Milwaukee Road, edited by Darrel Dewald, who lives in Alberton, Montana. The home-published magazine is full of information about the former railroad.

Our first issue carried news of Railroad Day, held every July in Alberton to celebrate the railroad that had built and sustained the town. We decided to attend and made reservations to stay in the small hotel there, a building formerly used to house railroad crews when Alberton was a crew change point.

We wrote to Dewald for details and as an afterthought asked him about the condition of the road into Avery. I recalled it as a narrow, primitive, and very rough dirt road perched precariously on the side of a mountain, going up and down steep grades in places that would not be any fun to drive. I distinctly remembered looking out a train window at the old road on the opposite side of a narrow gorge and wondering how anything but a packtrain could negotiate it.

His response was warm, friendly, and very helpful. "You can drive on paved road from St. Maries right up to the depot in Avery now." He told us of the many changes that had taken place since I had last been in the area.

We went to Alberton and enjoyed the Railroad Day parade (staged as only a small town can do) and found Dewald in his Baggage Car Museum, sitting in an old telegrapher's chair. Next to him was a full-size mannequin dressed in a Milwaukee conductor's uniform. He took us on a tour of the museum and pointed out photographs of scenes familiar from my childhood.

"Where do you want to go?" he asked when the tour was finished.

"Well, Avery, of course."

"No problem," he replied.

"I'd really like to see East Portal, too, but I suppose it's hard to get to a place so isolated," I went on. I remembered seeing the snowed-in section houses and hearing my stepfather talk about East Portal's legendary winter weather.

"It's only about ten minutes off the interstate now on a graded and improved road. From there you can drive right over the pass, down the old Milwaukee roadbed, and clear into Avery."

I couldn't believe our luck that the scenes I had longed to see for the past fifty years were nearby and easily accessed. I pressed him for details, asking questions about the difficulties involved in making the trip.

"No problem there. Lots of people drive it in cars—your pickup truck will be a snap. Drove it myself last week. Tell you what, I need to stay here while there are folks around, so I'll catch you later. Where are you staying?"

We told him and he met us there just before dinner. We sat around the comfortable front room and talked about the Milwaukee's final days and learned of his railroading activities. We shared with him our family background, which had given rise to the trip.

He took us totally by surprise when he said, "I knew your dad when I was young. I didn't know him real well, but I knew him. Being raised in a three-generation Milwaukee family I got to know or hear about a lot of Milwaukee people. My grandfather was an engineer and I'm sure he pulled your father's train more than once."

"I didn't think I'd find anyone who knew him," I said. "After all, he retired almost forty years ago."

"I'm sure there are probably some old-timers around who knew him, maybe even worked with him. I'll keep it in mind and ask a few folks when I run into them."

We didn't realize then how many contacts this man had and how much getting to know him would help our search. We got a hint the very next morning as we followed his directions and easily found the dirt road that led up a quiet draw as it climbed to the level of the Milwaukee right-of-way. There we took a short side-road to East Portal.

The mouth of the long tunnel through the backbone of the Bitterroots was just a few yards to our right. To our left was the straight path of the former trackbed stretching away to the east until it was lost to sight as it curved right around a timbered shoulder. Immediately across the right-of-way was what was left of the few remaining buildings of East Portal. Many had collapsed and those still standing were not in good shape, but I recognized them immediately. Then I spotted a heap of debris that had been the large brick substation that provided power to this stretch of the Milwaukee's electrified section.

Everything was in such bad shape that it should have been as disappointing and depressing as my visit to Cle Elum. But I was so excited to be back that the decay didn't register. Now having come this far, I couldn't wait to go over the pass.

The pass was interesting and as easy as Dewald had promised. As the road came down a steep hill and turned abruptly to meet the railroad right-of-way on the western slope of the mountain, we turned to the south and down the grade. It was a breathtaking loop that headed down one side of the valley and then reversed itself and snaked back on the other side and headed west toward Avery.

We went through tunnels—scaring out deer resting inside away from the hot sun—then at the point where further travel on the roadbed was prohibited, down a steep switchback and exposed Forest Service road. As we drove, signs of the old railroad could be viewed in every direction. We saw tall steel trestles, tremendous cuts through rock-filled mountain shoulders, and tunnels—all things which I had seen from the window of a train a long time before but were sights I had never expected to see again. We stopped every few minutes just to look at the panorama.

Upon reaching the floor of the valley, we drove for a short distance down the narrow gorge alongside tumbling Loop Creek. We were passing by the sites of early pick-and-shovel mines and railroad construction camps and cabins that had been burned out by the great fire of 1910, but we didn't know it then.

I took so many pictures of the dozen and a half tunnels between the summit and Avery that later I had trouble identifying them. I had taken notes, but I was so excited that often the notes were indecipherable.

"I'll never remember it all," I complained to Karen.

"Then we'll have to come back," she said with a grin. And she was right. We did come back, again and again—more times than we can count.

When the road following the old right-of-way exited from the canyon of the North Fork where it meets the main St. Joe River I recognized immediately where we were—this was Avery. I was so thrilled to be back that I didn't notice many of the changes at first. On later visits I would find much that had been lost or altered and would be disappointed to find so little left.

We browsed through the museum in the depot, walked around a bit, then decided it was time for lunch. The postmistress, peering through the window of her tiny office in a corner of the old depot (we discovered later that the window had formerly been the station's ticket office window), directed us to a small bar and restaurant across the river.

Too late for lunch and too early for dinner, we made do with odds and ends, including a large helping of homemade potato salad. It's not remarkable that we still remember the salad since we both agreed that it was the best we had ever eaten. A year later we went back for seconds and were saddened to find that the restaurant had burned.

Home again on Puget Sound we began to plan other trips. We decided to compile a set of photographs of every Milwaukee site that might have meaning to those who remembered and those who wanted to learn about the railroad.

At the same time we began to collect clippings from old newspapers telling about the railroad and forest fires, wrecks, famous passengers, progress, and finally the Road's slow death from economic strangulation. Carefully sought-out maps and railroad records, track profiles, old time-tables, and photographs gave us the tools to work with. And, as a parallel to this archival data, I began to retrace my own stored mementos for hints about the past. I talked to older family members, rummaged through boxes of family photographs, visited with a number of railroad old-timers, and searched my own memory as best I could. Finally, it was time to take to the field.

Our first trip was to the western slopes of the Cascades where the Milwaukee wound its way up to the long Snoqualmie tunnel. It had been dug through the summit mountain as a construction afterthought, forced upon the railroad to protect the highest stretches of track from snow so heavy that even the Indians warned settlers about it a century earlier.

We drove to a convenient Forest Service parking lot and left the truck, hiked up to the railroad grade, now a popular hiking trail, and set off eastward toward the summit. We soon were treated to spectacular views of the mountains and the interstate far below. The Milwaukee seemed to have had a knack for locating rights-of-way where good engineering and fine scenery went hand in hand. We walked across a trestle made famous in early railroad pictures of a tug-of-war between a steam and an electric locomotive—a clever piece of public relations designed to advertise to the public the assets of the electrification of a cross-continental railroad.

Climbing higher the roadbed skirted tall rock cliffs, some places clinging to the vertical mountainside with the help of timber and steel supports. Here the dirt road, with rails and ties removed, was replaced with bare ties still in place and open spaces in between. I recognized the spot where four electric motors (engines) had plunged to the valley floor during a derailment accident years before. I could still see the pictures of the smashed locomotives in my mind. The drop was almost straight down. My dislike of heights made it difficult to walk the ties with gaps between where I could see below for even a short distance.

"Just don't look down," Karen said, blithely strolling surefootedly across the bothersome stretch.

"If I don't look down, I'll fall for sure," I retorted. I made it across, tie by tie, but I'm very thankful it was one of the very few places we ever encountered anything like this.

Then, near where the station of Garcia had once been, we rounded a curve and suddenly came to Hall trestle, a gracefully curved steel bridge that stretched for nearly 500 feet across the gorge below. An entire section was missing from the trestle and the roadbed came to an abrupt halt at the edge of open space. The sight of the rest of the trestle, firmly in place a few yards away, helped not at all. For the moment our journey was stalled.

Disappointed, we turned to hike back (including again walking on the ties across open space beneath). The loop we had planned by railroad, trail, and highway was not available to us that day. Still, I felt the excitement of having walked the grade for the first time and having experienced the railroad again firsthand.

However, on the way home, as we discussed the trip, I gradually developed a feeling of disappointment. Something was missing.

"I don't think I feel as good about this as I thought I would," I said. My wife was perplexed. "Perhaps I expected too much," I said, more to myself.

When we returned home I developed my film and found some good images worth printing. Where to go next? We decided to follow the grade mile by mile across the state, but as I became more involved in making plans I found it difficult to sustain my motivation. It was a chance remark that helped me understand my funk. One of the old-timers at a meeting in Tacoma said, "It must have been nice to visit these places again."

Suddenly I knew what the problem was. I did enjoy everything connected with the railroad, especially the Milwaukee railroad, but what I really wanted was to go back and visit the railroad I remembered best from my youth, the railroad 300 miles to the east, stretching from the border of Washington across Idaho and into Montana. I was searching for a railroad that was more than steel and wood and belching smoke and sounds of whistles, bells, and laboring engines. I was searching for a railroad without rails—a constellation of scraps and pieces of memories and feelings that had stayed with me for over half a century. I wanted to experience again the depots and tracks as they were when there were people around them and I wanted to retouch the human side of the railroad, feeling again the unquestionable security of walking alongside a busy track with my father at my side.

Now I knew. Our travels must take me to the places where those experiences had first happened. I needed to return to the Bitterroots and retrace the miles I had traversed so many years before and link them to the present with recollections and memories. I was searching for a railroad of the heart and soul and spirit, a railroad without rails, and now I knew where I must go to find it.

2
TAKING A TURN

☞ My boyhood friends must have found the peculiar schedule that defined our family's activities difficult to understand. Their fathers were gone every day; mine was sometimes home all day and at other times away both day and night. Their fathers were usually available for evening activities; mine was available only two out of four evenings. Weekends were times for family outings for my friends; for me such outings sometimes occurred on weekends but just as often fell in the middle of the week. Their fathers had regular vacations; my father had none.

All this was because the railroader's work schedule was far less flexible than most other kinds of work, and my father was a railroad man. His work pattern, though varying slightly depending upon which train run he was on, was not a typical working man's schedule.

During the years I remember best, his routine was to leave town one evening and return home early the morning of the third day, having worked both nights he was gone and sleeping the day in between in the town at the other end of his run. Then he would be home for three days before repeating the cycle.

The days at home were interrupted by a half day of sleeping the afternoon before he left for work and the morning he arrived home. This meant that there was only one day out of four that Dad was free to do as he wished. My pleasure at having him come home in time for breakfast after a run was tempered by knowing that shortly thereafter my play was limited to quiet activities while he slept.

The earliest I can remember being aware of the negative aspects of Dad's unusual work schedule was when he was working on the evening I was crowned prince of my elementary school class. My moment in the sun was witnessed only by my mother. I recall feeling hurt, angry, and resentful despite the efforts of both my parents to explain. I didn't comprehend at ten years of age how rigid and unyielding his work schedule really was or how it was totally beyond Dad's control to alter it even for special family occasions. In those days, work schedules were designed for the employer alone.

His absence became a familiar experience as the gods of the permutations and combinations of dates and activities seemed to work against us over and over. Dad had to work during three different graduation exercises, four concert band performances, and three varsity track meets that I can distinctly recall.

Despite my interest in trains, it wasn't until I was old enough to occasionally travel with him that I began to see anything positive about his having to frequently leave home to go to work. At about that same time I also began to recognize that the unvarying routine related to his preparation for work and his approach to the work itself represented a genuine personal work ethic, deliberately applied because he thought it was the right thing to do. Gradually I assumed some of those same basic values and learned some lessons about being a good employee as well.

For years (perhaps not completely outgrown yet) I experienced guilt when I thought my approach to work was less attentive and dependable than his. However, the overall effect was salutary. It's fun now to think about his habitual prework routines and recall those instances when I was by his side, participating by getting ready to go with him. Preparations would start hours or even days before his departure for the train station, with several items of concern taken care of well in advance. These mostly had to do with dress and food.

He took great pride in his uniform and felt that wearing it as a representative of the Milwaukee Road entailed special responsibilities. He never failed to have his uniform cleaned and pressed and his shoes shined before he left for work. This meant frequent visits to the dry cleaners and to certain stores for shoe polish—always done before the day of his departure. He wore black high-top shoes to work ("for ankle support," he said, but Mother always maintained that, "old habits die hard"). He exclusively used one brand of black polish, which could be found only in certain stores he had long before identified.

I wish I could remember the name of that polish. I can't. But I can recall the style and size of the lettering on the round, flat cans, which were kept in a wooden box under the stairs in the basement, and how distressed he would become if the stores happened to be out of his favorite brand.

The routine on the day of departure was firmly established and never varied. Arising from his afternoon nap he would bathe (never shower) and would then dress, except for his dress shirt and tie, which had earlier been put aside to keep them fresh and clean. Then it was downstairs to get the shoe-shining kit. He would stand beside the stairs, one foot up on about the second step, and methodically shine each shoe.

If he was in a good mood, and he usually was, all of this might be accompanied by a whistled version of "I Love a Lassie" or "Danny Boy." If I was going along on this night's "turn" I shined my own shoes in the same fashion, minus the whistling, after he was through. He would usually stand beside me making suggestions about improving my technique.

As for food preparation the focus here was on his two lunches. The important status in which he held his lunch can be seen in the fact that no one ever, not even when he was really rushed for time, made his lunch other than himself. The lunch content, as with the rest of his preparation activities, showed little variance.

He liked his bread white, thick-sliced by hand at home, fairly hard-crusted, and preferably a day or two old so it was quite dry. Accordingly he usually went to a bakery at least a day or two ahead of his run. One large loaf was just enough for the separate lunches he prepared for the two nights he would be gone. He sliced each piece with slow deliberation (often still whistling), approaching the task like a draftsman entering a vital line on an important blueprint. Each precisely cut slice was then evenly covered with butter right to the very edge—no mayonnaise or other spreads for him. The contents, sliced as generously as the bread, were carefully placed and arranged upon the bread, were cut to fit the slice precisely. Each sandwich, when completely constructed was about two inches thick.

Of course, such a distinctive sandwich required an equally creative approach to eating it. Sitting on a box or a trunk in the baggage car while he ate, an edge of the sandwich was briefly dunked into a big mug of hot coffee and then the wet portion was promptly bitten off just before it could disintegrate into the mug.

For the first night's lunch, the choice was almost always braun-schweiger, available only in a real butcher's shop. Frank would sample his braunschweiger from long pieces hung from hooks in the butcher's cold room. Before making a decision he often tasted two or three samples sliced by the butcher from different tubes full of the flavorful and aromatic meat. I used to love to go along and get my share of samples, too. I learned to like the tangy lunchmeat when I was very young and still do. If I was going with him on the turn, Mother would prepare my lunch.

Dad's preference for the second night's sandwiches was limburger cheese, a particular favorite of his with the added advantage that the cheese would keep without refrigeration for the extra day and a half necessary. Limburger smells worse than anything I have ever even remotely considered to be edible. Indeed, it smells so bad that neither Mother nor I liked to be in the kitchen while he was making the sandwiches. He kept the cheese in the refrigerator wrapped in about six layers of wax paper inside a covered glass jar, and even then an occasional whiff of its noxious odor would meet you when you opened the door.

"It tastes better when it's not too fresh," Dad would say.

"How can you tell?" Mother would reply. "It always smells like it's spoiled."

Dad laughed at me when I turned up my nose. He would say, "Here, try it. It tastes better than it smells. When you eat this you know you really have cheese between your bread."

My second night's sandwiches were usually peanut butter and jelly, which occasionally was a stand-in for Dad, too, if he hadn't managed to lay in a supply of limburger.

These giant sandwiches, along with cookies, cake, or pie, cut and packaged in two pieces for the separate lunches, completed the menu. Each item was individually wrapped and carefully put into a paper bag and precisely placed in his grip, (yesterday's term for an overnight bag) which contained little else other than shaving gear, nightshirt, and a change of socks, underwear, and a fresh, clean shirt for the return trip.

Mother used to try to get Dad to add fruit or carrot sticks or cucumber slices to his lunch but never was successful. I believe he was a little afraid that the healthy-food aspect might get out of control at home if he yielded even a little bit, so he kept his finger in the dike, so to speak, and stuck with sandwiches and pastry.

However, the baggageman on his train, a jovial, stout, striped-overalls-wearing man named Persinger, but whom everyone called "Perse," used to bring such healthy items from his small farm acreage, and I noticed that Dad eagerly ate them along with the rest of the crew. They were always offered to me as well, and I can remember eating raw vegetables in the baggage car that I rarely touched at home.

With his nap taken, bath and shave over, shoes shined, and lunch made, only the eating of our evening meal remained for Dad to be ready to leave for work. We generally had a particularly heavy supper that night, and it was served a little early because he would be anxious to leave for the Union Station.

I don't know what railroad regulations required of train crews. I do know that Dad made sure he reported to work in plenty of time, always arriving well before any others in his crew. In fact, I never knew him to be late for any appointment, work related or otherwise.

In later years, particularly when I became old enough to drive, he sometimes would ride to work in the family car, but I cannot recall him ever driving himself. Instead, he carefully noted the bus schedules and arranged to be at the bus stop two blocks from our house well ahead of time.

Unless they needed cleaning, he left his uniform hat, coat, and vest at work, wearing only the uniform pants home as most of the uniformed train crew did. Still, he insisted on wearing a suitcoat on the bus to work, and it always bothered Mother that his pants and coat and vest did not match. When she would complain he would just laugh and say, "Well, they're clean," as she waved him off to the bus stop. I think this departing non sequitur annoyed her even more than the mismatched apparel.

When I got to travel with him I always felt that those hours we spent at the depot before departure were interesting and a major part of the fun. I began to understand his eagerness to get to those surroundings earlier than necessary.

The Spokane Union Station was a large four-story brick building, impressive with its giant green copper overhang reaching clear to the street and supported by large chains coupled to turnbuckles imbedded in the redbrick facade above it. It covered a hundred feet or more of the front sidewalk and clearly distinguished the building from those surrounding it. In my eyes it was something quite different from other railroad terminals in town, too. There were the Great Northern depot and the Northern Pacific depot nearby, but this was the Union Station! I felt part of an exclusive club when I entered its lobby and heard my footsteps echo across the cavernous room.

Inside, through the multiple large front doors, a marble-floored lobby contained ticket windows, some offices down a hall to the left, and a sloped passageway to the baggage checking counter across the lobby to the rear. On the back wall, stretching upward right and left from the center, two broad staircases led majestically to the floor above.

The second floor contained the main waiting room, almost as long as the building, a large open space with high ceilings, chandeliers hanging

Former Union Station at Spokane, Washington, built in 1914 and demolished in 1973.
The doorway on the right side of the second level opened directly out onto the platform
where my stepfather's train regular waited for us.
Inland Empire Chapter, National Railway Historical Society

from long chains, deep booming public address speakers, rows of church-like oak benches, and small open-fronted shops offering newspapers, souvenirs, and snacks for the traveler. From this room, through double doors in the back center, passageways with white-lettered information boards announcing arriving and departing trains led to several stairways up to the second level to the tracks.

These were the parts of the station the public saw. But when I traveled with Dad I gained entry to another part, a mysterious world of obscure, almost hidden, and mazelike passageways. Some of these were in the basement or even the subbasement. Others snaked along high screened-in catwalks stretching across the ceiling of the large freight and baggage room that occupied the rear portions of the building. These could be reached only by climbing long metal staircases bolted to the brick walls, and were scary to traverse.

By keeping my eyes open and remembering where we went, I learned how to bypass the checkpoints carefully established to screen the public from access to places deemed dangerous or off-limits for other reasons. In my teen years I used this knowledge to slip up to the platform at track level to be present when Dad's train arrived. Moving carefully and unobtrusively I always managed to do so without being challenged. The first time I did this Frank was surprised to see me and wanted to know how I got there.

"I came up the same stairs you use when you're going to your train," I replied nonchalantly.

"No one wanted to know what you were doing there?" he wanted to know.

"Nope," I answered with a confident grin.

"You'll catch it for sure if they ever see you," he said with a twinkle in his eye. "'Stay out' signs are there for a purpose," he added seemingly for effect, but he never told me not to do it or ever said anything more about it.

When we arrived at the station the night of a turn, we went into the basement to a locker room reserved for train crews, passing through the busy and interesting baggage room on the way. There Dad would put his controversial nonmatching suitcoat and vest into his locker, exchanging it for his uniform vest and coat. His large gold railroad pocket watch with the two separate hour hands, one for Pacific Time and the other for Mountain Time was carefully transferred to the special deep pocket in the uniform vest. (As a little boy playing conductor, often reaching into that pocket of the old vest he had given me, and pretending to check the time on a nonexistent watch was an important part of the role-playing.) When he was sure the watch was secure, he would take out his uniform hat and thoroughly brush it clean of any lint or dust.

When these items were in order he turned to a baggage cart in the middle of the room. On it rested a heavy wooden footlocker locked with a large hasp and padlock and labeled "# 7 & 8" on the end. Inside were a number of work-related items such as an extra pair of heavy leather gloves (or mittens in the winter), emergency flares (called fusees), and a small box of "torpedoes" (ravioli-shaped packets containing a noise-making explosive that could be set off by a train passing over it on a rail and which were used to signal a train to stop in an unexpected location). Also tucked away in the footlocker were extra lantern batteries and a .38 police special Smith & Wesson, which regulations required him to have on board because the train carried insured mail.

The only picture I have of my stepfather at work is this one taken at Missoula, Montana, on a spring afternoon in 1949.
Photo by S. Johnson

If the weather was cool enough, he would then take a work coat, made of heavy material like a sailor's peacoat, out of the locker and add it to the contents of the box. Satisfied that everything necessary was inside, he would relock the box and leave it for the baggage room handlers to routinely deliver to the baggage car of his train.

Next he would take an oblong and somewhat battered, medium-size leather suitcase from the locker, and laying it on the cart he would open it and check its contents. This suitcase, containing paper supplies and similar items related to train business, would end up on one of the pair of seats where Dad and the brakeman sat in the coach when they weren't busy elsewhere on the train. I liked to sort through the items inside. There were red-and-white station checks, small light cardboard tabs, which would be marked with station codes and slipped by Dad under the holders above each passenger's seat when he collected the tickets. Along with these were extra public timetables for passengers, forms for reporting routine and not so routine happenings, pencils, rubber bands, and paper clips. It also contained several technical manuals for reference and employee timetables, which contained details such as the number of cars that each siding could accommodate and which wayside stations had agents on duty at certain hours.

I was especially intrigued to find out that the box also contained some not-so-official items as well. These included pipe tobacco, sometimes a small bag of hard candies, and what interested me most—several popular *Detective* magazines complete with "real-life" photos of victims! After giving this suitcase a quick inventory it was also placed on the baggage cart alongside the wooden footlocker. Later it would be picked up in the baggage car by one of the train crew and placed on the front seat in the coach.

As a final step in his routine, Dad would put his civilian cap in his grip so he would have it at the turnaround stopover on the other end. The grip then joined the other two pieces on the cart, and we went on to other duties.

Our next stop was the dispatcher's office on the east end of the building several floors above. There Dad would complete the necessary paperwork for starting his run, working on the long green counter that looked into the office while I looked out the hallway window at the tracks below. Then he would pick up some report forms and lastminute supplies for handling unticketed passengers who might board from small stations where no ticket agent was available. Before we left I always was the subject of

friendly questions by the workers in the office and was invariably introduced by Dad, at which point I was expected to shake hands with everyone there. By this time, for more reasons than one, I was ready to head for
the train.

Dad's train, when he was working on the Spokane to Butte run, was a
local. The local was the ride I liked best because he had more time to
spend with me than on the grander but much busier Olympian. The
local, No. 8 eastbound out of Spokane, always sat on Track One, a dead-
end stub siding closest to and in view of the street. It was backed into the
stub siding so that the single Pullman car was closest to the station.

Besides the regular public access there was a back stairway leading to
this area. Its doorway was located so that it shows in many of the classic
photos and drawings of this old station, which has been long since
removed. Every time I look at the large engraved picture of the Union
Station that hangs in my den I am reminded of the two of us coming out
that doorway on our way to the train.

It was not unusual for us to arrive so early that the locomotive had not
yet been brought up from the engine yard. The station's platforms would
usually be deserted and quiet at this hour and no one else would be
around, except perhaps a car-man briefly working on one of the cars. Dad
would climb aboard and do a quick walk-through to see that the cars had
been properly cleaned. Then he would get a rag from the baggage car and
carefully wipe the handles on the steps to both the coach and the sleeping
car. I found out later these were not tasks expected of him by the railroad
but just another example of his thorough approach to his job. Sometimes
he would let me do the wiping job, and I felt very important as I worked
my way down the platform from door handle to door handle. I even
wiped the handles on the side next to the street (though these doors
would not be used in this station), hoping that someone on the street
below would notice me at work.

For the next hour he would sit in a coach seat with his feet up on the
seat opposite and read his magazines, often softly whistling to himself. As
long as I did not wander too far I was free to roam the aisles of the coach
and Pullman car and the platform outside these two cars. Occasionally, if I
was extra lucky, a freight train might slowly rumble through, offering me a
few moments of railroad action to watch.

When our engine arrived I was expected to be back on the train or with
my father if he was outside watching. From then, until we left, he wanted

me in my coach seat and out of the way of arriving passengers and plat-form workers who were loading freight and baggage, ice and water, and tending to other last-minute tasks. The last half hour of waiting seemed interminable, and I was always relieved to hear the "All Aboard!" call and to feel the train finally jerk into motion.

The activity on the trip itself varied. I sometimes rode on an engine or went down on the platform with Dad on the few longer stops such as at Avery, Idaho, where the railroad substituted electric power for steam on eastbound trains. But I knew that when lunchtime came in the middle of the night, I would be invited to the baggage car to eat my lunch with Dad and the rest of the crew. Essentially the only rules were to stay out of the way of the crew, not to go where I wasn't allowed (such as open platforms while the train was moving), and not to bother or annoy passengers in any way.

I was allowed to visit with the other train crew members if they had time, especially the sleeping car porter in the car behind ours who had lit-tle to do once everyone was asleep. I knew enough about his routine to wait until he had his passengers all bedded down before venturing back there.

Somehow it never occurred to me that he, too, might have enjoyed catching a little sleep. He was too polite and friendly to say anything. Many times when there was an unassigned berth, he offered me a place to sleep for the night, which I often accepted on the way home.

At the end of the first night's run we arrived in Butte, Montana, early in the morning. It only took a few minutes to close down the train and get checked in at the office in the Butte station, and then we would head into the lobby restaurant for a good breakfast, one of my favorite parts of the trip.

Then we walked a half-dozen blocks to the hotel, where Dad slept until midafternoon and I struggled to sleep or at least keep quiet enough so that he might sleep. When he awoke, Dad would shave and dress and then we would take a walk around town for an hour or so until suppertime.

Sometimes we would visit stores or look at some of the interesting mine-related activities that were scattered around the area. Other times we would sit on a sidewalk bench and watch the people go by as Dad told me stories about what Butte had been like when he first came west with the railroad in the early 1900s.

All this time, of course, I was anticipating my supper. We always ate in the same restaurant (more of Dad's habitual behavior), and I loved it

*The Milwaukee depot's tall brick tower can be seen for miles as the trains descend
Pipestone Pass. The restaurant, one of my favorite places as a boy, was on the first
floor on the left. The building still stands and is in use as a broadcasting station.
Photo by S. Johnson, Milwaukee, Wisc., Public Library Collection*

because they served my favorite restaurant meal. Yet to be introduced to
gourmet restaurant fare, I thought the epitome of dining out was a hot
roast beef sandwich with mashed potatoes and gravy and canned green
peas. I don't remember what Dad ordered, but my favorite was always on
the menu.

The trip home was pretty much a replication of the first night's pattern,
with one exception. While we were sitting quietly in the coach car in the
Butte depot waiting for our train's activity to start, the cross-continental
Olympian would arrive.

The Butte depot was at the end of a dead-end Y track, so long trains
such as the Olympian would pull past the mouth of the "Y" and then
slowly back into the station so passengers would be closer to the depot. I
looked forward to seeing the Olympian appear far down the track and

would be on the platform next to our train when it slid to a stop on the next track over. I liked to imagine that the people on the train would think that I was part of our train's working crew, so I would walk officiously up and down past our train appearing to be carefully studying the condition of various mechanical parts. The Olympian stayed a little over ten minutes, but it was an exciting interlude in the otherwise quiet evening as we waited for our own departure.

I was always glad to get home. I eagerly watched out the train window for familiar sites until finally we crossed Freya Street, from where I could see our house four blocks away. I already had any miscellaneous stuff I was carrying packed away in a paper sack and was ready for disboarding. My small suitcase was in the baggage car beside Dad's grip. It would be delivered to the train crew's room before we got there.

It didn't take long to get signed out at the familiar dispatcher's counter in Spokane, and we would quickly walk the two blocks to where we would catch a bus for the fifteen-minute ride home.

The very last part of the trip, and one of the parts I liked best, was waiting for us at home. Mother always called the dispatcher's office to get our exact arrival time. As we walked in the door I could smell the special breakfast she always had waiting for her "two working men," as she would say. We would eat sausage and eggs and homemade biscuits or pancakes with big dishes of home-canned Bing cherries while I told her about everything that happened.

After breakfast Dad would head for bed, and sometimes I would, too. It was easier to sleep during the day at home than in the hotel. Reliving the experiences, then and now, is almost as much fun as the real thing. Almost but not quite. ⌥

3
IF MEMORY SERVES ME RIGHT

☞ "And I'm telling you, the first place you could see those boards was when you came out of that reverse curve two miles below the section gang house!" The speaker was white-haired and walked unsteadily with the help of a cane, but his voice was firm and he pounded the table to emphasize his point.

"No, no, no. You're thinking of somewhere else, Abe. There wasn't any reverse curve anywhere near that place." He spoke just as assuredly though with fewer decibels, wiping up water that had spilled from his glass while the other emphasized his point on the tabletop.

"Well, I remember that."

I was sitting in a restaurant in Tacoma, Washington, listening to two very elderly ex-Milwaukee railroaders argue about the location and positioning of a set of signals relevant to a particular signal tower. They argued back and forth, obviously forgetting all about me and eventually forgot my questions, too.

"Do you remember Martha, the woman who worked that tower at night?" It was the table pounder asking the question.

"Of course. She used to open the window and wave at every train that came through. Friendly woman. Worked there a long time as I recall."

"She liked cake."

"She did?"

"I'll say. Seems as though she always had a piece of cake and a cup of coffee in her hands. When she leaned out the window to say hello she sometimes waved a piece of devil's food at you."

"Is that right? I don't remember that." He paused to reflect on the image of being greeted with a piece of cake. "She's dead now," he added.

"I suppose."

"Yup. Died seven or eight years ago . . . lived in Auburn for a while. Died in Cle Elum."

"Humph." The reply was accompanied by a resigned shrug. The argument was over.

I couldn't follow their recollections with memories and images as well as they were doing, but listening to them was a priceless experience. Through their conversation I was taken to a scene that no longer existed, a place I could visit in no other way. It was like eavesdropping on history. It didn't really matter about the signals, though that was the question I had raised. I hadn't known enough about the situation to ask about Martha waving with her hands full of coffee and cake.

Much of the enjoyment in searching out details about the old Milwaukee Road has come from the recollected perceptions of people such as these two old ex-railroaders. I had learned very quickly that my years of experience as a researcher and the skills I had acquired in seeking out important facts and data weren't going to be enough in this search. I needed more than academic and intellectual skills. I needed the insights that can come only from talking with people. At first I had thought I could depend upon my memory for such things, but I hadn't been involved in the project very long when I realized that my memory was neither as good nor trustworthy as I might have thought.

The first shock came from the irrefutable proof of geography. Things were not where I expected them to be. Tunnels seemed to be missing. Bridges, or the streams they spanned, had disappeared, depots mysteriously had been moved to opposite sides of the track. My wife grew weary, I am sure, of hearing me say, "But I remember it perfectly . . . it was right here." I, in turn, became embarrassed at hearing her say, "Is the tunnel you're looking for the one down the track behind you?"

The truth of the matter was that my own memory was not to be trusted. There were two things I needed to make the search successful. I had to have available a body of accurate facts and data. I could see it was a waste of time to just speculate about where something might have been or when an event occurred. And I needed to talk to people—folks who really knew, either from their own experience or from having talked to those who did. Getting the facts was going to take some hard work, but it could be done. Finding the people would take work, too, and I wasn't sure that I could find those I wanted to question.

Since my professional life had involved research, I thought I knew where to turn for facts and information. The library found copies of old magazines for me. My desk became piled with photocopies of newspaper clippings. That presented some difficulties in itself. My problem with researching newspaper clippings is that I respond to them with the same

I took this picture of the Columbian at Avery with my Brownie camera in the 1940s. Passengers often strolled the platform or visited the beanery in the depot while an engine change was being made.
Photo by S. Johnson

lack of discrimination that I show when faced with the stacks of inviting impulse items the supermarket places in my path just inside the front door. I browse, nibble, intellectually graze, and the first thing you know I have manila envelopes and file drawers full of clippings: each one interesting but not always relevant to my original shopping list.

But along the way I learned a great many things. Some were useful, some were not, but all were interesting to me. I had railroad trivia at my fingertips, trivia I was eager to share. I began to share them with understanding friends at social gatherings. For example I might say, "Did you know that the Milwaukee railroad started digging its big tunnel in downtown Coeur d'Alene the same week that Halley's comet came?"

Such bon mots of uncovered details did not always make me popular. But in the process of sorting the merely interesting from the important I soon became aware of other available sources rich with information: specialized magazines, brochures and flyers published by the Milwaukee Road, railroad union magazines, chambers of commerce promotional literature, and publications by other organizations.

Fortuitously, the search for some of these led me to the richest source of all—people. Initially I found only a few old-time Milwaukee railroaders. The passing years have taken many of these away. But those I found introduced me to their children or grandchildren or cousins, and to their friends. My circle of informed contacts broadened, and these friendly people began to fill in the gaps of information I needed. They described the panorama before the railroad's scenes had been enacted. It had been there when I was riding, of course, but I had been far too young to be sensitive to it and had missed most of what I might have seen and understood. Through their eyes I was being given a second chance to see what I had missed.

About the same time I met other people who were not only ex-railroaders but collectors of railroad memorabilia. One of these, Frank Kobe, had crewed on a variety of locomotives on the Coast Division of the Milwaukee and after retirement had started to collect railroad photographs.

He came to the bimonthly luncheon meetings of the Milwaukee old-timer meeting in Tacoma with first a handful and then a notebook and then even two notebooks full of collected photographs. He pointed out details of places he had known firsthand. It wasn't long before the depth as well as the breadth of his knowledge became obvious. I would ask him a broad question about a locomotive.

"Were there many of this type of locomotive working east of Spokane?"

He would sometimes answer with so much detail it was staggering. He would recite engine numbers and engineers' names, dates, and places. And, most important of all, he was willing to try to answer my questions.

By then I was taking my own photographs, building an archival set of how the old Milwaukee sites appear today. I photographed many places in which he was interested and we began to give each other copies of our photographs. It was Frank Kobe who introduced me to the gatherings of collectors, sometimes arena-size meetings, other times small intimate gatherings of people specializing in just one railroad, but always rich sources of information. I visited his home and found ceiling-high stacks of notebooks full of railroad photographs.

He even helped in our first abortive trip to the Milwaukee's grade near Snoqualmie. The gap in the trestle had stopped our progress, but before we retraced our steps I had checked my topographic map and found out that the trestle had been built across Hull Creek. I couldn't wait to talk to Frank Kobe about that bridge and its missing segment. When he sat down beside me at the luncheon the following month I was ready for him.

One of our earliest searches stopped abruptly when we came to this gap in the right-of-way at Hall Creek near Snoqualmie Pass in the Cascade Mountains of Washington. The missing segment was carried away by a landslide from a clear-cut tract on the mountainside above after the railroad ceased operating.
Photo by S. Johnson, Milwaukee, Wisc., Public Library Collection

"Tell me about the missing girders at Hull Creek trestle."

"You mean Hall's Creek?" he asked.

"I don't think so," I said a bit uncertain. Frank had often noted that his memory had slipped some. "It doesn't tell lies but it does forget where things are stored sometimes," he would laugh. I knew his memory left gaps, but I had also found that it didn't often make mistakes. I was hesitant to contradict him. It was just as well. The people to my right and across the table both agreed that the creek was called Hall.

"You just don't understand the way the Milwaukee worked," offered another with a twinkle in his eye.

"That's right," Frank agreed. The railroad didn't care what anyone else called a place. They named it whatever they wanted, and that's the way it stayed on all their records."

He was right—mostly right, I found out. Ever since the railroad had built through the Cascades it had disagreed with the state of Washington about the name of this particular creek and it didn't care what the state said. Or, as one of the other old-timers succinctly put it, "The railroad said it was not Hull. It was Hall and to hell with it."

In the St. Joe valley above St. Maries the railroad couldn't agree with the local residents or itself. They changed Elk Prairie to Calder because a single word name was easier for telegraph operators than a two-word name. Then they changed the name of a place that had originally been called Garcia to Zane because somebody pointed out to them that they already had not one but two other places on the mainline called Garcia.

Further complicating the issue, the early records were full of town sites listed on track profiles that never became anything more than some railroad official's wishful thinking about future development. We spent a lot of time looking for those places. We also spent a lot of time looking for two missing tunnels, but the effort was not wasted. We acquired a lot of useful information, but it was frustrating to spend time on a search only to have it resolved by someone telling us that the enigma was due to an arbitrary name change by the railroad.

Increasingly, we began to take longer and more adventuresome field trips, most of them in Idaho, exploring out-of-the-way places on both the branch and mainlines, growing braver about walking through dark tunnels and driving over high trestles. Each outing put more information in our files. We bought a handheld recorder to keep notes, then had to learn how to translate our own speech, which became slurred on the recorded tape as we bounced over rough roads or crawled through sticky black-berry bushes.

Sometimes memory-stimulating information would come from serendipitous encounters with original sources. In a shed off a side track of a small tourist railroad in Whatcom County, Washington, we were invited to walk through a well-preserved example of a luxurious passenger observation car. On a trip to New Hampshire, we climbed aboard and reacquainted ourselves with a classic "heavy" Pullman sleeper, which had been built in 1940. Though these weren't Milwaukee cars, they were very much like those I recalled from my youth.

As I walked through them, I tried to store away in my memory everything I was seeing. I had correctly recalled the big-ticket items: the brass-railed rear platform with the big drum light on the rear end of the observation car, the luxurious wood-paneled walls and the deep carpets, the fancy chandeliers, the muted soft-toned colors of the upholstery. What I had forgotten were some of the little details. The restrooms had little brass-edged slits in the walls for receiving used razor blades. Washbasins had foot-operated releases to close and open the drains in the bathrooms so that there were no sink handles to become wet and dirty. Private compartments had little latched doors at floor level, which opened from both inside the compartment and the outer hallway to be used as a repository for one's shoes upon retiring. While you slept the porter came and collected the shoes, cleaned and polished them, and quietly returned them ready for use when you arose. Every room had small circulating fans up in the corner, interesting additions to the central air-conditioning.

Twenty-five years after the last Milwaukee passenger train had rolled through Idaho and Montana I was traveling through Denver on Amtrak and went out on the platform to stretch my legs during our long stop there. A flash of orange from near the head of our train caught my eye. I walked down and found a nearly pristine Milwaukee Olympian Hiawatha Beavertail observation car sitting on a stub side track right next to ours. It was locked, of course (God knows I tried every door) but standing on tiptoe, I could see inside the same furniture and room layout I remembered so well from the day in 1946 when Dad first took me on a tour through the nation's newest and prettiest streamliner, which he had just shepherded into the Union Station as its conductor.

An unknown friend, hearing of my project from a third party, sent me a full builder's elevation plan of the type of Milwaukee steam engine I first rode out of Manito, Washington, for St. Maries, Idaho—a blueprint nearly ten feet long and three feet wide, rich with small detail. There seemed no end to the flow of memories that were coming back to me. They were mostly memories of things and places, but they were coming from people, too, because of their connections to the railroad or their memory of past experiences. This firsthand information took on special significance in my search.

It was always nice to receive a contribution through the mail, but as valuable as these contributions were, they were no substitute for being able to talk with the people themselves. Face-to-face contact came in all forms as the project developed. Owners of small collectibles shops learned of our interest and began to watch for the items we were seeking. My wife would call me from Seattle where a day's shopping trip had turned into a circuit of these shops.

"Do you have a Milwaukee Public Time Table from 1934?" she'd inquire. "I've found one at Mike's Basement Shop. He stuck it under the counter to save for me."

Some of the encounters were not only helpful but also fun.

One warm summer afternoon when I had begun to despair of ever finding and getting to all of the places I wanted to visit, I met a friendly deputy sheriff (of an unnamed Idaho county), standing beside his truck outside the town hall of a small Idaho village. I told him what I was doing, and he seemed interested and listened closely.

"Sometimes I can't find a place, and then sometimes, like now, when I do find it, access is prohibited," I lamented.

"I guess it would make a difference as to why the No Trespassing signs have been put up," the deputy said. "Most people turn out to be pretty reasonable when things are explained to them. Where are you talking about?" I told him and he reached into his car and pulled out a large county map, spreading it on the hood of his car.

I showed him the place I wanted to photograph, but the only access road was covered with No Trespassing signs. I explained to him that I didn't relish defending my railroad interests in front of a magistrate.

"Well, I can't exactly tell you to go ahead and trespass now, can I?" he said somewhat sternly.

"No sir, I'm aware of that. I'm just trying to figure out how to see that place and take pictures of it. Maybe there's a local person I can contact—obtain permission—or maybe there's another way into that place, a way that isn't posted."

He studied the map carefully, wrinkled his nose, and scratched the side of his neck with a curled, suntanned finger.

"Those are railroad company signs you're telling me about. But the Milwaukee doesn't own these tracks anymore, you know."

"I know."

"Still, the railroad office is a long ways away and I don't suppose they spend much time sitting around up here watching for folks like you. You don't look much like a vagrant or a teenager looking for trouble." He looked at my white hair and grinned.

"Are you suggesting—"

"I'm not suggesting anything. But let's look over these maps. If my memory serves me right, there used to be an old logging road across the draw from that bridge you're talking about." He traced its way across the map. "I can't imagine the railroad making the effort to climb up that hillside and post that road—that is if you can find it." He started to fold up the map, but I could see he was still interested.

"Never been there. I'd kind of like to see that myself."

"Want to come along?"

"I'm afraid I'm on duty, but thanks anyway."

He unfolded the map again, relocated the road on it, and traced its route with a pencil just to be sure I knew how to find it. When I shook his hand and thanked him it was with sincere appreciation for the law evenly applied with human understanding. It would have been fun if he could have come along.

Later, miles away from the village town hall, far back in the hills at the site of a former busy logging operation, I encountered another helpful person—this time by mail. I had traveled to the site not knowing what I would find to photograph and was disappointed to discover that while the small town remained, the mill and all evidence of the railroad were gone. Returning home I really regretted that this was one place I would not be able to photographically document. Then, hoping for a miracle, I wrote a letter of inquiry to the town clerk. I asked about old family photographs, old-timers who might have a photograph they would lend, anything that might help. Weeks later I received a letter from a kind woman telling me that the town didn't have a real town clerk, but that my letter had made the rounds of what town officials there were and had ended up on her desk.

She understood what I wanted but couldn't find anyone who had what I needed. She said she had started to write me with the bad news when she noticed an old photograph of the mill hanging on the wall of the town office. She took the photo from the wall, removed it from the frame, which had held it for some seventy years, and arranged to have it laser photocopied. I was able to enhance it further with some photo techniques. Another gap in my memory had been filled, and one more name was entered on my growing list of helpful people who went out of their way.

Sometimes memory failed. Several times we tracked down an individual recommended as being a good source of information about the railroad's past only to have them say, usually sadly, "I'm sorry. That sure sounds familiar to me but I just can't remember."

Even in such instances, though, we frequently were helped by an individual's recollections of the general atmosphere of a time or place. The outline of the picture we were trying to paint was usually well in place, but color and depth and personal perspective were needed to give the image life. Only people could adequately provide these.

As we visited a variety of sites, walking the right-of-way or trailing rail routes alongside many different roads and highways, we shared the experience with other people who had similar interests and were supportive of our project. The experiences were rich and varied. Sometimes they were carefully arranged interviews: other times the encounter was purely serendipitous.

One day we strolled the streets and lanes of Avery with two different men, each of whom had lived there for many years and knew it firsthand. On another trip, a former railroader and four very involved railroad buffs joined us as we traced the route of the Milwaukee's branch line to Elk River. Our caravan looked like an expedition. Two trucks, a multipurpose van, and more walkie-talkie and CB radios than we needed made the trip fun as well as productive.

An entire afternoon was spent slowly walking a piece of isolated trackbed looking for scraps of broken railroad pottery that might have been tossed from a train's dining car. Two more days were spent studying old city and railroad plat plans in the basement of the county courthouse in Coeur d'Alene attempting to trace the Milwaukee's route through a young growing city of sixty years ago.

In another instance we were invited to join a mixed group of historical society members and U. S. Forest Service personnel as we drove along usually closed sections of the right-of-way, taking with us a descendant of one of the original civil engineers who worked on the long St. Paul Pass

Avery in 1995. The depot still stands, but the tracks have been replaced by a paved county road. The flat area to the right, which was once the east yard with seven tracks, is now open field, gardens, and local residences.
Photo by S. Johnson, Milwaukee, Wisc., Public Library Collection

tunnel, high in the Bitterroots. We shared personal reminiscences of that family's significant involvement with the construction of the new railroad.

Seeing those scenes through the eyes of others, each deeply interested in their own way, magnified the experience to where it became almost overwhelming. We were surrounded by a vicarious rush of excitement, which grew to become a passion. Acquaintances became cohorts, cohorts became associates, and associations developed into friendships. Through it all, we all knew that the old railroad was still alive, and that what we were doing was going to help guarantee that it would live for a long time.

Those trips—some of them long and involved, others short, lasting only an hour or so—really encouraged us to move in two directions. We wanted to actively pursue our retracing of the remaining physical evidence of the railroad and we made plans for energetically doing so. But I also began to focus almost as much on retrieving memories—my own and those of others—for I now realized that these memories were going to provide the basic structure for what I wished to accomplish.

In the process I changed my perception of what memory is. I had started to capture the large picture—big memories in large and important blocks of time and place. I wanted to be able to scan that panorama and recognize that which was before me.

But these rich contacts with those who shared my interests made me realize that memory seldom is found in complete wholes and that recalled panoramas are seldom to be trusted. Memory is, instead, a collection of bits and pieces which begin to coalesce only when they are recognized as treasures to preserve and then are carefully and painstakingly assembled like pieces in a personal jigsaw puzzle. There is excitement in finding, but there can also be fulfillment in searching. I realized that the real joy comes not in knowing but in the process of rediscovering. The richest memories are not recalled, they are reconstructed as the searcher recapitulates the original experience, walking through an old scene as if it were new, greeting familiar faces as though they were newly made friends.

I have concluded from all this that the railroad never really died. There was no demise in the lifting of the rails and the bulldozing of proud buildings. These were sad events that happened to an old friend. But the railroad lives on because there are still memories of it, and the possibility always remains of rediscovering something we thought was lost forever.

During the early stages of this project, Darrel Dewald, a well-known ex-Milwaukee railroader who has already done much to preserve accurate memories of the railroad, wrote me one day that he had heard of a man who had my father's Milwaukee conductor's hat, complete with his name on the inside and the crimson rectangular logo pin still on the front. Throughout all these trips to sites and in our conversations with those we met, we kept hoping to find some direct physical reminder of Dad's presence—a signature on a preserved record book, a snapshot beside a train. We had found nothing so far, so Darrel's announcement was electrifying.

Several years have gone by now and the man and the hat have never been located. Darrel keeps trying, following first one lead, then another. I know Darrel regrets that he has not been able to locate it and I would, of course, love to hold that cherished item in my hands once more. But that doesn't really matter. What counts is that now I know that somewhere out there it exists. Somewhere, a person looks inside that hat and sees Dad's name and remembers. And Darrel remembers, and so do I. And that's what really counts. ◁

4
TIMETABLES, CARDTABLES, AND BASEBALL BATS

☙ Here's a recipe for potentially obnoxious behavior. Take one somewhat precocious ten-year-old. Season him well with loquaciousness and more than average self-confidence. Then provide him with a readily available and extensive source of detailed information. Finally, mix him into a group of curious but mostly uninformed adults who have found themselves in an interesting but unfamiliar situation.

From my point of view I can't really say whether I was guilty of being obnoxious when as an eight- to ten-year-old. I rode the Olympian and Columbian back and forth from Spokane to the Midwest on regular family vacations, but each of the above ingredients were available and the recipe had certainly been followed.

The youngest (by twelve years) of four children, I was raised as an only child for all practical purposes, since my older siblings had essentially left home by the time I was approaching ten. This, coupled with some health problems that caused me to be involved with sedentary pursuits, helped me develop my personal intellectual tools and verbal self-confidence earlier than usual and probably more than was good for me or pleasant for some of the adults around me.

Though I read everything I could get my hands on, including an entire set of encyclopedias from A to Z, my close association with the railroader's life and train travel caused me to develop a heightened interest in anything related to railroads, particularly the Milwaukee Road.

I quickly worked my way through simpler books and reference articles in the local library and graduated to perusing my stepfather's technical railroad manuals and handbooks. I also had access to many Milwaukee Road promotional pamphlets (the types of things now sought by collectors—including myself), Public Time Tables (with their distinctive Milwaukee orange covers) and the less flashy but more informative black-and-white Employees' Timetables, which were a wealth of information that somehow, in my youth, seemed especially mysterious and exciting because they were "not for public distribution."

In addition, though he did not often offer it unsolicited, Dad was a free source of information, always willing to answer my questions and in as much detail with rich background stories as I might wish. He was a good storyteller, which encouraged me to ask even more questions of him.

It had not really occurred to me that this information had great potential for creative play until I first rode the mammoth Westinghouse electric engine with my dad. During that first trip I quickly perceived that the throttle lever on an engine was very similar to that which I had seen motormen using on our local streetcars.

I would take an ordinary folding card table, turn it on its side with the two bottom legs open to hold the table up, and then move a chair in behind the table between the two open legs. I'd leave a folding leg in front of me, which I moved back and forth horizontally like an imagined streetcar motorman's throttle and another leg on my left, which moved up and down as a supposed airbrake lever. But I grew tired of playing streetcar motorman—the streets of Spokane, even when enriched by my fantasies, were neither very exotic nor exciting.

However, that initial trip on a real electric railroad engine broadened my horizons. I no longer was confined to the city streets riding a mere streetcar. Now I could lead my powerful imaginary engine back and forth along the Milwaukee mainline, over mountains, across bridges, through tunnels, hauling whatever kind of train I wished through any kind of weather, acting out any scenario I chose. But I soon tired of this play as well. It became apparent that my fantasy production could provide only a limited number of imaginary, unpatterned, and unrelated scenarios.

One day though, I happened to try and match the locations in a timetable to a map. Suddenly it dawned on me! I did not have to make up routes and create imaginary stations and events. A very fine facsimile of the real thing was at my fingertips waiting to be used. Now there was motivation not only to read these manuals, pamphlets, and timetables but also to study them, and I did exactly that. I read and reread and I memorized much of their content as I used the information in my fantasy play.

I graduated from the cardtable engine as I grew older, but I did not forget what I had read and repeated to myself time and time again in my play. I became a veritable walking encyclopedia of matters related to the Idaho and Rocky Mountain divisions of the Milwaukee Road and continued adding new details whenever I had the opportunity.

I knew how long No. 16, the eastbound Olympian, stopped in Butte (13 minutes . . . westbound No. 15 only stopped for 11 minutes), the elevation of Avery, Idaho (2,492 feet), the new name given to Saugas, Montana, after the fatal wreck of June 1938 (Susan, Montana), the length of the St. Paul Pass tunnel (8,771 feet), and even the locations and interesting names of the almost forty tunnels to be found on the Milwaukee in Montana and Idaho (such fantasy provoking designations as Eagle's Nest, Pipestone Pass, Dominion Creek, Beavertail, and Loop Nos. 1 and 2).

It was no secret to me that a train moving at forty-eight miles an hour would flash by a milepost every 76 seconds, and if one knew how to apply the equation (as of course I did) it was relatively easy to determine your train's speed. Nor was I at a loss to identify and locate the 14 electrical substations between Two Dot, Montana (named for the brand of George Wilson's cattle ranch, which predated the Milwaukee's arrival into the Harlowtown, Montana, area), to Avery, Idaho (named after Avery Rockefeller). I was fully aware that the Rockefellers had been early stock-holders and even company directors in the Milwaukee, and at least two other station sites besides Avery (Faith and Isabel in South Dakota) were named for Rockefellers.

I read about engines and passenger cars and remembered details and statistics. I had cataloged away in my memory such data as these: the drive wheels on a Westinghouse electric engine are sixty-eight inches in diameter and the entire engine weighs 567,000 pounds compared with a Pacific 4-6-2 steam locomotive, which weighs only 406,000 pounds including its tender.

I was familiar with the names of many of the Milwaukee tourist sleepers, several of which I had slept in myself, including intriguing and imagination-stirring names such as Sitka, Rushmore, Mystic, and Nisqually. As you can see, I absorbed a great deal of information, not all of it particularly relevant to anything important. At home by myself this background data was used only in my play. There was no reason to mention it to Dad who knew more about it than I did, and if I ever shared it with my mother in the midst of play, and I can't remember that I did, I'm sure I only received the cursory acknowledgment you might expect. But, put me in a place where there were people who were interested in such trivia and who were even the slightest bit eager to learn more about an ongoing railroading experience, and I was armed to the teeth and ready to hold forth at some length.

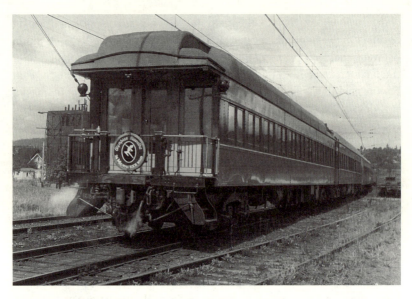

The observation car was my favorite place to ride as a small boy. I stood for hours on the open platform watching the scenery. I used the comfortable lounge inside to find people who wanted to hear about the railroad and sites along the way. The open observation platform disappeared with the advent of the Olympian Hiawatha streamliner in the mid-1940s.
Harold Hill Photo, Warren Wing Collection

I can remember many instances of being in the observation car or strolling down the aisle of our sleeper and sharing information with those who left themselves open to such contributions by innocently offering such open-ended queries directed to no one in particular as, "I wonder how many tunnels we have gone through" or "Do you suppose we ever get as high as Denver on this route?" If someone asked a route- or schedule-related question, the chances were very good that I had at least a partial answer. And if I overheard such a question, the chances were almost 100% that I would offer what I perceived to be a helpful response with no further invitation needed.

I can't recall how obnoxious I really was, but I suspect that I wasn't too annoying because I have no memories of rejection or unpleasant interactions. Perhaps my sincere interest showed through, and this coupled with my age caused people to be kind. In any event, the only specific instances I can remember at all are pleasant.

I remember one trip when I was queried at length by a Pullman Car conductor, an employee of the Pullman Company rather than the Milwaukee Road. This gentleman had just transferred to the Chicago to Tacoma run on the Columbian from some Midwest route, and much of the trackside trivia and background was new to him.

I never had much opportunity to share my information while riding on my father's train because it was a local and ran mostly at night. However, on the long trips to and from the Midwest we were on the train for almost three full days and nights. I spent as many of my waking hours as I could manage in the observation car. It was there that most of the opportunities for casual conversation occurred and there where I met the curious Pullman conductor when he asked me if I was enjoying the scenery.

I told him I was and he asked what I liked best. I explained to him that I had ridden this route many times and that there were so many interesting sites that it was hard to choose one as being the best.

"What about where we are now?" he asked as our train moved across a high trestle so curved that you could see the black electric engine disappearing into a tunnel ahead of us.

"Well, we're near East Portal, the start of the long tunnel underneath the Montana-Idaho state line," I replied. "That's an interesting place."

"Tell me about it," he said.

So I proceeded to fill him in on some details about the area, the reason for the tunnel, and some other general information I had stored away.

He was particularly interested in details about how the construction of the long St. Paul Pass tunnel on the Idaho-Montana border had caused the creation of a temporary community of some size at Taft, Montana, down the mountain below the eastern end of the tunnel. When I called his attention to how today's trains often entered this same tunnel dusty and dirty only to emerge at the opposite end freshly washed and sparkling clean from the overhead springs that splash through the tunnel roof and sides, he was amused and said it was the only time he had ever heard of a train taking a bath on the move.

I told him, too, of a trackside burial site just above Adair, Idaho, and not far from the western portal of that same tunnel. My father said that at this spot, marked only by a small cross stuck into some rocks and maintained by railroad section hands, supposedly was the grave of a person who had died in a fall from a flatcar headed for the safety of a tunnel during the disastrous 1910 fire. The fire had swept many square miles of the

Bitterroot Mountains, destroying thousands of acres of virgin timber and causing untold losses of homes, equipment, and human lives. It was popularly believed that this person had been one of the laborers who had helped rescue many others during the fire but had panicked and fallen or jumped to his death only yards from safety.

The conductor and I went out onto the open observation platform and watched for the gravesite as the train slowly made its way down the steep, curving grade. I remember the occasion distinctly because at the time I had little contact with Roman Catholics and this gentleman crossed himself several times as we passed the grave. It made an indelible impression upon me as I found his serious gesture to be quite mysterious and impressive.

Probably the most impressive experience I had as a preadolescent lecturer was on a westbound journey home from the Midwest when I had a full day of repeated observation-car contact with a well-dressed businessman. Mother had warned me to be careful about strangers but no one on a train ever seemed like a stranger to me. We first met while standing on the sunny platform at Three Forks, Montana, where we were both enjoying an ice cream cup from the famous creamery there. He initiated the conversation with the ice cream and how interesting it was that such a special feature was offered on a transcontinental train ride. This was his first trip west on the Milwaukee and he was impressed.

I agreed and suggested to him that he was in for a treat this day because he was about to encounter a whole list of interesting and exciting trackside features.

"Like what?" he asked. That was more than enough to get me started on my travelogue.

"Well, like the Lewis and Clark Caverns [if I remember correctly they were called Morrison Caverns in those days]." We would see this interesting place very shortly after leaving Three Forks as we entered the scenic Jefferson Canyon just a dozen miles or so down the track.

"Say," he said, "how about you and me sitting together in the observation car and you can point out the sites to me? Would you mind being my guide?"

Mind? I was delighted to have found a ready and eager receptacle for all the data I had collected. We sat together for hours discussing interesting details about what we were seeing, and with my mother's permission he even took me to lunch in the diner. In every way he was correctly polite

I introduced a new Pullman conductor to trackside points of interest from the observation car platform. He introduced me to Catholic rituals, crossing himself repeatedly as we passed this 1910 fire-death grave near Adair, Idaho.
Photo by S. Johnson, Milwaukee, Wisc., Public Library Collection

and well mannered and seemed genuinely interested in both what I was saying and my enthusiasm.

Late in the afternoon as we descended out of the Bitterroots and approached Avery, Idaho, he asked me how and why I had acquired such a range of information. I explained to him how I had read and studied the various sources available to me and how my stepfather had shared many interesting details with me.

"Well it's obvious you love trains," he commented. "But what about other things young boys like? Do you enjoy sports? Do you play baseball or other games?"

I had always been embarrassed about the limitations imposed on my physical activity by my illness and seldom ever mentioned it to anyone. As I look back I can see where my studious behavior was a compensation mechanism I applied broadly until the doctors released me from my restrictions in midadolescence. However, this man had been so pleasant and his interest seemed so genuine that I briefly explained to him that most of those activities were not available to me and told him why.

"But are you interested in them—in games and more strenuous things?" he asked.

"Of course," I said. "Sometimes at home we go see the Spokane Indians play baseball, and I like to read books about sports and other adventurous things."

"Have you ever read Richard Haliburton's books about his exciting trips and adventures?" he wanted to know.

I told him I had not and he took a piece of paper out of his pocket and carefully wrote the author's name and some book titles on it and then handed it to me. "Here, try these," he said. "I think you'll find them great reading."

I took the paper and thanked him for his interest.

"If you don't play ball I don't suppose you have much in the way of athletic equipment, do you?" he asked.

"No, I don't," I said.

"Any baseball bats?"

"No."

"Do you know who Babe Ruth and Lou Gehrig are?" he asked.

"Sure," I said. I knew about Ruth's home run records and knew at least that Gehrig was Ruth's teammate on the New York Yankees.

"Have you ever been to a big league ballgame?"

"No."

"Would you like to go?"

"Oh, yes, of course."

"Then why don't you ask your mother if you might not go see the Cubs play in Chicago during one of your train layovers there? I'll bet she just might take you to see a game. Look," he said as he handed me another slip of paper, "here's a telephone number you can call from the railroad station in Chicago to see if there are any seats available at Wrigley Field."

I thanked him again and vowed to follow up on his suggestion about the ballgame.

"Just one other thing," he said as the train slowed for the stop in Avery. "If you'd like some baseball bats I'll send you some. How about a couple of special souvenirs made of polished walnut . . . one with Ruth's name on it and one with Gehrig's?"

I was thrilled and thanked him profusely, rushing off when the train stopped to tell Mother of my good fortune. She listened with interest, "That was very nice of him, but don't be disappointed if he doesn't actually send the bats. Sometimes people mean well and promise things and then forget," she cautioned me. I was sure that he would not forget. I just knew that he was being truthful when he said he would send me the promised souvenirs.

Three weeks later my faith in him was justified. A long package arrived in the mail and inside were the two bats exactly as he had promised. Alongside was his business card with his name, which unfortunately I have forgotten. However, I remember very well what was printed below. In flowing script it read:

President
The Spaulding Company
Manufacturer of Fine Athletic Goods

He had told me the truth about the bats. I found out later that he had also been right about Mother taking me to the ballgame because on our next trip to Chicago we did indeed take in a game at Wrigley Field. And, as it turned out, he was telling the truth about the Haliburton books, too. They were great reads.

5
NOW YOU SEE IT;
NOW YOU DON'T

Except for one thing, the inside of our garage looks pretty much like anyone else's. If you were to do a quick inventory you would find shelves of odds and ends along the back, garden tools and a lawn mower in a front corner, and a small workbench along one side. But if you were to examine these mundane areas more closely, you would see that they do not contain a typical garage sale collection of miscellaneous items.

In one box you would find an unusual collection of insulators—green and white and amber telegraph line insulators—most from the Milwaukee, but some from the Alaska Railroad and other lines across the country. Among these you would also find distinctive insulators designed to isolate the killing charge of the 3,000-volt trolley wire used by the Milwaukee's electric engines. There are also a few unusual insulators used on catenary support pole lines and in various types of railroad signal equipment. Hung on a wall are some pieces of heavy twisted cable with insulators still on them, held there by stubbornly tight nuts and bolts that have so far resisted my efforts to loosen them.

A really thorough search would uncover a small box carefully tucked away on a back shelf. The box, surprisingly heavy for its size, is full of track nails. These heavy short spikes with flat heads the size of a quarter and displaying an embossed date, were pounded into ties by section hands to identify maintenance dates and facilitate replacement decisions. Only a few of those I have are Milwaukee. These I found at collector shows. Needless to say, they were not collected when I was with my step-father even though he was the one who first showed me track nails. Sometimes, on late-afternoon walks in Butte, before heading for the station for the return run to Spokane, he and I would walk along a track and look for these tie nails, trying to see how many dates we could find. At that juncture I never considered removing one and would have encountered very stern fatherly resistance had I even broached the idea.

On the floor of my garage, underneath a long, low shelf, are bricks. I find myself unable to avoid collecting bricks from the piles of rubble remaining at familiar railroad sites. I have bricks from East Portal, Drexel, Hyak, and Avery, among others. My wife frequently asks what I'm going to do with them, but I consider such utilitarian queries irrelevant. One collects bricks so one will have a piece of history, a legitimate and worthwhile end in itself in my opinion. No plans for use are necessary, though occasionally I have suggested that if I had 200 or 300 more I might be able to make a terrific fireplace—if I had a place for another fireplace.

But, it is under the workbench that I have stashed my most precious treasure trove. Tie spikes! Surely no railroad buff can resist at least picking up and looking at a tie spike found along a favorite piece of trackage. My wife and I discovered, as the two of us walked most of the Milwaukee right-of-way across Idaho, that there was a veritable bonanza of tie spikes in the grassy shoulders beside the ballasted old roadbed. When I first picked one up and carefully laid it underneath the seat in the truck, I was closely interrogated.

"What are you going to do with that?"

"Save it."

"For what?"

"Not for something, from something."

I explained my acquisitive motives in detail. Before I had been able to return to the old right-of-way, others who got there first took many of my memories home with them. Trolley and telegraph poles were cut off. Depots destroyed. Substations demolished and carried away. Rails lifted and melted for use in unromantic ways. Even fourteen-foot-tall automatic block signals had been spirited away in the dark of night. I was pursuing my own private crusade to at least save something. Tie spikes seemed a good place to start. They were small enough to handle, could be linked to specific locations and, most important, they were still available if you looked for them.

Fortunately we became aware, shocked at even our own behavior at times (or at least temptations), that our interest in collecting for the purpose of preserving really was not far removed from looting. Finding so much of the railroad's physical entity destroyed or looted made us sensitive to the need to preserve some of these important artifacts in some way. Not only had many things disappeared over the years since the railroad stopped running, but items, important, unusual, and historically significant, were still disappearing at a surprising rate.

Trees growing in the track tells it all. Only these switches and a single switch stand, the snowplow building, and a few section-hand shacks remained at Haugan, Montana, in 1992. One year later the switch stand had disappeared. Two years later the rails and most of the building were gone, too.
Photo by S. Johnson, Milwaukee, Wisc., Public Library Collection

The steps taken to create the Trail of the Hiawatha along the former roadbed and register it as part of the nation's historical treasury was of legal help. But the problems are not simplistic, and effective solutions are elusive. Enforcing a ban on removing or defacing items within a protected zone is difficult if not impossible. There are too many miles and too few personnel to effectively carry out such enforcement. Unfortunately, railroad buffs (ourselves included) find it difficult not to carry souvenirs home. The cache in our own garage is proof of that.

Some of this "pick it up and carry it home" behavior comes from a well-intentioned and emotionally laden personal desire to have a piece of what once played such an important role in this area. Many people have developed a strong rationalization for such behavior. Nevertheless, over time I have come to view it as looting.

"I want to save it from those idiots who take it away and then throw it in a box somewhere so that no one else will ever see it," is the way the argument goes. I believed it when I said it but later began to perceive that the boxes in my garage was stronger evidence for abuse than preservation.

Adding items to a private collection is not the only motivation. Some of this behavior rises from anger. Among those who have a long-standing emotional attachment to the old railroad, there is a persisting strong undercurrent of resentment and anger over the chain of events that led to the railroad's disappearance. I have seen this anger in a meeting of the Milwaukee old-timers, stimulated by some chance remark. As the participants feed off each other's hurt, sometimes anger rises and swells until it buries logic, personalities, and habit patterns beneath its contorted and nonproductive weight.

It is easier to understand the intensity of this anger if personally present. Sitting in a Milwaukee old-timers' meeting, experiencing the depth of their hurt and witnessing the depth of their anger, can be heart-wrenching at times.

Usually the meetings have a quiet air of camaraderie among these treasured, former railroaders, who are the only remaining evidence of the Milwaukee spirit. They always formally note those who are ill or who have passed away since the last meeting (sometimes a shockingly large number), and as they do so a sadness sweeps over the group. This is followed by a surging tide of anger that in turn gives rise to a stubborn refusal to yield to any person who might rob them of more of their memories. "It should never have happened," they frequently complain as they speak of the death of the Milwaukee. Sometimes, the lament is accompanied by tears, brusquely rubbed away by those who are not used to crying in public.

Nothing that has come after their loss is compared favorably with that experienced before. Even the quality of the food they eat at their meetings is measured against the past.

"Not like the meals the beaneries served!"

"Or the diners either, by God."

Their anger builds as they relate the injustices they perceive in the loss of the railroad. "Interstates. Airlines. Humph! The railroad carried people and goods better than any of these." "Low profits? Personal greed by those who served to profit from doing the Milwaukee in, I'd say."

These are rigid and sometimes illogical opinions, but they stem from honest emotions. It doesn't require a crowd to generate these emotions; similar feelings are encountered among individual ex-railroaders. Who could expect to successfully counter such feeling with the argument that one should not carry home a piece of what no one else has yet stolen?

The sadness I feel at the loss of my stepfather is magnified a thousand times in these people who see themselves and their friends dying without even the warmth of knowing that the memory of the railroad will remain after they have gone. They are faced with the reality that the evidence of their life's work is being permanently erased from the sight of even those who search to find it. At the same time, it is these very people who would argue most vehemently against the plundering of such treasures. Their pain has given birth to a paradox of reactions that is difficult to resolve through logic.

My search for scenes to preserve on film presented us with many paradoxes. Much of the old railroad line was not included in the segment listed in the protective National Register. One might think that such failure to protect would guarantee the ultimate destruction of remnants of the right-of-way. This is not necessarily so.

Parts of the old road (such as the trackage remaining between Plummer and Bovill or that between Plummer Junction and Spokane) have been kept in use by other lines who purchased the right-of-way at the end of the Milwaukee's life span. The locomotives seen there are not Milwaukee, and the familiar colors and logo are missing. However, there is a welcome serenity in knowing that the railroad's spirit lives on in some form, even if through a reincarnation of different colors and markings.

In other places, preservation activities are clearly active. The mainline east of Seattle is a heavily used hiking trail, and a piece of track and a train car stand at the Grant-Kohrs Ranch, Montana, preserved as part of the National Park System. In Deer Lodge, Montana, an electric locomotive, refurbished and repainted through the efforts of a group of Milwaukee supporters, sits near the former right-of-way, resplendent in its fresh coat of orange paint.

Other groups are hard at work to preserve tunnels, trestles, depots, and substations in various places. The attitudes of private citizens who own parts of the old right-of-way range from total disinterest and insensitive acts (such as so thoroughly reshaping the terrain as to completely obscure its former character and its artifacts) to careful reuse of the area in ways deliberately planned to maintain the memories of the old railroad. At one very isolated place, miles deep inside the boundaries of posted land and seldom opened to tourists or railroad buffs—historians or not—are several miles of right-of-way with old telegraph poles still standing, complete with their insulators still in place. The landowner has decided to leave the relics stand as they are and has been forceful in keeping collectors away.

The pace at which physical artifacts can disappear is amazing as we discovered time and again. It was a constant surprise to us as we traveled the right-of-way in Washington, Idaho, and Montana to find major structures and contours disappearing almost literally overnight.

Long before the Milwaukee ceased running, the sturdily built snow sheds protecting the right-of-way alongside five-mile-long Keechelus Lake were landmarks for motorists on their way to Snoqualmie Pass in western Washington. The railroad right-of-way follows the western shoreline while the highway hugs the eastern shore. The mountainside rises steeply behind the railroad route and midway along the lake several long snow sheds were built to shield the line from the snow slides that periodically rumble down the slopes and into the lake. The long snow sheds served as markers for the right-of-way on the opposite shore.

A mainline railroad grade is never steep and we enjoyed riding bikes from Hyak down the length of the lake and back, going through the massive sheds built of hewn foot-square timbers twice, once from each direction. Often seen from across the highway half a mile away, we had been excited to see them firsthand close by on the right-of-way. Photographers love them—every angle presents an interesting image. Their rugged presence marked by angled dovetailed beams is a testimony to the artistry of those who built the railroad.

It was a hot summer day when we last visited the site and we stopped to rest in the coolness of one of the sheds. We leaned our bikes against an upright and gazed out at the view. The azure blue of the reservoir blended warmly with the greens of the forest and the grays of the rock cliffs on the mountains. The faint hum of highway traffic, a pleasant undertone almost like bees in a clover field at this distance, drifted across the water. The shadowed coolness was refreshing.

"It's like being in a cave with windows," I thought, and my wife, with her artist's eye, stood quietly to one side, scanning the view before us. I let my memory drift back to boyhood trips on the Olympian from Spokane

These snow sheds, visible for miles across Lake Keechelus near Snoqualmie Pass, Washington, were removed by the state in the mid-1990s to save maintenance expense. They originally sheltered the right-of-way from the thunderous avalanches that frequent the area's steep slopes.
Photo by S. Johnson, Milwaukee, Wisc., Public Library Collection

to Seattle. This same scene, viewed in comfort from the window of a Pullman berth, reminded me of our nearness to our coastal destination after an all-night trip.

Now long-lost images and sounds returned, lingering for only a fleeting moment but with the sure certainty of vivid recall. Heavy brown wooden uprights passed in a rhythmic quick-step march before my eyes, left to right, one after another, as the train carrying me to Seattle rolled through the shed. My vista of lake and mountains was interrupted in a flashing pattern like a movie film run too slow, and then the bright sunlight returned as we swept out into the open. Before I could adjust my eyes to the remembered change in light I heard a distinctive, hollow, echoing roar. Buried within the booming sounds was another rhythm, a syncopated allegro beat that I immediately recognized as the patterned click of wheels announcing their progress from one rail joint to another. Then memories of sights and sounds were gone and only the quiet view, now cast in the hues of a sweet melancholy, remained.

I understood the origin of the memory that had momentarily returned, but was puzzled for a moment over the auditory recall. Then I remembered. These were sounds generated and heard in only one circumstance: only minutes away from this spot, only a mile or two along the grade, the right-of-way turned sharply toward the nearby mountainside and plunged into the long Snoqualmie tunnel. There total darkness allowed sound to be the sole sensory conveyor of meaning. I was hearing again the sounds of my train in the tunnel, sad but pleasant memories triggered by the sights from these beautiful old snow sheds.

We photographed the sheds several times. Then one day we went back again, and they were gone. Now all that can be seen from the highway is a long scarred piece of mountainside that signifies only the intrusive hand of man. The railroad's signature has been erased.

We learned that the sheds had been removed from the hiking trail because of maintenance cost. The reasoning was sound and the logic good, but the pain of a personal loss remained.

Almost the same thing happened to us in Montana. On our first return to East Portal, several old buildings were still standing. They were ramshackled and in disrepair but in good enough condition that we were able to walk inside and look through the glassless windows at the same mountains the section foreman and his family had viewed when this was their home and the railroad paid regular visits to their doorstep.

On a return trip, only a year or so later, two of the buildings had collapsed. A year later another had gone down. The last time we visited the only remaining indications that there had been buildings here were piles of rubbish standing in a tumbled row. The experience was made even more unpleasant when we discovered that someone had with thoughtless malice attacked the long curving snow shed, which sheltered the tunnel portal itself, using a chain saw to cut out an entire beam.

We were glad that we had returned to East Portal earlier, in time to see some of these old buildings before nature and men destroyed them. But we were angered that we had to rush to see what should have been permanently cared for as an important historical relic.

Not all the visits to places where the railroad artifacts had suffered from the passage of time and the thoughtless work of men were unhappy. Some were good visits, resulting in pleasant experiences and the discovery of things we didn't know existed. In an instance or two the results were humorous and the visits fun to remember and laugh about.

On the western slope of the Bitterroots is the site of Drexel. It is directly above the St. Regis River, across from interstate 90 but not easily reached from the highway without a lengthy walk. A substation once stood at this place, frequently memorialized by photographers because of the way the roadbed rounded a sweeping curve in front of the small cluster of buildings gathered around the big brick power house. The tall trees along the tumbling river and the panorama of mountains offered a splendid backdrop to the classic image of a mighty locomotive leaning into the curve—a curve that allowed the train behind the engine to be visible at the same time. Steam, electric, and diesel trains have all been photographed at Drexel. I remembered Dad's local stopping there in the cool of very early morning on its way to Butte. My orientation to its location was based solely upon its place in the timetable. Trying to return there I was afraid I would be unable to recognize the spot. We accessed the right-of-way some distance away and walked in the direction of where Drexel had once stood.

"There it is! This is it," I excitedly cried to my wife and son who were along on my first revisit there. "I'd know that curve anywhere."

Much was unchanged. The curve and the river and the trees were the same, but the wooden buildings were gone. The substation had been reduced to a large heap of twisted steel and broken bricks. Salvagers had not even bothered to remove the debris. We walked around looking, hoping to find some shard of pottery or a piece of an insulator, which would tell more of what life must have been like here. Suddenly a shout rang out from my oldest son.

"Look at this," he yelled. We ran to where he was on his hands and knees, cautiously leaning forward and looking down into a round black hole. Shining our flashlights into it we could see it was an old well or cistern, meticulously walled with precise rows of brick. The walls funneled upward in a graceful arc as the well became smaller toward the top like an old glass milk bottle. A small rock dropped into the blackness below could be heard hitting water far below, obviously below the level of the river a hundred feet or so away.

"Was this their drinking water do you suppose?" my wife asked.

There was no way at the moment to know, of course, but this discovery so excited us that the next hour was spent lifting up every piece of easily moved debris, searching through the tall grass by the riverbank, and generally combing the area for further discoveries. We questioned some former Milwaukee railroaders, but they didn't know a well existed, or didn't remember. Those who did remember had no idea what it had actually been used for, although some thought it might have been the source for a water tower for steam engines in pre-electric days.

Two years later, as unexpected as the discovery of the well had been, at an old-timers meeting a friend handed me a photograph showing Drexel as it was years before.

"For your collection," he said, not realizing how interested I was in the site.

The pump house was clearly visible.

"Did they get their drinking water from this well?" I asked the group of old-timers gathered around to see the picture.

"Maybe they did, but I wouldn't have," offered a grizzled old-timer, leaning forward to see more clearly.

"Why not?" I asked innocently.

"Look at the other buildings," he answered.

Then I saw what he meant. I had seen the large substation, of course, and had also noticed the two houses used by the operators and their families. What I had missed were the two smaller houses with crescent moons cut in their doors, connected by a well-worn path to the big houses, and too close for comfort to the well house. At first I thought I had answered the question about the use of water from the discovered well. Then the same man who had questioned drinking that water, said, "'Course, you never could tell what some of them substation folks would do. I always figured all that electricity sometimes did funny things to them switch pullers." The others all laughed and he laughed with them, but I wasn't sure whether he meant that last remark.

Sometimes the speed with which artifacts disappeared amazed us. There is an isolated stretch in central Washington where the track cut through two high banks near the edge of a meandering stream. When we first walked there we spotted a very unusual site—two automatic block signals were still in place, standing opposite each other to cover trains moving in each direction. The following year we revisited them because it had a special attraction to my wife, who often sees beauty where I overlook it.

On our third visit, not long after the previous one, we found the signals gone. No trace or sign of them remained. Whoever had taken them had removed every vestige of their being, unbolting them from the concrete bases that supported them and carting them off to some unknown destination. Hopefully they will end up in a museum somewhere, but who can tell. We stood and looked and then walked away. We haven't gone back.

Sometimes we were surprised in a more pleasant way. On a return to Cle Elum for a district meeting of Milwaukee buffs and researchers, I went back to the substation that had so depressed me earlier. I wanted to set up a camera on the top of the truck so I could shoot above the level of the chain-link fence for a better photograph. I found the gates open and introduced myself to a man who was standing in the yard. He was friendly and interested in my work and told me he was the owner of the building.

"I'd like to put it back together somehow," he offered. "The problem is, I don't really know where to start. I can't even keep glass in the windows," he complained. A glance at the building with its broken windows and pitted brick confirmed his problem.

"That would be a great project," I said wistfully. "I wish there were some way it could be done."

"Well, maybe . . . someday. I haven't given up. Would you like to see inside?"

Ecstatic, I went inside to find piles of neatly stacked bricks, pieces of machinery from the hoists and trams that had been used to move the now absent heavy generators. The lever for closing the contacts between the main power lead and the trolley wire was still in place in the operator's bay, as were the rows of insulators high on the wall and along the ceiling.

The place wasn't the same as it had been, of course. Some of the machinery was still there along with banks of insulators high on the walls, but the big transformers were gone, and broken bricks and other debris made a sharp contrast with the well-kept polished concrete floor and humming machinery I remembered. A rescued pile of brick stood alone in one corner of the main room. But despite this, it made me feel good to see that someone was trying to keep things from disappearing. Since then, I have heard that plans to restore both the substation and the depot are proceeding, a nice ending to my despondency when I first saw this place from the outside.

I believe it was the sense of futility that bothered me most. I could think of little that anyone could do to change the overall situation. Even with a great deal of effort and expenditure the task seemed insurmountable, as evidenced by the shots fired through the chainlink fence at the Cle Elum substation.

It was not a simple task, but we wanted to help. We bought commemorative bricks to help repair a depot, wrote letters of support, and donated photographs to support the dedication of a piece of the right-of-way to a commemorative trail. We sent photographs to the Milwaukee archival collection in the Milwaukee, Wisconsin, public library, but even these efforts did not alleviate our sense of helplessness.

"Things are disappearing faster than anyone can save them," I protested to my wife. "It won't be long before everything is gone just like the people who made all these things important."

"I thought we had decided that the people weren't really gone," she said. "Isn't that what we are doing—keeping the memory of these people present in the minds of those who learn about them?"

"Of course," I replied. That was the best answer to the tragedy of disappearing artifacts. "Keep the faces and deeds alive instead and it will guarantee a permanence not possible with wooden and steel artifacts."

And so, our odyssey continued.

6
DEPOTS

Early one morning on a chilly fall day in 1901 my grandfather boarded a train in Independence, Missouri. He was on his way to a evangelistic preaching assignment 250 miles away in a small town in Illinois, a town he had never visited. After a full day's journey he arrived to find a lonely and deserted platform waiting for him. The smoke curling up from the single stovepipe at the end of the depot was the only sign of life.

Carrying his grip he entered through the single wood-paneled door and found the agent working at his cluttered desk beside a telegraph key and a wire basket full of papers. As he relates in his diary, Grandpa quickly discovered that the agent was a rich source of information.

He was hungry, so Grandpa asked the agent where he could get something to eat. The agent told him how to find the local general store where he could buy some apples, his favorite food, for his dinner. The agent knew where the church was and how to get there so he could meet his scheduled preaching assignment just an hour or so away.

Grandpa started out the door but the agent hailed him back.

"No reason to haul that grip around 'less you want to. You can leave it in the baggage room. It'll be safe here."

"Thank you for your kindness," Grandpa said to the man with the black sleeve protectors and green eyeshade. Then he started to walk to the church, but on the doorstep he paused, and as an afterthought, stepped back inside the small depot.

"Perhaps you'd know where Brother Jensen lives. He was supposed to meet me here but . . . " The man did know, of course, and drew a map on the back of an envelope for my grandfather so he wouldn't get lost.

"I was fortunate to have met this repository of useful information, Grandfather wrote, "since later, upon arriving at the church I found I had confused the dates and was a day early. It would have been a long wait for Brother Jensen if I hadn't had that map-bearing envelope."

Reading through Grandpa's diaries, written at the turn of the century, one gets a clear picture of the importance of the railroads and their accepted role in everyday life. Depot buildings seemed to be the focus of that service. This helpful station agent apparently was no exception, and more than one depot, staffed by railroad representatives who took their role in the community seriously, served the townsfolk of their villages well. Grandpa certainly made use of these services. He writes of walking from his house to the local Missouri Pacific depot to meet an arriving friend. While at the depot he made arrangements to ship some of his daughter's belongings to her new home in Texas, sent a telegram to his son who was exploring a new business venture in the Oklahoma Territory, and discussed the weather in Iowa with the incoming train crew and station attendants.

It is obvious from his diaries that these varied uses of the local railroad station services and personnel were commonplace and usual. The local railroad depot was a dependable and consistent resource in communities where phones and other means of ready communication were as yet rare or unknown. The depot was an important building in a community at the turn of the century.

Depots and stations carry a special nostalgia for railroad buffs. Though decrepit and ramshackled, their yards overgrown with weeds sprouting up through the platform and missing swaths of roofing shingles, they remain the sole reminder of a departed time, the only evidence of a railroad's presence. In most instances, less permanent rights-of-way, signal towers, and even the rails themselves have long since disappeared. Occasionally a depot still stands.

The railroad depot's distinctiveness of form and use has led to preservation and protection of some of the finer examples. The towered Missoula, Montana, station is one of these. The Milwaukee Road has long since departed but the fine brick station is still there, well preserved, and in use in a variety of community-related ways. On the wall beside me as I write is a photograph of Dad in his conductor's uniform. I took that picture in 1949 as his train paused for a few moments in Missoula. Tucked away among our snapshots is a picture of my younger daughter taken years later at nearly the same spot, standing on the base of a preserved railroad signal in front of the same station in 1980. The signal now stands in the middle of a park where once the bright orange Olympians paused to leave and pick up passengers, mail, and freight. Behind it the depot still stands as a common denominator for the years that have come and gone. It is a friendly storehouse of the memories of many families such as ours.

The Missoula, Montana, depot, a classic design, is now used for community functions. The tracks ran down the middle of the road to the left of the depot and under the highway overpass beyond. One of the automatic block system signals has been preserved and can be seen to the left in the photo. The former right-of-way is a bicycling and hiking path.
Photo by S. Johnson, Milwaukee, Wisc., Public Library Collection

A few miles away is a more humble but equally good example: the wood-sided station at Alberton, carefully restored and painted, its grounds well tended and its graceful lines unchanged. The town's name remains on the name boards at each end of the station though no tracks are there to bring trains so that passengers may read them. But the depot is in regular use as the small town's community center.

In earlier days these railroad stations, many of them fine examples of specific period architecture, were the center of much of a community's contact with the outside world. While my brief contact with them as a young boy was not nearly so involved, I did build a treasury of memories that reflects in some small way, this personal relationship between an inanimate structure and the people who use it. And, in an instance or two, these experiences were microcosmic examples of the encompassing role they must have played years before in a culture now fading from our memory.

Milwaukee trains Nos. 7 & 8, which my father worked during the war years and on which I rode with him overnight between Spokane and Butte, were not glistening, romantic streamliners. They were short, three-car consists—and old cars at that—designed to carry on the daily work of pickups and deliveries. These paid the railroad's bills but took so much time they couldn't be included in the crack Olympian's workload without devastating its fast Chicago to Tacoma schedule. All the piecemeal work went to Nos. 7 & 8. These services were much like those performed by the railroads of yesterday, tasks that supported the everyday needs of people scattered across the countryside.

Much of the work I observed while riding on Nos. 7 & 8 involved frequent stops at stations where people waited for the supplies we brought. These places, such as St. Maries, Idaho, were interesting in their own busy ways, full of people and activities and things to see. I enjoyed them, but it was the isolated, lonely stations that were really exciting.

One of my fondest memories is not of a single station but of a number of small, so-called whistlestop stations in the mountains of Montana and Idaho.

Most of these places are clearly listed in the Milwaukee Employees' Timetable for the Rocky Mountain and Idaho divisions with the footnote, "No agent or office." This simple caveat reminded train crews that should there be work to do at this site—freight to be loaded or unloaded, cars to be set out on a siding, or messages to be communicated—they were on their own. No on-site personnel should be expected and no nontrain crew assistance was likely. The names of these entries in old timetables form a litany of mysterious places, forgotten in detail but clearly recalled nevertheless: Marble Creek, Stetson, Kyle, St. Joe, Falcon, Pedee, Bryson, Tarkio.

Their names are remembered, but they have become blended into a common stereotype that is hard to separate into clear pictures of specific places. They carry individual images in my mind, clear and distinct even though unlabeled. I have fond recollections of an excitement and strong camaraderie fleetingly passing by in the darkness outside an open baggage car door as the baggageman dropped packages by the trackside. Sometimes there was a quick shout of greeting from someone in the

In contrast to the impressive Spokane, Missoula, and Butte station buildings Kyle, Idaho, was an isolated stop in the Bitterroot Mountains with never more than a cluster of small frame buildings. This is how the Kyle station and some of those who used it looked in 1910. Later that summer, these buildings were destroyed in the great forest fire that swept the area.
Darrel Dewald Collection

darkness or even the wave of a hand faintly seen in the glow of a kerosene lantern. More often than not there were only the dim shapes of small trackside buildings, dark or at best lit by a single bare bulb hanging beneath a tin reflector over a closed door. Deserted in the middle of the night, these places were indistinct blurs by the side of the track.

Sometimes the train stopped briefly while items were unloaded and placed in a shed protected by a padlock which could only be opened by a key the train crew carried. Often, items were simply left beside the rails, safe by virtue of the deserted and isolated nature of the place, waiting to be picked up by someone hours later after day had broken.

I met a woman who had been raised in a railroad family, married a rail-road man, and who was now working as a cohost with her husband at the Montana Hotel in Alberton. She told me of living in section-hand build-ings at Falcon, one of these isolated sites sitting alone in the shadow of a mountain. Falcon had a depot according to the timetable, but it was really nothing more than an extra large storage shed with no other amenities.

"Most of the time," she told me, "we had supplies dropped by the train. We would climb the steep hillside on a switchback path and carry the items back down to our living quarters. It was hard work, especially when it was cold or wet, though sometimes easier than trying to go 'out-side' for things—easier than hiking clear down to the road in the valley.

"Sometimes though, we'd get bored with being cooped up and we'd take the track scooter to Avery just for the ride and to get a warm dinner in the beanery. I'll never forget one of those trips. My husband, our baby, and I had made the trip down to Avery fine and were on our way back to Falcon. It was cold riding on that gas-powered track-walker's machine, but a lot better than walking and we were all bundled up. It was only twelve miles and it went by pretty fast. This time, though, a few miles above Avery on the upgrade in one of a string of tunnels there, we ran into ice on the rails."

I understood what she meant. Most of the tunnels dripped some from springs above. In the winter condensation turned into icicles. Sometimes this dripping water would freeze on the cold steel of the rails, not a hin-drance to the trains, which simply crushed the ice with their weight, but a potential problem for the very light four-wheeled, motor-scooter cars.

"We tried for quite a while to break the ice, but we just couldn't do it. We tried to push the scooter over it and on through the tunnel but that didn't work either. Nothing worked. Joe got concerned about the possibility of an unscheduled train coming through, so he had me take the baby and walk back outside the tunnel. It was rough going over the icy and rocky roadbed with only the reflected headlights of the motor scooter to guide us but we made it."

Her husband sat quietly and nodded at the story she was telling. "It was pretty rough going," was all he said. She continued.

"Joe finally gave up and backed out of the tunnel downgrade, lifting the scooter off the track at the tunnel mouth where we were waiting. We sat huddled together for warmth in the darkness for quite a time until finally a freight came through and knocked the ice off the rails. We put the scooter back on the track and followed the freight into Falcon and made it okay, though I was tired and the baby was crying. It was exciting but not much fun on a cold night, and we were glad to get home."

Living in those places must have been an uncomfortable, hard life but one with special adventure attached. I could understand how a visit to Avery with a chance to sit and talk with others at the depot over dinner would have some appeal, but I'm not sure it was worth it in this instance.

Many of my recollections of depots are about the peculiarities of the place itself, but some are related more to things I personally did there.

I think of East Portal, Montana, in the winter with the trackside buildings buried in snow over their eaves, snow so deep that pathways had to be tunneled from trackside to their doors. In Milwaukee, Wisconsin, I remember the surprise at finding the trains at street level immediately in front of your eyes as you came into the lobby from the street. I loved boarding the already quiet sleeper there, speaking in hushed tones as we moved quietly between the long rows of dark curtains behind which previously boarded passengers already slept.

Large urban stations have a character all their own. I have been fortunate to have visited some of the largest—Grand Central in New York City, Union Station and LaSalle Street in Chicago, and Union Station in Washington, D.C. Each is spectacular, but the one that impressed me the most was Union Station in Kansas City.

The gray stone station, which is still standing but used for other purposes now, is large. In its day, as you went to your train you walked through a very large lobby with ticket counters and various shops and restaurants. Across that room was a series of large portals opening into a city-block-long concourse. Covered by a several-story-high, glass-paneled roof, this immense room had row after row of wide oaken benches, placed, as I remember, not like church pews but back to back in lines running left to right across the concourse with a wide aisle down the center.

On each side, every fifty feet or so, were double doorways like entrances to a church. Each doorway led to a stairway down a long double flight to the track level below. Above each doorway was a lighted panel sign bearing the name and number and departure time of the train residing on that track. Many of the famous names of railroading were represented including the Super Chief, the Eagle, and the train we were to board, the Southwest Limited. To one side of the door was another information panel bearing the names of the major places served by each train. Of most interest was the sign announcing our train, listing the mysterious places we wouldn't see, hidden from our sleeping eyes as we passed in the night. It was a list of intriguing places with names that sounded strange to a young boy: Excelsior Springs, Chillicothe, Ottumwa, Davenport, Savannah, and Beloit (where my stepfather had worked on Milwaukee freight trains as a young man before coming west).

We passed through Kansas City's Union Station regularly while visiting relatives during our annual summer vacations. We would arrive from Chicago on the Milwaukee's Southwest Limited early in the morning and on return depart for Chicago in the evening after dinner. It is the departure experiences I remember best.

Consistent with my mother's careful nature, arriving early was important. "Better safe than sorry," my mother invariably said. I didn't object; I liked the ambience of the huge gray buildings. I didn't mind that Mother encouraged those who brought us to the station to go home rather than wait for the train to depart.

"You have so far to go," she would say.

Our routine pattern after they left never varied. The first stop was at the ticket window to verify our tickets and sleeping car reservations. Next was the baggage check-in, and last was finding a seat close to the doorway. There we could see when the sleeping car conductor would allow reservation holders to board the train, though we knew that this would not occur for another hour.

Then, with Mother's careful rules having been clearly stated and restated, I was allowed to venture about the station as long as I reported back every few minutes. I visited the magazine stand and the candy shop, strolled a little farther on and read the menu on the wall outside the fancy restaurant and sneaked a peek inside. The next port of call on my journey was usually a return to the baggage counter to watch passengers check in their bags, many different sizes and shapes bound for all kinds of interesting places. Sometime during the evening I would make a circuit around the room to count the number of doorways. If I was lucky one of the doors leading down to the tracks would be open and I could peer down the long tunnellike stairwell and see a whiff of steam float across the platform below. It was important to include at least one trip to the massive men's room though.

All of these activities consumed time yet the minutes still dragged slowly, but at last there was the thrill of hearing the booming public address system announce our train. Getting on a train is always fun but it is hard to equal the bustling excitement that came from doing so.

Although I've driven past the Kansas City Union Station many times since, I've never perceived it as just a building. I see instead a palace that once housed a magic carpet of dreams upon which an excited young boy could change mere travel into unforgettable adventure.

It was from this station that I boarded a train for New York, leaving home for my first permanent job. I was now an adult, but the mystery and excitement were still present. I was trading old horizons for new, and in the excitement I felt the conflict and adventure of uncertainty combined with expectation. Trains carry one to a destination without the traveler having to worry about crossroads and the decisions they present.

I have a host of memories of stations and depots connected with food. Like any young boy, I loved to eat. If the time of day matched the train's schedule appropriately, depots were a rich source of food. Many stations had simple lunch counters that offered what amounted to yesterday's version of fast-food service. This consisted mostly of prepared sandwiches, fruit, sometimes hot soup, and desserts such as pie, cake, and paper cups full of ice cream.

There were predictable opportunities for eating at stations on the Milwaukee main east-west line, and I had them all located. Eastbound out of Spokane on the Olympian, some sort of snack at Avery was a must on our schedule. An engine change was required there so the stop was longer than most. If we bought sandwiches we fed scraps of crust to the trout in the trackside pond next to the platform. The tracks disappeared over time as did the trout. For years, only the pond, dry of water, and a deserted station remained as a reminder of a busier and nicer time. Today the few remaining residents of Avery are trying to restore the depot, and one of their first projects was to put water and fish back in the pond.

Westbound, the opportunities for depot eating were better because of the schedule. Mobridge, South Dakota, was reached after dinner was over and no fast food was available in the station but we could get something from the on-train vendor. We'd eat as we watched the local Indians dance in their native costumes. A colorful blanket was spread on the station platform to catch the coins tossed by the tourists.

However, the really great place to stop was Three Forks, Montana, which was famous for its creamery. From its own building immediately next to the station every possible delicious dairy product was available.

I usually opted for ice cream or chocolate milk, sometimes even a milk shake. Mother preferred a glass of cold buttermilk. It was fun to watch the dining car chefs and waiters lean out of the loading door of their car, talking and joking with dairy workers as fresh milk and ice cream were loaded onto the diner. Those same dairy products always seemed to taste far better on the open platform than inside the train.

In the late afternoon our train stopped at Butte, where a full-service restaurant offered lots of possibilities but was a bit too intimidating for me at that age. Nevertheless, this depot and its restaurant elicit memories of food. When I rode on Nos. 7 & 8 with Dad we arrived at Butte in time for breakfast. Immediately after signing in at the office we would head directly for the restaurant, stopping briefly at the newsstand for a morning paper and pausing by the slot machines, legal in Montana, while I unsuccessfully entreated Dad to try his luck.

"Please?" I would implore.

Invariably I got the same sermonlike response.

"No one wins at these. They are the devil's own playthings put here to steal the working man's hard-earned money." With that we were always off to the restaurant. Dad wasn't about to "throw away" a quarter.

Breakfast never varied. My stepfather was a man of regular habits including ordering breakfast. I had no objection in this instance, however, since I considered our early morning depot meal to be a delicious feast. Dad had coffee while I had fruit juice. Then we would have a short stack of pancakes (buckwheat for Dad but regular for me) and a side of either ham or sausage. Sometimes we would end up with a piece of pie. Dad loved pie for breakfast, a taste Mother never understood, but which I thoroughly endorsed. I always ate until I was stuffed and loved the novel experience of sitting on the revolving round stools at the counter and watching the cooks work in the kitchen just beyond.

One memorable morning I started my usual plea as we passed the slot machines.

"Please?"

Dad stopped abruptly and said, "All right. I'll tell you what. Here is a twenty-five-cent piece (a significant amount of money for me at that age and time). I will give it to you for your own. You're too young to play the machine. But if you want me to, if you want to waste your money and throw it away so you won't be able to buy anything else with it, I'll play the machine with your quarter and lose the money for you."

To his chagrin, the morality-shaping moment of decision making was wasted. I didn't hesitate a second.

"Do it!" I urged.

Carefully he put the quarter in the slot and pulled the handle down. I stood on tiptoe, eagerly watching the three reels spin and spin and then stop one by one. I was wide-eyed as first one, then a second, and finally a third red cherry appeared. With a clatter, a pile of quarters spewed from the machine and into Dad's cap, which he had hurriedly thrust under the payoff opening. I was ecstatic. He was disgusted.

"Judas Priest!" he exclaimed.

"What can I spend it on?" I asked eagerly.

"Save it for college," he muttered. "We're going to the hotel and get some sleep."

Neither Dad nor I mentioned it the rest of the trip, but I noticed he had to grin when I told Mom about it. Even now, the sight of that station, which still is a prominent landmark in Butte, brings to my mind the memory of his warm smile, the three red cherries, and the pile of quarters.

Some years later, after I had grown, married, and sired a son, the circle of depots came full circle in my family. Frank and my son, Dennis, stood on the Missouri Pacific depot platform in Independence, Missouri, the same platform my grandfather had written about in his diary over fifty years before. Frank stooped down and took the four-year-old by the hand, and together they boarded a passenger train for the ten-mile ride into Kansas City's Union Station. A grown man now with a son of his own, Dennis still remembers and speaks of the trip, an experience the other children never had due to their age and their grandfather's death. I often wonder if there might not have been friendly family ghosts of yesterday standing on that same platform that evening, enjoying perhaps one last visit to that familiar place.

Most railroad depots are no more, but the effect of the roles they played remains—a stalwart wood-and-stone welcoming committee, seemingly an unassailable friend. But when I left such warm surroundings, the sight of the depot growing smaller and smaller until it disappeared brought sadness: It was a reminder that I was leaving a special place behind, a place I might possibly never be able to visit again. How true this has proven to be.

7
THE TWO GREATEST SHOWS ON EARTH

☞ Not too long ago I visited a railroad exhibit and on one of the tables was a fine layout with a model circus train being switched and unloaded in the process of setting up the Greatest Show on Earth. The scene was exactly as I had experienced it as a boy. All the fascinating cars were there, loaded with animals and the myriad paraphernalia of the circus, splashed with painted scenes and figures in every color of the rainbow, emblazoned with that name no circus-goer can ever forget, Ringling Brothers and Barnum & Bailey Circus: the Greatest Show on Earth.

I stood there watching for almost an hour, immersing myself in the scene, once again hearing and seeing experiences from my childhood: I smelled the sweet odor of fresh wood shavings and heard the clank of chains dragging behind the working elephants, who were covered with dirt that they would blow away with their trunks every minute or so.

"They don't make 'em like they used to," certainly applies to almost any aspect of contemporary railroading, but one of the saddest examples of this steady erosion of the "good old days" is the disappearance of the circus train.

I was very young when I went to my first circus, probably only four or five. During those trying depression times so many years ago my mother sometimes lost patience with the railroad and the demands it placed on my stepfather and therefore on our family. No extra board call or dispatcher's request was ever turned down, when the railroad beckoned, he came.

Exasperated, Mother used to say to him, "Railroading is your whole life. You have no other interests!"

She was nearly right even in her deliberate exaggeration, but there was at least one other interest almost as strong in this man's heart: the circus. And when the circus and the railroad were lumped together, well that was something really special!

During the waning but still lean years of the 1930s depression, there was never much extra cash around our house. Even loose change was carefully counted and saved, set aside for important essentials such as food and housing. Clothing was used until worn out and the table was set with plain fare. Pleasures for the family were those that came cheap or at no cost at all—fishing from the local river, hunting for wildflowers, or exploring new routes on the streetcar.

Money was rarely spent on any form of entertainment, except when the circus came to town each summer. Then the pennies, nickels, and dimes came out of the round tin Prince Albert tobacco can in the cupboard where they had been saved one by one throughout the year. At least two (sometimes three if it had been a better than average year) circus tickets were then purchased from the advanced sale booth at the corner drugstore near our house.

These were almost always matinee tickets because the afternoon show was cheaper than the evening performance and there was seldom extra money for souvenirs or candy or popcorn. Even so we enjoyed the show and we always came back to the grounds at night and walked amidst the tents and along the shavings-covered midway, strolling with the crowd between the long rows of barking sideshow hawkers backed up by rows of lights blinking off and on and giant garage-size painted posters boasting of the wonderful sights that might be viewed firsthand beyond the mysterious canvas-shrouded entrances.

Imagination had to suffice for me, however, for neither money nor my parents' opinion allowed me to see any of these delights.

"It's all a big come-on, a phony," Dad used to say. I believed him, I guess, but grew up disappointed that I never was allowed to check out the freaks and other wondrous sights for myself.

On the other hand, the main show itself, which took place under the canvas big top, included all the traditional excitement, and I experienced it all. I loved every whistle-blowing, band-playing, hyperbole-exaggerated, clown-filled minute of it and I remember it well. And I also clearly recall that my parents seemed to enjoy it as much as I. That definitely added to the fun. But even then, as young as I was, I could appreciate the sacrifice and effort my parents put into assuring that with at least one of them, I always got to go to the circus—a privilege not shared by all of my schoolmate chums.

In addition to the glamour and glitter of what our hoarded coins had purchased came a series of other exciting circus-related experiences which cost us no money at all! I remember these most fondly and in greatest detail and recall them with a nostalgia that the show itself does not

We always watched from the top of a boxcar as the circus train unloaded. It was the best seat in the house.
Circus World Museum, Baraboo, Wisconsin

match. These I treasure, more than the performances themselves, perhaps because I shared them intimately with my parents.

You had to get up early if you wanted to even vicariously help the circus unload and set up. Circus trains arrived in town very early, indeed, not waiting for those who wished to "sleep in."

The circus came to our town on any one of four railroads. Because my stepfather knew the railroaders and because the sidings that the circus used to get to the tent-site grounds were often Milwaukee Road tracks, he knew the arrival time and the route to the sidings which the circus trains would take.

We had no automobile in those late-depression days, so Frank and I rode the streetcar to where the trains would be switched off the mainline and onto the siding route. There we would watch as the larger cross-country steam locomotives were replaced by switch engines, sometimes breaking the train into several smaller units more easily handled and spotted on the designated sidings.

At the circus grounds we would be only two of many among a crowd of curious observers. But here, at this early hour, there was seldom more than a handful of spectators, and I felt that somehow we were privileged overseers of this important operation.

Sitting on an empty flatcar, or sometimes high up on a boxcar with our legs dangling over the edge, we would watch with interest, most of our attention drawn to the boarded-up cars. We would sit and speculate what might be inside of these mysterious cars. Perhaps they contained wild animals or gaudy, gilded bandwagons. Our interest was especially caught by the cars loaded with bales of hay that stuck out through the cracks—food for the elephants that we knew were inside their own special cars nearby, waiting to be unloaded so they might go to work.

It was particularly exciting to spot the elongated flatcars, which carried the long slender poles, painted in concentric rings of red, white, and blue. These included the poles for the main tent itself, the home of the five performing rings of the largest traveling show of its type in the world.

As soon as the yard crews got the trains into workable sets on the siding, we clambered down from our perch and quickly left for the circus grounds—we didn't want to miss seeing those poles unloaded or those boarded car sides removed.

Sometimes as many as three separate sections of train were needed, and they didn't all get into town at the same time. Even when we got to the circus grounds at this early hour we would most often find some circus cars already there. Usually the first section to arrive would be a passenger train, a collection of various types of dormitory and Pullman cars. This section sometimes arrived in the middle of the night since the performers retired to their sleeping quarters on the train almost immediately after the previous evening's performance.

Once loaded, the dormitory train slipped out of town for the next day's performance site even before the big top came down and well before some of the other tents, equipment, and animals were loaded. The last section to leave the site of yesterday's show carried a few plain dormitory cars that provided transportation and sleeping quarters for the workers who completed the final stages of the show's breakdown.

The early arriving passenger cars (sometimes as many as a dozen or so) were painted brilliant white with trim in bright circus colors and the show's name emblazoned on their sides. Dad explained in detail that these were special cars, built by the Pullman Company, specifically designed and constructed for the circus. Except for the gaudy coloring, they did not appear to be any different from regular Pullman cars when viewed from the outside. But inside, the sleeping quarters varied greatly, ranging from long lines of dormitory bunks in some cars to small two- and three-room suites for the stars and circus brass in others.

Whenever possible this dormitory section was placed near the performance tents to make the trip to and from the big top and sideshow tents as quick and easy for circus performers as possible. While waiting for the working equipment cars to arrive we would stroll as close to these dormitory cars as we could without intruding. I was always full of questions as to which ones were the animal trainers, which were high-wire performers, and how to distinguish the clowns from the others. My stepfather would answer with what had to be speculative answers but I was more than satisfied to assume that he was right.

The only thing that took priority over the location of dormitory cars was the No. 1 working section. This important collection of flatbed and boxcar type railroad cars carried the ticket wagons, the main tent, the big top, several equally important auxiliary tents for the sideshows, and perhaps the most important working tent and equipment of all, the commissary.

Commissary equipment and supplies were the first to be unloaded. Local provisioner trucks and wagons were already on hand, waiting with fresh milk, produce, and ice. By breakfast time, the portable iron wood stoves were going full blast, and coffee was steaming. Pancakes, eggs, and bacon all were ready for the work crews.

I remember the tantalizing smells of breakfast cooking as we watched the show unload. Cold peanut butter sandwiches were a poor substitute for bacon and eggs at that hour. And, to a youngster, there was a very special glamour in the idea of eating a plate of sizzling bacon and eggs from a bare plank table in a circus tent. My lunch, no matter how carefully and lovingly prepared, could never successfully compete with that!

But even as some of the crew ate, strings of more cars loaded with all manner of things were rolled into place and the unloading and setting-up process commenced. The sidings that held all these cars were standard industrial tracks serving a variety of small factories, warehouses, and other consumers alongside the circus grounds. Dad always looked for an empty standing boxcar in a place where we had a view of the whole unloading process.

Boosting me ahead of him, we climbed the steel-runged ladder up the side of the car and eased our way onto the board strips forming a walkway down the center of the top of the car. I was always eager to sit down as soon as possible because the top seemed extremely high to me. Sometimes, to my displeasure, we would climb up on one car and walk down the length of it, crossing to a second and sometimes a third car until we found the spot Dad felt was just right. I realize now those long steps from car to car were routine for him. I wonder though if he knew how frightened I was to make those leaping steps even with my hand firmly in his.

I used to worry, too, despite all his assurances, that some switch engine would come along, couple to the car we were on, and take us off at high speed to some unknown destination. These two concerns were the only negative things I can remember about the whole experience, which even at that was worth the risk.

"Just don't look down," Dad used to remind me. The reminder wasn't needed.

When the circus train cars were properly spotted at their planned location, the work crews quickly moved to set large planks as unloading ramps at the free end of the first car in line. Then they used more planks to bridge the open spaces between the cars. When finished they had created what amounted to a long narrow roadway consisting of a series of flatcars connected by a few boards.

Elephants, horses, and a few tractors pulled the cars along the artificial roadway to their prearranged locations. I used to wonder if one of the wagon wheels would miss the narrow plank bridge, tumbling a car to the ground, and freeing a ferocious tiger or two. But such accidents never seemed to happen.

The bin cars full of canvas and smaller poles were unloaded early in the process. Then the center poles for the main tent, the menagerie tent, and the sideshow midway tents were dragged off one by one by the elephants which were fitted with wide leather harnesses.

The big top, the largest tent on the lot, was always the first to go up. By this time workmen had driven color-coded stakes indicating where the main poles were to be placed. One by one the poles were dragged to those locations with their heavy bottom ends at the precisely designated spot and their tips along the same axis.

Then large metal rings with ropes attached were slipped over each end of the poles. Teams of elephants pulled the ropes until pole by pole the framework for a tent arose. As the poles reached a vertical position, guy ropes were secured to hold them in place and large sheets of canvas were laid out on the ground around the poles.

Dozens of workmen laced the pieces together until the canvas lay like a giant covering over what would soon be the floor of the tent. Other workmen, swinging large sledge hammers never missing the stake heads, were busy systematically driving hundreds of stakes into place around the perimeter of the canvas so that it might be lashed down firmly once in place.

Finally the exciting moment came. Elephants were hitched to lines attached to the top of the poles where they ran through pulleys and then back down to the metal rings that now lay on the ground around the base of the poles. Now, as a cry of command was yelled by the tent crew chief, the mahouts urged the elephants outward in every direction like rays extending from each pole.

Ponderously and slowly but steadily and smoothly, the elephants moved outward and the canvas began to rise, lifted upward around the poles by the rings, rising higher and higher. I can remember clapping my hands and cheering with the gathered crowd of onlookers as the tent grew and took form.

At a second command the elephants stopped and dozens of workmen, assisted by local boys working for the price of a ticket, grabbed lines hanging from the edges of the canvas. Others slipped shorter poles into holes along the lower edges of the canvas and as the lines were tied down the main tent structure was up and secure.

Once the big top was up, the tent crew hurried away to raise more tents. And then a parade of what looked like chaos but actually was a carefully orchestrated performance began.

Wagon after wagon of equipment was towed into the tent. Giant performing rings were set up; seats were put together from a thousand separate pieces; banks of lights and safety nets and harnesses for the trapeze and tightwire performers were assembled and raised to their proper places in the top of the tent. Numerous wagons and dozens of workmen came and went from every direction, dropping off and picking up loads of materials, equipment, and supplies.

Load after load of clean white pine shavings were strewn on the hippodrome track around the inside of the tent where the audience would sit. Then, just when it seemed we would be able to stay and watch the performance itself, the sides of the tent were closed with long bands of canvas walls laced to the tent edge above and staked to the ground below. Any further look was going to require a ticket.

At this point we would usually climb down off our boxcar perch and follow the workmen as they raised other nearby tents. We were careful not to be stepped on by working animals or to step in the steaming reminders left behind by these same beasts.

Sometimes we would try to find the great piles of hay where the elephants were fed. The elephants, like the workers, ate in shifts so that work might continue at a steady pace. We would find a convenient place to sit, usually on a bale of hay out of the way, and watch the giant beasts use their trunks to stuff their mouths with hay. At the same time workers would be using hoses attached to a tank wagon to wash them down, and it was obvious that breakfast and a shower at the same time was an elephant's delight.

Often the grounds were situated so that city water could be directly provided through hoses attached to fire hydrants. But on occasion it was necessary to bring the water to the grounds in railroad cars. Sometimes tankcars were used but often an engine tender, unattached from its own engine but filled to the top with water, was hauled in to fill the water wagons.

The process was always a sloppy one and the place got muddier and muddier as water was spilled and mixed with the churned up dusty earth. I can remember stepping in this mud and going in over my high-top shoes much to the dismay of my stepfather. I also remember that getting dirty while watching the circus unload was so routine that we always had to make a quick trip home for a bath before returning for the afternoon performance.

Though I was irresistibly drawn to all the many species of circus animals it was always the elephants that fascinated me. Perhaps it was because many of the animals I saw in other local exhibits such as the town's small zoo or the sportsman's show were similar to those carried by the circus. But the elephants were something totally different.

Some of the things I remember about them are peculiar indeed. I clearly recall listening to the rumbling of their digestive systems as they stood in their stalls. As I fed them peanuts I noticed the inside of the tip of their trunk was pink rimmed with black with a mottling of black dots scattered throughout the pink. I also remember the extraordinary length of the elephants' eyelashes and the small wisp of hair at the end of their long tail. And their skin had deep wrinkles or crevices and was covered with a thin coating of long black hairs.

With such distinctive recollections it came as no surprise to me that some 20-plus years later when I took my oldest son to his first circus, a small single-tent show, he returned home bursting to tell his mother of his experience. Foremost in his mind and what he wanted to share first was the size of the elephants' droppings and the fact that one of the show's three pachyderms had obliged him by leaving a pile of fresh droppings in the straw immediately in front of our seats where they could be observed and studied for most of the afternoon.

There are many other circus experiences that cannot be duplicated today. One is the circus parade. A sampling of the glitter and excitement was walked through the downtown streets complete with some animals in wagon cages, the circus band, and lots of painted clowns laughing and tumbling and throwing pieces of saltwater taffy to the crowd. It was always a conflict whether to leave the spectacle of the assembling circus at the grounds in order to watch the parade. Some years we stayed. Others we went. In each case I always worried that we had made the wrong choice and wondered what I was missing.

The glamour of the circus and its connection with the railroad was not lost on me. I knew that the circus needed and used the railroad. Not understanding how railroad men's assignments were made I eagerly antic-ipated each year that my stepfather might get a call from the dispatcher to work the circus train. Such an event would, in my eyes, have given me about as much peer status as a kid could handle. Unfortunately it never happened, and I realize now that Dad knew it wouldn't but didn't want to spoil the fun of my anticipation.

The thrill of the circus did not depart with the show. If Dad's work schedule permitted, we would go back to the circus grounds the day after the show and walk over the ground where the tracks of wood shavings and scattered debris clearly outlined where various tents had stood. Once in a great while we would find a broken trinket discarded by a vendor, but these finds were rare because a hundred other kids were also scouring the grounds.

The second activity was more personal and longer lasting. Before I got my first bike I had an extra large, black-and-red tricycle, selected to match my lengthening legs. I used to tie my wagon on behind, and ride around the block on the sidewalk, which had become my personal railroad track. I had established a number of different station and siding sites marked by a particular bush, driveway, or telephone pole. I would trace the route of my private version of Dad's train route for hours, meeting other trains, loading and unloading passengers, and picking up and delivering mail and baggage.

This was always fun, but for several weeks after circus time it took on additional excitement. Now I was no ordinary train: I was a circus train. Perhaps even *the* circus train! And my wagon was now loaded with sticks and pieces of rope and cloth, stand-ins for poles and rigging and tent canvas, and I personally brought the circus to each and every whistle-stop on my circular route through the neighborhood.

As I grew up I was able to verbalize my thrill of the circus and to thank my parents for introducing me to it. I don't believe I ever did tell them about my private, tricycle-powered railroad, but I think they may have guessed, because one year Dad brought home some cardboard circus posters and suggested I could tie them on my wagon.

I used those posters over and over until they simply fell to pieces. I wish one had been saved. I would frame it and hang it on my wall in a prominent place. Looking at it daily would give me the same thrill someone else might get from looking at a treasured original Picasso knowing that they had gathered sunflowers from that same field even at the moment the artist was preserving the scene on canvas. Some experiences are as priceless as a precious masterpiece. ⌐

8
NOTHING COULD BE FINER

☞ All my life I have loved sweet corn. As I've grown older I have become more demanding as to its quality, but not so when I was a young boy. I can remember visiting a relative's Missouri farm and persuading the lady there to boil up some feed corn ears for me. She obliged, and much to the amusement of the adults I slathered the ears with butter and salt and ate away, naive but happy.

I suppose that corn was tough and probably relatively tasteless by normal standards. But to me it was a treat. And to look out the window at over fifty acres of such corn standing in the fields next to that farmhouse suggested to a small boy from the city a storehouse of culinary riches that emulated heaven.

If anything could improve the delightful taste and satisfying crunch of a fine ear of corn it could only be to eat it in a very special place. I can recall several instances when what might otherwise be considered a rather mundane menu stands out in memory as much as any eight-course, five-star repast: a lunch of peanut butter sandwiches, slightly smashed plums, and a not very high-class bottle of red wine consumed while perched high on a rocky crag of Poke-O-Moonshine Mountain in the Adirondacks; chunks of dry roll, warm cheese, and grapes munched on a windswept mound of prairie grass beside a road in South Dakota; and thinly meated tiny crab legs boiled in an old bucket on a gas burner on the stern boards of a lobster fisherman's boat, enjoyed while laying-to, rocking in the swell off Jonesport, Maine.

My mother forbade me to order sweet corn on the diner of the Milwaukee Olympian—a source of major frustration and disappointment to me when I was young. To really understand my mother's stance, today's traveler would need to know what the Olympian's diner was like in contrast to plastic-tray and paper-cup Amtrak railroad food.

The dining car was specially built to run with a softer yet more stable ride with less sway than other passenger cars in order to make eating more comfortable and serving less sloppy. It was also a place of elegance; the showpiece car of any deluxe train of the time. The narrow hallway along one side of the car through which you entered the diner had highly burnished wood-paneled walls from floor to ceiling on one side and wide windows on the other. There were stainless steel handles across the window so one might use them for balance if necessary and not be tossed from side to side while negotiating this passageway.

If the car was busy, as it often was, you might spend ten or fifteen minutes in this hallway, waiting to be beckoned to the small hutchlike table where the impressive dining car steward waited.

The steward was the maître d' of the dining car. In his traditional railroad uniform of dark blue or black, with a sparkling white shirt and conservative tie, he would welcome and seat you, greeting you as though you were a long-lost friend. Friendliness was his hallmark and this, coupled with his obvious authority, made him a mysterious though warm and friendly figure in my eyes. Stewards didn't wear caps as did the conductor and the brakeman, so you could see their hair. My memory is that all stewards had wavy gray hair, blue eyes, and smiling faces, but I suppose that might not really be so.

As you stepped out of the hallway into the dining salon, it was impossible not to be impressed with the grandeur of the car. The long row of decorative lights above the wide aisles immediately caught the eye. Before the more simplistic art deco designs became popular, the chandeliers were ornate and fancy, a marked contrast with the utilitarian lights in other cars. Paradoxically, the railroads were quick to boast when they added electric lighting, yet designers were told to make the electric chandeliers look as though they held candles or gas flames. The windows were large, and even the tables and chairs were impressive. White linen covered each table with its sprig of greenery and a fresh flower, and the chairs were heavy and upholstered.

Though seating arrangements varied somewhat, it was common to have tables for four on one side of the car and tables for two on the other. Tables were always formally set and as the meal progressed, fresh linen was used whenever soiling occurred. If the linen was not soiled too badly, fresh linen was simply laid on top of the old. As a result, if you ate late in a dining session, you would often find the tabletop luxuriously soft with several layers of heavy linens.

The setting was glamorous. China was always preset with a full place serving for each person, which later would be whisked away if not

Today's diners do not match the luxury or the menu of the Milwaukee's Olympian Hiawatha of the late 1940s. But even those luxurious fittings did not match the polished mahogany and linen tablecloths in the cars they replaced in 1946. Courtesy of the Milwaukee Road, S. Johnson Collection

needed. The pattern was created for each train. Some sets were rimmed in soft green edged with stripes of gold, others were a soft rose pink with graceful birds winging around the edge or across the center. Some trains featured the famous Milwaukee flying winged Hiawatha or the tilted red rectangle logo in the center.

Silverware was plain but very heavy and was typically engraved with a logo or the Road's name. Table service included silver-plated sugar and cream sets and salt and pepper shakers. Glasses were especially heavy with weighted bottoms for stability and during some periods had the Milwaukee logo engraved on their sides. Coffee, tea, and syrup were served in a heavy, wide-bottomed silver-plated container, fashioned in a design of style and grace.

It was to such a setting that my mother and I would come for dinner or perhaps an occasional breakfast. Lunch was handled with cheaper snacks or lunches brought from home or purchased in a depot beanery.

Though my mother's background was economically humble, graceful living and personal social style had been well taught in her home and she intended to pass it on to me. I was well drilled in a long list of tableside faux pas to avoid. Please and thank you were standard parts of my vocabulary and I was urged to use them regularly, but especially in social situations. I very early learned where one's napkin went while eating and which fork or spoon to use. As a consequence, my manners were reasonably good for a young boy—at least in intent. Saying "Excuse me" when I dropped my fork full of mashed potatoes and gravy on the floor evidenced good training, but it did not satisfy my mother's goal of being quietly unobtrusive.

Among other lessons in my litany of table manners I had been specifically instructed on how to graciously eat a buttered ear of corn. The rules were relatively simple and easy to understand: Use only one hand, never two; take only one or two bites at a time and always in a row along the ear (like a typewriter, not round and round the ear like unwinding string from a ball); and wipe your mouth with a small corner of the napkin after each bite, putting the ear on the plate while doing so. Showing finesse in applying the rules was something else. For some reason, whenever we entered this car of quiet luxury and elegance the one thing I wanted to eat more than anything else was a hot buttered ear of corn.

Mother allowed me to order corn on a diner only once. It was a total disaster. The problems started when the smiling waiter laid out our order. The corn sat on its own special small oblong silver dish to one side, hot and steaming. Obviously one had to eat it very carefully or wait for the corn to cool. I chose to combine the two approaches, waiting a short time and trying to handle the corn with care while still quite hot. Mother did not notice this risk-taking decision.

My initial problem followed immediately. Hot corn, rolling slightly back and forth in harmony with the swaying of the car, does not retain butter well. I had applied the butter correctly with my knife, buttering only two or three rows of kernels at a time as I had been taught, but the butter did not stay put. It slipped down each side and ran in beautiful golden streams of sweetness onto the plate below. Giving up, I decided I would eat it, partially buttered.

At this juncture a second difficulty arose. The ear had tiny silver handles stuck in each end. I had never seen these before but I quickly ascertained their use. I had been taught to use only one hand at a time to hold an ear. Here were two handles challenging me to use both hands. I figured that the railroad had a corn eating strategy different than my mother's, but I didn't know which form of etiquette to use.

I picked up the ear using only one hand, leaning carefully forward over my plate as I anticipated the first sweet bite. Butter ran down the ear and onto the table linen as the corn tipped to one side, deflected by the pressure of the bite. I could not grip the little silver handle tightly enough to keep the ear horizontal. I quickly recovered and returned the ear to the plate. Mother was still oblivious to the catastrophe developing beside her. Analyzing the situation, I decided that it was worth breaking the rules to avoid the mess. I picked up the ear of corn again, carefully holding both little silver handles this time.

Another problem developed. No longer did the butter drip on the table, it ran down my chin and onto my shirt front. I immediately let loose of one handle and grabbed for my napkin, managing to staunch the flow and reduce the rivulets on my shirt to yellow stains. However, in fending off this disaster I had lowered the ear while holding it to one side (on the side away from my mother, of course) and in so doing, I moved it slightly into the aisle space. The steward, moving down the aisle leading other diners to their table, brushed against it.

He didn't notice this but the people following him did because his nudge removed the corn from the handle and it was rolling down the aisle. The first in line, a woman in a dress, stepped back quickly to avoid the tumbling missile. The man behind her did not see her stop and was knocked back a step when she bumped into him. Temporarily losing his balance, he put out a hand to steady himself, unfortunately he put his hand into another diner's full plate of food.

Somewhere during the melee, the ear of corn rolled under a table and disappeared. The outcome of the situation wasn't exactly bedlam but it was pretty chaotic, causing several people to become involved for a moment. Attentive waiters and a concerned but ever-confident steward quickly calmed things down. Mother, though aware of the excitement, still hadn't recognized my role in it.

A few minutes later our waiter stopped at the table and smoothly asked, "Would the young gentleman like another ear of corn?" Shocked at the disaster I had created, I mumbled, "No, thank you," and burst into tears. Mother was distressed but did not fully understand. It was the steward, attempting to soothe the feelings of an embarrassed eight year old and defuse the situation, who explained to Mother.

"Do not be concerned, madame," he said. "The corn is difficult to eat under these circumstances and I am sure your son did not mean to drop his in the aisle."

Now Mother understood. She did not show anger nor did she punish or scold. She simply never permitted me to order corn in the diner again. Never!

Despite this experience I remember eating in the diner with great fondness, I recall with delight the close companionship with my parents there, experiencing a special occasion together. Whenever I think about the pleasure of eating on the diner, I picture myself there with one of my parents enjoying a fine meal. It is a comfortable, relaxed, and happy memory.

I ate in the diner more often with Mother than Dad, he had his own distinctive peculiarities about ordering in the diner as I found out on a trip from Milwaukee to Spokane during my freshman year of college. I met Dad in Milwaukee as he headed back from a visit with his siblings in Wisconsin and we caught the Olympian home. Dad was on vacation and I looked forward to the ride on this impressive luxury train, now a sleek streamliner, and to the companionship with him, some of which I presumed we would share in the diner.

Our train left in the late evening, so our first meal aboard was to be breakfast, but I overslept, so that meal was eaten alone. Lunch was at our seat in the tourist sleeper because true to family tradition he had brought a lunch. That was alright with me as the Wisconsin cheese and sausages he brought made a better lunch than those I had been used to taking with us on the train anyway.

Dinnertime arrived and we answered the first call, following closely behind the white-coated dining car worker who traversed the train gently tapping his three-noted chime and announcing, "First call for dinner. The dining car is to the rear."

We were promptly seated by a steward who obviously knew my stepfather well, calling him by his railroad nickname, Feebee. Laying out menus he welcomed us, chatted informally with Dad a couple of minutes, and then said, "I've never had a chance to serve you, Feebee. This meal is on the Milwaukee Road and me."

I was elated. My family's frugality had taught me to always look for the Chef's Special or some similarly reduced item on the menu. It was apt to be meat loaf instead of roast beef or breaded chicken steak instead of T-bone. Sometimes the menu simply read, "Meat, fish, or egg entrée of the chef's choice. Inquire of the steward." Such mystery entrées did not, in my opinion, hold much hope of a very sumptuous surprise. And, there was another shortcoming. The Specials came with a preselected simple dessert like vanilla ice cream and a cookie instead of a choice of pie à la mode or a sundae. I always enjoyed my food, but still envied others' meals, which obviously came from the higher-priced side of the menu. Higher prices in those days meant a dollar and a quarter for a full four-course meal complete with beverage. Given my father's salary, that amounted to a significant splurge for dinner.

Now, I ignored anything in the menu close to a Special and turned to the page where à la carte listings included oyster stew, boiled fresh spareribs with escalloped potatoes, steak, and similarly luscious items.

Dad picked up both meal order cards and prepared to write out our order.

"Do you want meat or fish? he inquired.

"Steak. With baked potatoes and asparagus and selected relishes and potage Parmentier and chocolate sundae and iced tea," I eagerly replied. I didn't even know what potage Parmentier was but was willing to find out at the railroad's expense.

"I think the special only offers scrambled eggs and chipped beef or broiled Great Lakes whitefish with new potatoes," he replied, glancing again at the menu to make sure. "Iced tea is available all right, but no sundae. Vanilla or chocolate pudding cup, though," he added.

FOR VICTORY
BUY
UNITED
STATES
WAR
BONDS
AND
STAMPS

WAR
CONSE
Please write
pay only on
which you
Employees

Good Morning

CLUB BREAKFAST

BREAKFAST NUMBER ONE — SIXTY-FIVE CENTS

Choice of Juice - OR - Fruit and Cereal

Rolls, Toast or Muffins

Coffee   Tea   Milk

BREAKFAST NUMBER TWO — EIGHTY-FIVE CENTS

Choice of Juice - OR - Fruit - OR - Cereal and

Choice of

Filet of Fresh Fish, Tartar Sauce

*Emince of Chicken, Green Peppers

*Bacon or Ham and Two Eggs

Rolls   Toast   Muffins

Coffee   Tea   Milk

*Due to conditions beyond our control, it is sometimes necessary to make a substitution

FRUITS AND JUICE

Tomato Juice   Grapefruit Juice   Orange Juice   Vegetable Juice

Half Grapefruit   Baked Apple with Cream

Jumbo Prunes   Lemon with Water   Sliced Orange

CEREALS WITH CREAM

Quaker Oats   Bran Flakes   Cream of Wheat

Shredded Wheat   Rice Krispies   Corn Flakes

Grape-Nuts   Shredded Ralston

Form 3115 L 84
2

*An Olympian luncheon menu from about 1945. Though I longed to try those items on
the right side, we always selected the less expensive items from the left side of the menu.
S. Johnson Collection*

ING
ASE

desired;
check on
order.
orders

IS SOMEONE WAITING

For Your Seat?

BREAKFAST A LA CARTE

FRUITS AND JUICE

Vegetable Juice, 25	Grapefruit Juice, 25
Sauerkraut Juice, 25	Tomato Juice, 25
Orange Juice, 25	Orange Juice, Double, 35
Half Grapefruit, 25	Baked Apple with Cream, 25
Sliced Orange, 15; Two, 25	Jumbo Prunes, 25
Lemon with Water, 10	Individual Strained Honey, 15

CEREALS
All Cereals with Cream, 30

Quaker Oats	Shredded Wheat	Cream of Wheat
Corn Flakes	Wheaties	Bran Flakes
Shredded Ralston	Rice Krispies	Grape-Nuts

FISH
Filet of Fresh Fish, Tartar Sauce 50

EGGS — OMELETS
Boiled, Fried or Scrambled, 30

Omelet, Plain, 35   Poached on Toast, 40

BREAD, TOAST, ROLLS

Assorted Bread, 15	Muffins, 15	Dry Toast, 15	Rolls, 15
Milk Toast, 30	Cream Toast, 45		Ry-Krisp, 15

BEVERAGES

Coffee, 15	Tea, 20	Milk, 15	Chocolate, 20

All prices listed are our ceiling prices or below. By Office of Price Administration regulation, our ceilings are our highest prices from February 1, 1943, to April 10, 1943.

Records of these prices are available for your inspection at Dining Car Headquarters 2801 West Grand Avenue, Chicago, Illinois.

Service rendered outside of Dining Car Twenty-five Cents Extra Per Person
Steward will furnish an envelope for patron desiring to mail this menu

B. J. SCHILLING, Superintendent Dining Cars

Suggestions for the betterment of the service are invited

F. N. HICKS, Passenger Traffic Manager, Chicago, Illinois

"But the steward said—" I protested.

"I heard him," Dad said. "But one should never pretend to be something he is not. We always eat the Special and there's no reason to change."

"But he's paying," I cried.

"I know. But we shouldn't take advantage of his generosity. It was nice of him to offer to pick up the check and we'll let him do that and thank him for it. But what we eat will be our typical meal, not something extravagant just because someone else is paying for it," he said calmly but firmly.

I knew better than to argue. My one and only opportunity for eating like a first-class passenger on the Olympian fled with the steward's departure from our table. I was very disappointed, angry even, and found the whole affair a disappointment, which annoyed me the rest of the trip.

I suppose Dad perceived my pique, but he never said so. It was several years later before I understood the importance to him of not only his integrity but also the need to be consistent in such integrity.

I had lost a steak but learned a lesson. Man does not, even on a diner, live by bread alone—unless it is included in the Chef's Special. ◄

9
TALES ALONG THE
RIGHT-OF-WAY

Sometimes after midnight, when the passengers were few and the freight stops were far between, there was time for Dad to sit with me in the coach where the lights had been dimmed so passengers could sleep. We would sit there side by side, and often Dad would tell me stories. I never asked directly for a story, but I certainly knew how to get him started on one and looked forward to his tales—not only the new ones but also the retelling of those I had heard many times before.

"I wonder if . . . ," I would offer in an inquiring voice, broaching a question about a potential topic such as train wrecks or homesteaders or the building of the railroad.

"Well, let me tell you about that," he would say, and the story-telling session was under way.

Most of the yarns he told were true. Many were about his own experiences or about things he had heard firsthand from others who had been involved themselves. A few of the tales were tall and not meant to be taken literally. But he never specifically labeled a story as fact or fiction. I don't remember ever hearing him say, "Now this is true" or "I don't think this really happened, though it's a good story."

But I could usually tell by the cues he gave me. Sometimes I would question him, "Really?" His laugh in response would give him away if he was relating a myth, though he would go on with the story just the same. If the episode he was describing was true, he didn't have to say "Of course" to my questioning. Instead, he gave a shrug of his shoulders with his head leaning slightly to one side, which immediately gave his words total credibility.

A few of his yarns were of his early years as a young trainman and brakeman near Beloit, Wisconsin, before he came west. I must have urged him a dozen times or more to tell me the story about his little finger, scarred and permanently bent because he had carelessly handled an old-style ring-and-pin coupler on a rainy night outside Milwaukee during his first months of railroading. As he told the story I would reach out and touch his finger with mine. The scar was shiny and hard like a polished callus, and the joint, bent at an angle, was stiff.

Many of the stories, particularly the true ones, were about railroading, of course. Some were funny, and a few scary or sad. Passing through a particular segment of the right-of-way would prompt him to remember some of the things that happened there.

Once he joked about how hard it was to restart a long freight train headed upgrade at Adair. It had stopped in a sleeting rain, which made the tracks slippery.

"The engines dumped sand on the rails," he said. "Sometimes so much sand that we would have to refill the hoppers from extra bags carried on the train or pick up some more at the next section gang stop. Once in a while we would even back down the grade a ways to get the train straightened out or the engine on dry rails in a tunnel where the traction was better."

"Did you always get started without calling for help?"

"Oh, yes. But, some nights the weather was so bad—like tonight," he said dramatically while pretending to look out the window, shaking his head in mock dismay. "On that kind of night—this kind of night—we might have to get everyone off the train to push."

"Really?" I readily took the bait when I was small.

"Can you imagine how hard it is to push a train?" he asked, ignoring my query.

Then, noticing where we were, he paused and changed the focus of his story.

"After the big fire in 1910, a lot of the trees were gone and the mud and snow slid down the mountainside more often than before. One of those nights when it had been both snowing and raining, a big slide came down right here at Adair, just about where we are now. The section gang crew were in the section houses alongside the track, right next to the long slope leading down to Loop Creek."

"Were you there?"

"No, I was on a run east of here that night, but I heard about it right away. Word got up and down the line pretty fast and the tracks were blocked."

"The men must have been scared," I said.

"They probably didn't have time to be scared," he said after a moment's hesitation. "Three, or perhaps it was four, I don't recall exactly, were killed in the slide."

"Wow," I exclaimed, impressed with the story and feeling a little uneasy about where we were.

Not all the railroader's battles with the weather were as solemn as the Adair episode. One of his stories was particularly meaningful to me, not only because of what happened to him, but because it directly affected me in a manner a child doesn't forget.

The winter of 1933 was unusually unkind to the Bitterroots. Early heavy snows, then unseasonably warm winds and rain sent water in torrents down every mountainside watercourse, large and small. Rivers rose rapidly, until they were bank-top high and then continued to rise some more. Railroads, which often follow the rivers through rough terrain, were hard hit. On the eastern slopes of the Bitterroots the Milwaukee ran along one side of the St. Regis River, with the Northern Pacific tracks on the opposite bank. Being slightly lower in elevation, the Northern Pacific was the first to shut down operations as the river overflowed and washed out hundreds of feet of NP roadbed.

The Milwaukee continued to run its trains for a day or so longer, slowing with caution through places where the railbed might have softened. Then, with the westbound Olympian only a few miles away from where the climbing grade would begin to take the right-of-way, well above the reach of the river, the fifteen-car passenger train was temporarily halted at the substation of Drexel.

Drexel was located on a bank that normally rose 10 to 15 feet above the river. This day, however, the river was almost even with the top of the bank, and there was considerable concern for potential disaster . With the NP closed down it looked like the same was in store for the Milwaukee. The crew was anxious to be on the move, to get away from the danger of the rising river. Dad was conductor on that Olympian.

"We had just been cleared to move on to Haugan and Saltese when telegraphed orders arrived countermanding that and telling us not to proceed west of Drexel. A major slide had come down ahead of us and there was no way to get through," Dad told me, pointing out the locations of the stations on a map in a timetable.

"I thought it best to back up to St. Regis where we could transfer the passengers out to highway transportation since the NP wasn't running either. But just when we were ready to do that, word came through from the dispatcher's office that track walkers had reported that other slides seemed imminent behind us as well as in front of us and that the trackbed

Pre-Christmas floods in 1933 devastated the railroads. My father shot this picture from near where he was temporarily marooned by high waters both in front and back of his train. Note the mainline rails curving into the river (upper left edge of photo). S. Johnson Collection

looked too soft to hold the train in other places. We were marooned for sure."

I remembered that day because we were in Spokane, our tree and holiday decorations were up and we were getting ready for Christmas, happy that Dad was due home the day before Christmas. We knew the weather was bad in the mountains but a call from the local dispatcher's office advised us of the Olympian's specific problem and the probability of considerable delay.

"He's in no danger at Drexel," the dispatcher told Mother, and we'll keep you posted about the progress of the train. But I wouldn't count on him being home for Christmas," was the disappointing message. At Drexel, Dad was having problems of his own.

"We were concentrating on keeping the boiler in the engine going so we would have heat for the train. Other than being delayed and nervous about the flooding, the passengers were all right. They were being fed reasonably well and at the railroad's expense. There seemed to be sufficient food in the diner and in stores at Drexel to take care of that problem," he

Northern Pacific tracks, across the St. Regis River from the Milwaukee right-of-way,
were wiped out by the 1933 flood and were never rebuilt. The NP chose to buy running
rights over a stretch of Milwaukee track instead.
S. Johnson Collection

went on with the story. "But one of the baggagemen came back and asked
me to step outside in the vestibule where he could speak to me in private.
There he told me the bad news."

"We've got a body, a dead man, on board," he explained. "A corpse in a
casket, and it's pretty warm up there for it to keep good."

Dad chuckled when he told this part. He explained how ordinarily
they might have just set the casket outside in the cold, but the weather had
warmed so much that it was too warm outside, too.

"We had to do something," Dad explained. "I finally decided we
would just carry the casket up the side of the mountain above the high
water. Then we'd walk the mountainside, returning to the track where a

gas speeder car could come to carry the body on into St. Regis. The trouble was, I didn't have a big enough train crew to manage the portage. So I just went up and down the coach aisles recruiting every strong-looking man we could find. I got over a dozen volunteers and we dressed up warm and got to work."

Leaving just enough train crew behind to manage the train and its passengers, Dad and the others turned into a team of slipping and sliding pallbearers over almost a mile of mountainside until they reached a spot where a speeder could take on the load. Some of the bearers waited there for a ride into St. Regis while others went back to the train with the crew. Eventually, many of the passengers chose to hike out via the same route, but Dad and his crew stayed with the train for six long days.

The dispatcher who phoned us at home had been right. Dad didn't make it home for Christmas. In fact, he was exactly one week late, and that year we celebrated Christmas and New Year's on the same day. It was a long week for a five-year-old.

Some of the experiences he told me about were very funny, although they might well have turned into tragedies instead. Floods were a common experience along the St. Joe River. One time Dad's train was between Avery and St. Maries heading west. The river had been rising, and orders had warned of the need to be alert for rising waters. Dad told me the story early one morning as we ran over exactly the same stretch of track he was describing in his story.

"We stopped without warning in between stations," he told me. "I knew something was wrong and got off and hurried up to the head end. I could see then why we weren't proceeding. The water was lapping at the ends of the ties."

"I guess we'd better back her into Avery," the engineer announced, leaning out his cab.

"I was just about to tell him he could start backing as soon as I could get someone on the rear end to look out for problems in that direction, but when I turned to head back I saw the trainman had already dropped off the rear end when we stopped—to protect us from that direction, just as he was supposed to do—and he was now standing back there waving a fusee quickly back and forth. (A fusee is a flare with a nail in it so it can be lit and stuck into the earth as a warning signal. All trainmen carried a canvas bag of emergency tools including fusees.) Now that red light swinging back and forth means just one thing to a train man—Stop! So I told the engineer to sit tight for a minute and headed back to find out what was happening."

"What did you find?" I asked just as Ross, Dad's brakeman, sat down beside us, listening to the story, too.

"Well, the trainman came forward as fast as I went back and when we met he told me the river was rising behind us and had completely covered the tracks."

"What did you do?"

"Ross and I went back up to the engine and we talked it over with the engine crew."

"'We sure as hell don't want to sit here either,'" the engineer told me. "'This fill's so soft that if the river rises much more we're likely to roll over on our side.'"

"'What about ahead?'" I asked him.

"'It's about the same, no worse I guess, but the river sure ain't going down any!'"

Dad said they decided to go ahead anyway; it wasn't a comfortable option but the only one they had. They knew that a change in terrain about two miles ahead would put them on safer ground. He described how he and Ross cut long poles from alders growing by the side of the tracks, using an ax from the emergency tool kit on the engine. With Dad on one side and Ross on the other, they knelt down on the step on the side of the engine's pilot. As the engineer eased the throttle open, they poked the sticks into the ballast ahead of them to make sure it was still firm and that the rails, which were now covered with water, were still there.

"My arms got so tired I didn't think I could lift them," Dad laughed.

"Longest two miles in the world," Ross put in. "I wanted to walk ahead of the train, but your dad wouldn't let me," he added.

"You could have tripped on a submerged tie you couldn't see and broken your leg. I would have had more explaining to do to the railroad than any man would want. Besides, if something had happened to you I'd have had to wade through that cold dirty water to help you."

As we passed the spot, they pointed out where they had stopped on higher and firmer ground and told about how the track behind them had indeed washed out later that same day.

"The superintendent was so excited he didn't know whether to give us a medal for saving the train or fire us both for taking the risk of pulling her over that soft roadbed," Ross said.

"That's about right," Dad agreed. "But if it rains today, you find someone else to pole this big gondola along. I'm too old now," he laughed.

One of the impressive things about having the conductor as a father was knowing the authority he had. It was he who said when the train should stop or go. He assigned tasks to the other crew, he was in charge and I reveled vicariously in his power, making far more of it than he did. I knew as well that in the locked wooden box in the baggage car, rolled up in a leather belt full of cartridges, was a loaded .38 Smith & Wesson police special. The trains carried mail under contract to the federal government and this automatically made the conductor a representative of the government, responsible for protecting the mail. Regulations required that the weapon be available to the conductor if needed. It went along on every run he made, but to the best of my knowledge it never came out of the trunk let alone out of its holster.

It didn't matter to me as a young boy that train holdups were pretty much a thing of the past. I still had visions of desperadoes, probably on horseback, dragging logs onto the rails and setting them afire in order to stop the train to rob it of freight and mail. Every time I went along I asked to see the revolver. Dad would open the trunk and let me look in to see it but did not ever permit me to touch it. I was sure Dad was ready to use the gun if necessary, but I am certain he never would have considered it except as a very last resort, and perhaps not then. He hated violence and anything connected with it.

This is not to say that he was soft or easily dissuaded from supporting what was right. My stepfather was a strong and capable man who displayed values he held very strongly. For example, children—particularly young children—could do no wrong in his eyes. As a consequence he conceived of no more vile sin or wrongful behavior than to mistreat a child. He was often stern with me, and sometimes laid down rules or made judgments I thought too severe, but I never felt his hand in anger. I was not surprised, therefore, on one particular trip, at his reaction when a man and a woman began arguing toward the rear of our coach car. Their loud voices, particularly the man's, were easily heard and bothersome to other passengers, some of whom were trying to sleep. A young child with them whimpered but did not cry.

Dad moved back to them quickly, but quietly, and I could see he was telling them to keep it down. They obeyed his directions for a few minutes and then the man started to yell again. Once more Dad moved back to the scene, repeating his cautions to be quiet. Over a period of about an hour he made three more trips, with about the same results.

Later I noticed that he was keeping the arguing couple in view, glancing their way every few minutes. They had lowered the volume of their argument at least to the point where we couldn't hear them from where we were, but it was still going on. All of a sudden, with no warning, Dad was moving toward them again. This time he grabbed the man by the arm, jerked him to his feet, and before the man could protest, Dad had his arm up behind his back and was leading him forward. The two of them disappeared into the vestibule leading to the baggage car. I really wanted to follow to see what was happening but knew better than to stick my nose where it didn't belong.

A few minutes later the train slowed, then stopped. The sky was just beginning to lighten and I could see that we were at some sort of isolated, non-agency stop with only a locked tool shed beside the track. As I watched from the window, Dad and the man descended from the train, Dad leading him by the arm over to the shed. There Dad pushed him to a sitting position on an old nail keg. Shaking his finger in the man's face, Dad gave the engineer the highball and the train started to move even before Dad moved to the steps. With a couple of quick steps he reached the train and swung aboard and once inside closed up the hinged floor and door. I could hear it bang shut as I watched the man stare at us from his nail-keg seat, the train moving away, leaving him alone and sitting on a very uncomfortable nail keg.

Dad came back and sat down. The brakeman walked by and quietly said something to the woman left behind. Dad picked up his paperwork and started up where he had left off. I could stand the suspense no longer.

"What happened?" I asked.

"I gave him some time to cool off," Dad replied. "There'll be another train or someone with a speeder car along in a few hours. He probably won't be in a better mood by then, but at least he won't have anyone to hit."

"Did he hit her?" I was disappointed I had missed the real excitement. "No."

"But you said—" I began.

"He hit the little boy. Twice. Now read your book," he said somewhat gruffly and returned to his work. I found his anger a little frightening since it was so unusual, but I was very proud of him.

All kinds of people rode the train. In those days it was a mainstream mode of transportation and you could expect to find characters of every type aboard at some time or another. Dad had great patience with people, but there were several behaviors he would not tolerate aboard his train. These included drunkenness, any kind of assault on another passenger, or loud annoying behavior. He handled problems quietly and with tact, but he handled them firmly and well.

When I was a teenager, Mother told me a story that he probably would never have shared with me. I never told him that I knew about the incident.

"You should never question anyone's honesty unless you are absolutely 100% sure they have erred," Mother announced to me one day when Dad was away on a turn.

"I don't think I do," I replied, puzzled at her raising the topic.

"Well, don't ever do it. Never! It can hurt someone very deeply. Someone questioned your stepfather's honesty and he's had a difficult time dealing with it. He's the most honest man you'll ever meet and he can't stand someone thinking otherwise."

"What happened?"

"A lady apparently lost her purse and thought it was left on the train. She went right back to where she had been sitting but it was gone. She asked Frank about it and he looked and so did the other train crew, but it wasn't found."

"And . . . ?"

"Well, when the purse wasn't found, she wrote to the railroad accusing Frank or someone in his crew of stealing it."

"What did the railroad do?"

"That's the good part of the story, though he was still very upset over the whole affair. The superintendent wrote back to the lady and sent us a copy of the letter. Here, let me read part of it to you, the important part.

> We are of course very sorry that your purse was lost and are hopeful you will find it somehow. However, we cannot take seriously your accusation that the conductor was involved in its theft. He has investigated the incident and advised us that there is no evidence of theft by any railroad employee. There is no reason to doubt his word. This man has worked for us for over 30 years and if ever there was an individual who could be completely trusted it would be him. I know him personally and

consider him to be one of the most honest and trustworthy individuals I have ever met.

It was easy for me to understand how Dad would have been upset. I was angry and hurt on his behalf. The railroad superintendent's evaluation of my stepfather was accurate. Dad wouldn't pick up a dime off the sidewalk without looking for the person who dropped it.

That honesty, which I greatly admired even as a youngster, didn't keep him from stringing me along on a tall tale, however. There were several he enjoyed telling and I often asked to hear them again and again, even after I realized that he was telling me something he didn't believe himself and didn't expect me to accept as true either.

"Tell me about the Frenchtown ghost," I would say.

He would laugh and agree. "In the early days of the railroad, there were not as many people living in the valleys and draws along the tracks. Going through some of those places was pretty lonely, especially at night. Just east of Frenchtown in the Clark Fork Valley, was a stretch none of us liked at night. I always worried about having some sort of problem along there and having to get out and walk along the tracks in the dark. It was a very lonely place in those days. But we really became worried when several different train crews began to report seeing the ghost of a woman sort of gliding across the valley as though she were trying to walk up to our tracks and climb aboard."

"Did you ever see her?" I would ask.

"I'm not quite sure—I think I may have once or twice. It was hard to tell what you are seeing when you were so afraid."

"Who was the ghost?" was the question I always asked at this juncture.

"That's a funny thing. Some people thought it was an Indian princess who had died of a broken heart at a sacred council grove nearby. Others thought it was Huson Annie, a very friendly lady who used to welcome tired and weary travelers to her cabin near Nine Mile." (I suspect the story had been cleaned up a bit here for my young ears.)

"Who did you think it was?"

"I kind of leaned toward Annie. The ghost-lady that folks were seeing didn't have the look of an Indian princess to me."

"I thought you said you weren't sure you saw her," I would interrupt.

"I said I wasn't sure," he would counter.

"Go on."

"Well, this ghost would float out of the door of an old log cabin across the valley and then drift across the river until she got right up next to our tracks. When the engine would come roaring past her, she would just disappear. Poof. Gone. Just like that!"

When I was little, I am sure I sat wide-eyed contemplating the fact that soon we would be going along that same eerie stretch of track. Years later, less naive, I would try to get Dad to level with me.

"Come on, tell me the truth. Where did this crazy ghost story start?" He would just laugh and shrug his shoulders.

I was almost out of high school before he finally told me the rest of the story.

"The truth of it is, I really did see the ghost. Not once, but several times."

"Come on. Don't give me more of that stuff," I retorted.

"No, I did. Honestly. I really did. I never believed the Indian princess or Huson Annie stories, but I saw the ghost. Not once, but several times. Many times."

"You're still putting me on."

"No, I'm not. I'm telling you the truth."

"All the truth?"

"Uh . . . maybe not everything."

"Tell me everything."

"Along that valley the Milwaukee and the Northern Pacific tracks run parallel, though often on opposite sides of the river. The valley was full of old snags, some left over from logging, others from forest fires. On a foggy morning the place sure looked eerie enough with all those weird shapes floating in the fog. When an NP train would come in the opposite direction at night, its headlight would backlight those snags. Then as the two trains moved along, one eastbound and the other westbound, the shadows moved and made it look as though the snags themselves were moving.

"In the early 1930s a rancher moved in there and pretty well cleared out most of that land, dragging stumps and snags out to be burned in a slash pile. He burned down the old cabin, too, but not before an engineer on one of our freights happened to notice that the headlight from an NP train would shine into the cabin through a back window and out the front door, changing position as the trains moved, just like the shadows of the snags. As he watched this, the ghost came out the door but disappeared immediately. Without the fog there was nothing for the light and shadow to play on and so, no ghost.

"He told everyone else about it and lots of us checked it out. He was exactly right. The rancher heard about it, and being a superstitious fellow, he decided to burn down the cabin anyway, 'just in case.' He did, and the ghost was laid to rest . . . except in the minds of curious little boys," he ended, laughing heartily.

I felt admitted to the halls of adulthood when he let me in on the secret. The tale was a good one and I enjoyed telling it to others, including dozens of young teenagers around campfires at youth camps where I worked as a young man.

The Frenchtown ghost has not been seen for many decades now. Still, it is not unpleasant to consider that the departed early residents of the valley might have wished to hang around in less corporeal form. It is a pretty spot, no longer lonely, the kind of place anyone would hate to leave while there are so many good stories yet to be told. ⌘

10
QUIET IS REQUESTED

☞ Mystic. Rushmore. Nisquall. Sitka. Mount Rainier. There was romance in the names of Milwaukee Road sleeping cars and adventure in riding them, especially when they were footnoted with such labels of distinction as "varnish" or "heavies," the pride of the railroad.

Taking the sleeper was more than romance. For a youngster, it was a special treat, a memorable luxurious alternative to riding coach. Boarding a sleeper of the westbound Olympian at the old Everett Street station in Milwaukee, Wisconsin, was an experience never to be forgotten. It arrived in the evening, late enough for the skies to be darkening. Above the train the only light was from smoke-stained bulbs high in the old open-air train shed over the curving tracks, which were at street level. The Olympian, freshly arrived from Chicago where it had started its 2,000 mile journey west an hour or two before, always sat on track No. 1. As we walked along the cars searching for the sleeper that was to be ours, the smell of oil-and-grease-covered steel stimulated the nostrils. Drifting, freshly condensed steam added a touch of moody suspense to the air. Workmen scurried about checking journal boxes, water levels, air hose connections, almost silently as what little noise they made was lost in the open space of the shed.

We found the vestibule window holding the sleeper identification card matching our ticket—car A, or sometimes a number, like 110 or 115, depending on the train. While boarding was always exciting in itself, starting off on a trip at night was especially so. Boarding our car in silence, the quiet was so noticeable it seemed mysterious. All outside noises were muffled, car lights were dimmed. Heavy privacy drapes separating the berths from the aisle created a long narrow passageway that made it seem as though we were walking through a dark green velvet tunnel. Every sleeping car had a reversible cardboard sign hanging at the end of the car. On one side it said, "Have you forgotten any belongings?" On the other side was printed, "Quiet is requested for the benefit of those who have retired." The quiet side was always face up when we boarded in Milwaukee, the directions from the porter spoken in a near whisper.

Separating the curtains of our berth, we found the headboard lights already on and blankets incitingly turned down. Puffed pillows with white, crisply starched pillowcases still carrying the smell of a warm iron were tucked up against the headboard. Every detail seemed to say, "Comfort!"

We hurried to retire and usually were tucked between the sheets before the gentle nudge that made the heavy curtains sway told us we were on our way. The first sensation of movement was as exciting as though the engineer were publicly announcing, "Let the westward adventure begin."

I fully appreciated the comfort and adventure of riding sleeper-class since I had seen my share of nights on coaches. Today's streamlined coaches routinely feature comfortably soft, wide reclining seats and in some cases even offer passengers pillows for sleeping beneath the indirect lighting that is dimmed for the night. When I was a boy the coaches were different. Most of the seats were nonreclining, semisoft bench seats with stiff unfriendly fabric, not unlike a Victorian horsehair upholstered couch. Individual seat lights were too dim for comfortable reading but too bright for sleeping and bothersome to your neighbor who was trying to sleep. And, coaches were busy and noisy. In those days, trains served many short-trip passengers as buses do today. On most trips, day or night, there were frequent stops for passengers. This meant a rather steady stream of people going by with lights being turned first on then off for the convenience of departing or arriving passengers, and the conductor or brakeman going up and down the aisles announcing each station stop several times. Sleep did not come easily and was not very restful when it did.

Passengers in coach and sleeper classes were not considered equal. The passengers were aware of this, but it was emphasized by the railroad itself by offering better amenities, special privileges, and, of course, higher fares for sleeping car accommodations.

Travel dollars were not plentiful in our family. Though we were lucky enough to have a small steady income throughout the depression years, we never had much extra money and frugality was both a virtue and a necessity. We could afford to ride the train because we traveled free on passes. Railroad lingo identified us as "deadheads," or nonfare-paying, pass-using passengers. With these passes we were able to make trips to visit relatives, which would have been impossible had we been required to buy a ticket. But passes typically carry some limitations. In those days they could be used only on certain trains (usually the less luxurious ones), and did not cover sleeping car fares. Even with the magic pass it took money to ride the sleeper.

Nevertheless, when we made overnight trips we almost always slept in a sleeper. Mother insisted that she was "much too old" and had "given too much to the railroad already" to sit up all night in a straight-backed coach seat. So, we usually paid the extra fare, but not without some careful planning to make it affordable.

First, there was the choice of type of sleeper. The Milwaukee Road, unlike most railroads, operated not only regular Pullman sleepers (called Standards and served by Pullman Company employees even when part of a Milwaukee train) but also its own sleeping cars, which it labeled as Tourist or Touraluxe cars.

I could never see much difference between the two except that Pullman passengers had access to the observation-lounge car and Tourist passengers did not. This distressed me greatly as a small boy and I learned to circumvent it later by sneaking through the Pullmans to the observation car without asking permission. That is, I did this when I was traveling with my mother alone. My stepfather, long a Milwaukee conductor, believed in following the rules on duty and off. I never tried it with him along and certainly never when he was the conductor on the train!

The layouts of the Standard and Tourist cars were the same. Usually the Pullman sleepers were somewhat newer but not always. Pullman cars were typically located farther back in the train, behind the diner with the tourist cars usually immediately behind the coaches and in front of the diner. Theoretically, the farther your car was from the locomotive the better the ride. If this was so, I never noticed the difference.

I recall that the color schemes were always different. My clearest recollection is that Pullmans had shades and tones of gray while Milwaukee Tourist cars had browns and greens. The importance of this, except to delineate a difference, escaped me then as it does now. It may have been coincidental.

Pass passengers were welcome to ride either Standard or Tourist, provided they paid the necessary extra sleeping car fare. Tourist fares were costly for out budget, but considerably less expensive than Pullman fares. Still, with careful planning, and my mother was a planner, fares could be reduced considerably and quite legitimately. You simply needed to know the ropes.

All sleeping car fares were figured differently than regular train fares, and still are, for that matter. A typical train ticket provides passage from point A to point B. Sleeping car fares purchase sleeping space for the passenger for a specific period of time (such as a day and a night), such costs being in addition to the regular A to B ticket price. Thus to ride the sleeper one must have the A to B ticket plus a sleeping car ticket.

The simplest way to handle the whole thing was to buy two A to B tickets—one for the train travel (the pass could be used for this) and one for the sleeping car space. However, in doing this, the passenger was paying the extra sleeping car fare for the daylight hours to sit on a seat not terribly unlike those in the coaches.

"That," my mother firmly declared, "is a waste of good money." To avoid this extravagance, she would carefully study the timetable noting our itinerary and locate a station stop approximating some hour near bedtime and another somewhere shortly after our typical hour of arising. Then reservations would be made so that we were buying sleeping car space only for the nighttime hours thereby avoiding paying the additional tariff during the day.

This worked fine—in principle! There were some decided disadvantages, however, and an occasional glitch, the worst being when all the space had been sold. The part I disliked the most was having to load up and carry our belongings back and forth between coach and sleeper twice a day. Carrying all our luggage along narrow aisles on a bouncing and weaving train was not easy. You banged your knees as well as those of the person in front or back of you, and more than once we encroached on the physical space of passengers as the train gave an unexpected lurch.

Our typical entourage for two consisted of a medium to large trunk (checked through in the baggage car though always a delivery problem at our destination); at least one and often two suitcases apiece, always kept with us at our seats just in case—of what my Mother never defined—and several cloth carryall bags, as well as a paper sack or cardboard box or two containing lunch, magazines, a deck of cards, crossword puzzles and a miniature first-aid station of tissues, aspirin, iodine, bandages, and laxative tablets (Carter's Little Liver Pills as I recall). Everything but the trunk had to be dragged to the sleeper at night and back to the coach in the morning. Usually finding two seats together in the unreserved coach section was not difficult. There were times though when we had to sit apart for at least some of the day, and I really hated that.

The Milwaukee ran its own Touralux sleeping cars on the 1940s Olympian. The slanted ceiling wall folded down to make a second berth, an upper over the lower constructed on the seats below. The two berths together comprised a section. Courtesy the Milwaukee Road, S. Johnson Collection

I was embarrassed by the public pilgrimage, sure that everyone would know what we doing to save money. I was almost sure I could hear people whispering behind my back. Sometimes I even had to make more than one trip to move all the luggage, and that made it even worse. I also hated to leave the sleeper status-symbol seats during the daylight hours when status counted most. Status was mostly wasted at night when you were hidden behind heavy privacy curtains and no one else knew you were there. My reluctance and unhappiness counted for naught, however, and for years we traveled on Mother's system. I was exceedingly thankful as I entered my teen years, when Mother said, "We can afford a Tourist sleeper all the way now." In reflection I suspect our budgetary situation was largely unchanged. However, Mother was older and the trips back and forth had become harder for her.

Even when we decided to travel on the sleeper, there was still the question of which "space," as sleeper car accommodations were called, to occupy. One of the first pieces of insider information I learned from my railroad-sophisticated parents was that you do not experience the same kind of ride throughout a train car, especially noticeable if you are trying to sleep. Sleeping cars typically had 10, 12, or 14 sections arranged in pairs directly opposite each other across the aisle. In addition to restrooms, some sleepers also had some private compartments or roomettes at the end of the car. The number of these special rooms determined the number of regular sections in the space remaining in the car. If you knew the configuration of the car and its assigned number for a particular run, you could decide which berths to reserve.

Accordingly, we always made reservations in person at the Union Station, never by phone or mail. The points to remember in making a selection were never get a seat (or berth) over the wheels. The ride is both noisy and bumpy there. Get something in the middle of the car, along about sections 5/6 or 7/8. Also, determine which end of the car would have the bathroom that matched the gender of the person who ordered the ticket and select berths accordingly. Equally important was to locate the position of the designated cars in the train, so by car selection you could shorten the walk to the coaches (in my younger years) or the diner.

When I was little, Mother and I shared a lower berth. This was never easy even though I was small, because Mother was not. As I grew I graduated to an upper berth. This meant an additional expense but not double the cost of a lower since uppers were cheaper and purchasing a whole section (an upper and a lower) was cheaper than purchasing the two separately. At first I was thrilled because I had my own private bed. I could sit up late and read by the tiny lights in the wall at the head and foot of the berth—a privilege severely limited by my mother when she had to share both sleeping space and light with me. I also had the fun of ringing the bell for the porter so he could bring the small portable ladder for me to climb up into the berth, an exciting event in itself. However, I quickly discovered that my new found freedom and privacy had a high price. I had no window!

When I shared a berth I was always placed on the inside. Though I ran the risk of being jammed up against the side of the car, the inside position had its own advantages. It was next to the reading light. It was also right below the long net-hammock strung from one end of the berth to the other so passengers could store small items at arm's reach. That was where the books, crayons, and sometimes pieces of candy were kept—significant assets to consider.

But best of all, it was next to the window! I always tried to wake up early so I might slowly and quietly slide the tracked window shades up an inch or two. Then I could sit up on an elbow and watch the scenery go by. Accomplishing this without waking my mother wasn't always easy since the shade had a release that required the squeezing together of two levers. Sometimes the levers stuck, and when the release gave, it was with a jerk which sent the shade flying to the top. Being awakened by a screeching shade and a blast of light at 6:00 A.M. did not please my mother.

But to think that I had reached the age where the decision to open the window shade and watch the scenery from the comfort of my berth was mine and mine alone, was very exciting. So, you can imagine my disappointment when I found that an upper berth has no window. It was time to execute a change in sleeping habits or be imprisoned for what seemed like an interminable time in the morning without a window. Either my mother had to wake up earlier or I had to sleep longer. Unfortunately I was unable to change either.

I still like to watch scenery from a train berth. On a recent trip I boarded an Amtrak sleeper at 1:00 A.M. and quietly lay in bed with the shades up for almost two hours watching what few dimly lighted scenes could be seen in rural Nebraska at that late hour. Watching the scenery go by while you are snug in your own bed has to be one of the best parts about riding a train, but having your own private berth is no big deal if you haven't got a window. You can be sure that as an adult I have never reserved an upper berth!

Contemporary sleeping cars feature a long hallway down one side of the car with the various sizes and styles of accommodations. In this newer arrangement passengers can only look out windows on one side of the car unless they open a door or pull back curtains to see out the other side across the hall. Vistas have been sacrificed for privacy.

Increased privacy has always been a touted feature of sleeping car travel but it was not always as private as in today's sleeper (unless you rented a roomette or a compartment). Most sleepers were laid out along a section design. A section consisted of two facing unmovable bench seats separated by polished wooden panels from the sections before and after it. This separation supposedly offered a modicum of privacy, but you were still on open-door terms with your neighbors directly across the aisle.

Each sleeping car section represented two berths. The lower berth gave the person holding that space riding rights to the seat facing forward. The backward-facing seat was to be occupied by the individual holding upper-berth space. Mother always had the forward-facing seat. I didn't mind because I had no problems with "riding backwards," but sometimes I did wish I might see where we were going instead of always looking at where we had been. And too, if you wanted to see the engine on a sharp curve, and what boy didn't, you had to be looking forward. Whenever possible I would slide into an empty forward seat and enjoy the purloined view.

When not watching the scenery I found other things to do. Sleepers of that era had a window for each seat, not a long vista window like now. On the panel separating the two windows was a button like a small doorbell. Underneath the windowsill were three-inch slots in the wall. The bell summoned the porter, who would supply a table with a lacquered finish matching the polished woodwork of the curved upper sides of the car. The table had a leg at one end and two hooks at the other that slipped into the slots under the window much like the take-down tables in today's travel trailers. Although we usually brought our own entertainment, upon request the porter could usually produce a deck of cards or a timetable that listed not only stations but rivers and tunnels and all kinds of interesting things. Sometimes he could even find us a magazine (though often a detective story issue, which my mother wouldn't let me read), and frequently he had a newspaper available or some informative publicity literature put out by the railroad.

But the thing I most liked to hear my mother request was a towel. The towels were bright white, folded neatly, with an orange stripe along one edge upon which was printed "The Milwaukee Road." There was nothing very special about the towel itself, though. My excitement came from knowing that mother always asked for a towel when she was ready to break out the lunch we invariably packed. Though we occasionally ate in the diner, to do so for every meal was considered unnecessary and frivolous. Instead, Mother packed a lunch—a real lunch. And when it was time to eat it, she spread it out on the clean white towels as though it were a picnic on the grass.

I loved the lunches, and I liked the fact that the brief partitions between sections allowed us to eat in semiprivacy from the people ahead and behind us though squarely in view of those across the aisle. Mother was sensitive to this and tried to time our lunches when our aisle neighbors had gone to the diner. But for me, if I had been forced to choose between privacy and lunch, the sandwiches would have won every time.

I can clearly recall sitting there watching the telegraph poles slide by, a drumstick in hand, and a cup of ice water from the cooler at the end of the car in front of me on the table.

Today's trains, with their electronic intercoms, microwave ovens, private drinking fountains, and similar niceties, are missing an important ingredient—they have eliminated the romance in traveling.

While riding the train today I feel as though I have been inserted like a coin into a machine that delivers services. I feel used rather than served. As an individual I am no more or less important than the automatic thermostat on the compartment wall, the vertical-sliding venetian blinds across the tinted window, or the portable shortwave radio the conductor carries strapped to a hip. I am only a cog in an impersonal system designed for something other than the individual.

It was different years ago. I recall it clearly: lying in my upper berth between crisp fresh sheets and soft tan blankets, carefully turned down and smoothed for my comfort; soaking up the pleasure of a smuggled detective magazine while munching a meatloaf sandwich; luxuriating to the accompaniment of the click of rail joints under the wheels of an otherwise quiet car. No wonder I slept so well. Somehow I knew that those wheels were singing their reassuring song just for me. ⌁

11
THE OSPREY AND THE EAGLE

In childhood my eyes perceived things differently than they do today. The Bitterroots appeared to be unbelievably tall and rugged, stretching to unimaginable distances in every direction. The St. Joe seemed to have two faces, unalterably molded and cast by the land surrounding it. It was either a flooding torrent racing down a nearly impenetrable rock-lined gorge or a dark bottomless stream, silently intimidating in its noiseless flow through the meadows. My inexperienced spirit was not yet tuned to the wonder of the St. Joe Valley's true beauty. I saw but did not appreciate the majesty of the cliff, the perseverance of the cataract, the relentless pursuit of the diving falcon. And most of all I did not understand the joining of the forest's strengths with the personality of those who had walked there.

Just before I left my childhood, my father began to tell me of the people of the St. Joe. I found it easy to imagine tepees with coils of smoke drifting overhead, surrounded by huge firs and pine—towers of red bark and green boughs stretching nearly as high as the mountain peaks. I could imagine the forest providing dense hiding places for hordes of wild creatures of every imaginable kind. I was introduced to homesteaders, miners, loggers, and railroaders and accepted them as reality. But I still only dimly perceived what the land and its people were like.

When I returned as an adult, almost 50 years later, it was apparent that my childhood memories had deceived me. The mountains were smaller and less threatening, the river was friendly and understandable, the timber more related to a complex ecology of natural life and death which I now recognized. But, this was not disappointing. Rather, the change in my perception and awareness was fulfilling.

Now I perceived something I had missed altogether in my youth. I stood at first one site and then another, silenced and humbled by the overpowering beauty inherent in the land. What had passed unnoticed before now stood in bold relief producing an awe, reflecting the true nature of the land and its people.

I also saw the limitations that the harvests over the years had placed on the natural resources and the importance of preserving what remained. This beauty, splendor, and majesty were wedded with history and an epic story of dedicated people working long hard days to establish something worthwhile. I wanted both the place and the people's efforts to be preserved.

As I slowed my pace to appreciate a distinctive characteristic of the valley, I paused to reflect on the source of this new appreciation. Thinking back on our experiences together, I realized that Frank laid the foundation for such feelings. Now, sensitive to this contribution he made to my development, it is easy to recall the many instances when a piece of that foundation was put in place. I am surprised I hadn't recognized this earlier. Perhaps there is a magic moment when understanding for certain basic truths occurs. If such a moment is accompanied by a journey to the proper place the results can be life changing.

Frank was a storyteller. Sitting in the quiet of the coach as we headed toward home during the early morning hours of his run we would watch the mists rising from the water of the gentle St. Joe and see the meadows come awake. Much of the time we would be searching for deer who stood with their heads high, turned toward us, ears forward, watching in careful nonchalance as our train went by. Once in a while, if it was a special morning and we were very lucky, we might catch a glimpse of a black bear walking through the alders—an unusual blend of power and gentleness in a single creature. Sometimes we would see herons fishing for their breakfast, standing knee-deep in the shallow water of Benewah Lake.

It was during these times that Dad told me of the Indians who once came to this valley from far distances during the summer to search for the root of the camas plant. The treasured root would be roasted in pits and then ground into a pulp to be formed into cakes, which could be stored and eaten later. They were relished for their flavor, which hinted of licorice. They gathered eggs from wild bird nests along the shores of the ponds that dotted the delta of the St. Joe River.

He also told me about their gathering and preserving of the area's abundant huckleberries. I learned about pemmican—strips of venison dried with berries and nuts to provide a food source which could be stored for the winter. Sometimes Dad would bring a jarful home for pie, a gift from one of his Avery friends. As a family project we even tried to make pemmican ourselves one year, substituting beef and pork for venison and local

This long wooden trestle carried the Milwaukee across Benewah Lake near Chacolet, Idaho. Homesteaders in prerailroad days walked around the lake to a landing near this spot to catch steamboats for Coeur d'Alene and St. Maries at Silvertips Landing. The bridge is still in use by the St. Maries River Railroad.
Photo by S. Johnson, Milwaukee, Wisc., Public Library Collection

domestic berries for the wild huckleberry. It was tasty and fun to eat, but we never found the knack of drying it correctly so it would keep moist without molding.

On some stretches of the trip, where the tracks twisted around sharp curves to follow the wandering river as it neared St. Maries, our train would slow enough that we might sometimes see a trout rise to an insect floating downstream. Watching these elusive fish leap in rivers nearby, almost close enough to touch, was an exciting experience for a boy who loved to fish but seldom had the opportunity. Sometimes a fisherman would be fly-casting as we went by, and Frank would tell me how the trout once had been so plentiful in the St. Joe River that they were caught commercially and shipped to Spokane and Seattle for restaurants.

I liked the Christmas-like suspense of seeing Dad walk through the back door, home from his run, carrying something wrapped in a roll of newspaper. Friends along the right-of-way were always giving Dad things to bring home to our family. He would carefully wrap them in a discarded morning newspaper, tied with rough brown twine borrowed from the big ball in the wooden box in the baggage car. I quickly learned that when he carried that roll of twine-tied newspaper it meant fresh fish for breakfast, venison steaks for dinner, or perhaps enough huckleberries for a pie. Every other year or so he would be given elk steaks, something the family considered a special treat.

One unforgettable fall morning Frank brought home a large roast of bear meat given to him by a man who lived alone in an old cabin across the river from Avery. With a wide grin Dad put the larger than usual newspaper-wrapped package on the kitchen counter. He fumbled in his coat pocket and pulled out a folded piece of paper and handed it to Mother. Carefully written in pencil on the back of a discarded freight invoice were the directions the donor had given Dad for cooking the meat. Mother was skeptical but willing to give it a try.

The details of the recipe are vague now, but I do remember it was immersed in salt and vinegar water for several hours, rubbed with spices, covered with slices of thick bacon that dripped their rich fat down over the dry meat, and then slowly roasted for a long time. The whole family enjoyed this special treat and we looked forward to having it again sometime but Dad was never given another bear roast.

Huckleberries were brought home much more often, an occurrence that did not particularly elate my mother. Although huckleberry pie was a very special treat, fresh huckleberries do not smell quite like cooked huckleberries. I never found the fresh smell unpleasant, but mother did. The huckleberries almost never would make it directly into the kitchen, but instead were left in the garage before Dad came in with the news of their presence. Mother's response was always the same.

"If you think I'm going to pick over those tiny foul-smelling berries you're wrong. If you want to spend your time getting all the leaves and stems out of them and staining your hands purple, that's fine with me. You prepare them, I'll make the crust and have all the ingredients ready. You can put them in the pie plate, cover them, and bake them."

Before Dad could agree to the conditions, which he always did, she would invariably add, "I'll eat them but I won't fix them!"

She would eat the pie along with Dad and me but never with the relish we did. There was no doubt her dislike for the odor was genuine.

After Dad retired and he and Mother lived in the Midwest (not an area known for producing many huckleberries) I would sometimes bring them a blueberry pie, telling Frank that blueberries were very much like huckleberries. He ate it and enjoyed it, but I knew it fell short of his favorite. Mother would eat it, too, but even then she had the last word.

"They don't smell like huckleberries," she would say.

Frank's interest in the natural things of the mountains he crossed by rail so many times was wide and varied. Some were easy to understand and appreciate, others not.

Coming to the area in 1908, he had lived through much of the early speculation about the mineral riches, particularly the speculation over the veins of gold possibly held by these mountains. He knew many of the old prospectors and had watched mine shafts suddenly appear and then just as quickly disappear beside handbuilt log cabins on the slopes along the railbed. He had observed the struggles of larger operations as they sought to find the mother lode by panning, digging, and placer techniques. Few of these ever shipped a single bag of ore, and the mountains retained whatever secrets they held.

He knew of the low success rate of these early prospectors and lectured me on the value of financial prudence. His personality certainly was not that of a gambler. I heard cliché after cliché used to explain his philosophy. "There is no free lunch," "Most get rich schemes are just schemes—no more," "If you are going to be gullible, someone will always find you and use you," and "Lady Luck never gives a sucker an even break."

Perhaps I was too young to be sensitive to how out-of-character his decision to hunt for gold seemed to other members of the family. His decision to hunt for gold suggested an exciting adventure to me. But now as I reflect on that experience, I find it hard to understand. I have no idea where his interest in that mine was born. I don't know and have never asked whether it was his idea or if he was drawn in by others. Perhaps I am protecting an image of his invulnerability. It doesn't matter. In any event, he bought some land and hired some help. Many family members—my older brother, my sisters, and family members by marriage—became involved. They dug shafts, shored their sides with timber, and spent many hours searching for gold, which was seldom found.

I was very young at the time and largely unaware of what was actually happening. I only have a scattering of incomplete memories about those days spent in the deep woods near Superior, Montana. I remember crawling under a table with my mother, for protection from falling rock, when a dynamite blast was set off nearby. I have an image of small wooden airplanes, hand carved by my brother during the quiet evening hours when there was little else to do but rest from a hard day's labor. I would watch him work while the family sat around a rough-hewn table and talked about the mine and speculated on others who might have been in the area years before. To me it was like an extended camping trip with intriguing bedtime stories every night.

One of the things they discussed was the possible history of the flumes which still existed in the area. God, how I remember the flumes. The woods abounded in flumes in those days: flumes to transport water for mining, flumes for carrying water to a distant camp, flumes for logging. I've seen remains of them in my current explorations and respect the skill used in constructing them and the role they played in logging.

There was one flume that stretched high across what seemed to me to be a bottomless gulch. Only a trickle of water flowed through it, so we walked along its bottom using it as though it were a special sidewalk with sides. My family members joked and laughed as we crossed. I was scared to death, frightened I might fall out, fearful that the bottom of the flume would break through, worried that a sudden stream of water would surge through from some unknown source carrying me to some dreadful, unimaginable fate. I cannot think of the mine without remembering that dreadful crossing over the yawning gulch below.

I have one other memory of those days that always leaves me with an uneasy feeling of disappointment, emptiness, and loss.

Dad could not find much free time to work on the mine. He contributed more by providing financing and arranging to deliver supplies—dynamite, groceries, clothing—dropped off at the depot on the days his run took him through the nearby town of Superior. Sometimes we were able to schedule the work at the mine so we could drive to the depot and be there to meet him when the train came in, to say hello and exchange a few words during the minute or two the Olympian paused there.

On this particular occasion we planned to drive to meet the train but for some reason we arrived later than we expected. We knew we were cutting it close and drove as fast as the twisted road and the rattletrap car would allow. But, as we came over the crest of the hill where the road dropped to the trackside and depot below we could see the train was beginning to slowly edge away from the depot, picking up speed as the black Westinghouse motor pulling it applied all the power 3,300 volts could deliver. I remember leaning out the window yelling at my father and waving, and just as clearly I remember him standing on the steps of a coach car, holding on to the grab iron with one hand and waving to me with the other. Watching that observation car round the curve down the track and disappear from sight as we sat in our car on the station platform remains one of the saddest memories I have. I shall never forget it. Thoughts of the mine have carried negative overtones for me ever since that sad summer morning.

Dad used to tell me of the homesteaders' ingenuity in utilizing the natural resources around them and enjoyed doing so himself whenever he could. He chopped wood for our heating needs on the acreage we owned, and looked forward to picking fruit from the trees in our backyard. He also collected pine pitch. Any time he was near a pine tree with a few minutes to spare he could be found carefully examining it for globs of yellow pine pitch—sometimes hardened into an amber resinlike substance, other times sticky and runny and inclined to permanently attach itself to whatever it touched.

He always carried a small pocketknife so when he found a particularly nice piece of the stuff he could cut off part of it and pop it in his mouth.

"Good for the blood. The pioneers used it," he would say to me, grinning as he offered to share, a teasing gesture he laughingly knew I would refuse.

The rest of it would be slowly scraped onto a clean piece of bark or a rock, which he would then carefully store away somewhere in a reasonably safe spot such as in the baggage car or the coffee cans in our garage. At the first hint of a cold or sore throat he would go for the pitch, mix some of it with a few drops of turpentine and honey, and swallow it. I only tried it once and it was the grossest thing I ever tasted. From that day on I was careful about mentioning to him any of my ailments that carried even a hint of a possible sore throat.

Dad collected rocks, too—small flat rocks that he used for sharpening his pocketknife. If he was at home and had nothing to do, or was whiling away time at work—perhaps waiting for a "meet" with another train—he would look for a flat rock and sharpen his knife. I must admit the knife was sharp but it embarrassed me when his brakeman would good-naturedly accuse him of stealing every flat rock the Milwaukee hauled in for track ballast.

Frank's peculiar habits created unusual learning opportunities for a youngster, nothing like most children's introduction to the things of nature. I took notice and remembered the stories he told me. He introduced me to a variety of people, experiences, and ways of life I might otherwise never have known. In the last half-dozen years as my wife and I have walked, biked, and driven through mountains and valleys, I have appreciated them more because of Frank. I have found myself contemplating whose footsteps I might be following, whose eyes first observed the view I was admiring, and why they stood where I was now standing. I have found myself looking for pine pitch on the trees and picking up flat rocks.

Dad explained that humans and nature were meant to live together in a special way that resulted in happiness. He firmly believed in a working communion between all living species.

The Kwikiutl have a legend that the owl has special powers that tell it the time of every man's death. If you are in harmony with the natural world, when your time comes you alone will hear the owl call your name. It is a beautiful image of personal communion with nature and one I appreciate, having seen the Kwikiutl's land, the misty fjords of Southeast Alaska. There the silent virgin timber stands with dignity and meets the water of an endless rushing sea giving rise to wondrous tales.

But I have also walked the banks of the gentle St. Joe and watched the osprey and eagle sail and sweep over those beautiful waters that have shared their unfathomable flowing beauty with the equally beautiful spirits of those who came to this place when it was unspoiled. Men and women with skin of red and white and yellow and black gazed in wonder at this valley from the windows of a sunset orange railroad coach gliding between stream and mountainside on rails of steel.

The sight of the osprey and eagle, as unfettered as were their ancestors in these same skies, stir me as the owl did the Kwikiutl. Perhaps they carry with them the vision of all those who came before. Perhaps those who soar in spirit with them see us in return and long to be remembered even as we watch. Perhaps the cries we hear are a roll call of those who went before, a recitation of their names for anyone who will listen. ⚞

12
RIDING THE HEAD END

I placed my toes squarely on the white line that marked the safety clearance distance from the rails, which ran in three-foot-deep valleys through the massive concrete station platform. Then I stared down the tracks through the dark, focusing on the signal block gleaming in the mouth of the tunnel, slightly downgrade and a quarter of a mile from where I stood. Its green eye stared back and then blinked to yellow announcing that the westbound Olympian was rolling into the inner yard, less than two miles away. I knew that in a few seconds the yellow would turn to red and the twelve-car train would follow the pounding black locomotive as it steamed into the east portal of the tunnel, which burrowed underneath the brewery, warehouses, and manufacturing plants. Then the engine would gather its superheated steam-generated strength for a final half-mile laboring climb into Spokane's Union Station where I stood waiting to test my courage.

Busy city traffic crossed over the Division Street bridge in full view above the tunnel mouth, but I never noticed it. I trembled slightly, shivering with excitement. The bull's-eye signal light turned to red. It was followed by the flashing white beam of the locomotive's headlight, first bright and blinding, then suddenly softened, dimmed by the engineer as it approached the station platform.

As it drew near I could hear the regular, clocklike striking of the engine bell, two to a second like a double-time swinging of a hurried pendulum. The sibilant sound of escaping steam and the complaining squeal of wheel flanges binding against the curve of the approach track screamed through the night. Then all these competing noises were drowned, silenced by the deep throated growl of over 200 tons of locomotive pointed directly at me, less than a hundred yards away.

As the sweating engine with its six-foot-high drive wheels thundered by, a mere thirty-six inches away from my face, the entire platform trembled and shook in obeisance. The noise was deafening and I was caught up in a cataclysm of sound and movement. I was powerless to react, helpless to resist. It was a fantastic feeling!

Above the roar I could barely hear the yell of reprimand from the engineer who nevertheless grinned at me and lifted a gloved hand in greeting as he swept by. He understood my youthful enthusiasm in being involved in this test of courage, standing close to the monster that answered his hand and will. He knew that I was paying homage not to the engine alone but to him as well.

The roar quickly faded into the distance, replaced by the steady, friendly sound of six-wheel roller-bearing passenger trucks sliding effortlessly across rail joints. The final grinding grasp of brakes against the wheels brought the Olympian smoothly to a stop.

Railroad traffic was extremely heavy in those wartime days. My stepfather, not as young and spry as he used to be with about thirty-five years of seniority as a conductor, usually arrived home tired and sleepy after his three-day round-trip turn to Deer Lodge, Montana. Knowing that a call from the extra board to handle a troop train or to ride a helper engine to Manito was likely to rob him of his regular rest, I used to meet him at the Union Station with the family car so he would not have to ride the bus home.

I used my thorough familiarity with the station's layout to obtain access to the routinely prohibited platform, which was elevated one story above street level. That way I could be there when he stepped off the train. I was always glad to see him and looked forward to experiencing the busy excitement of the arrival of the heavily loaded Olympian, aware with pride that it was "his train," that he was in charge.

Standing and touching that white safety line, I was accepting the challenge of the giant locomotive for sole ownership of the track and all its environs. I enjoyed the heady rush of fear that accompanied it and the bravado I felt in seeking and accepting that fear. I never shared with my stepfather my participation in this personal duel or the feelings I experienced with it. I knew he would disapprove of my taking chances that he would not have taken with over 40 years of firsthand railroading experience.

It has been almost 50 years since I toed that white line but I have never forgotten it. If I were to have the opportunity today, I would do it again. And I would probably still be frightened, and, even now, I would not tell anyone else about it.

The first time you stand next to a locomotive, its actual size and bulk come as a surprise. These machines are so large, so strong, so independent and impersonal, so aloof until we come to know them well. Because I was introduced to trains by a warm and caring stepfather I seldom found any of my railroading experiences frightening. Engines, however, were an exception. I always perceived these monstrous machines in a state of awe and with a sense of respect. Still many of my fondest experiences with trains, railroading involved locomotives.

Most of the times the engine was only a segment of a larger experience, a symbol of something else I enjoyed, an appetizer before an extraordinary meal. This is the way it was at the Union Station. The closeness of a steaming locomotive in a secure and comfortable building, and a close relationship with a man I both admired and loved, joined to create a special bond.

Though I frequently rode with my stepfather on locomotives, there are two specific instances I particularly recall. One of these involved a steam locomotive. The other was on a Milwaukee electric motor, a massive piece of machinery that the railroaders called a quill because of its unusual drive-train design.

My first ride on a steam locomotive was in the 1940s, on an early summer day. I was about thirteen and was riding with my dad on the morning eastbound Olympian out of Spokane, Washington. Our train was being pulled by a new Northern, a lighter and not as powerful version of the old dependable S-1's and S-2's, quickly built and put into service during the war years to help with the extra burden of war-related traffic. The grade for the first twenty miles east out of Spokane was steep. When the consist of heavy passenger cars was a large one, as on this day, the Northern needed help. Consequently, a dependable Pacific-class helper engine headed our train in front of the Northern as we left Spokane.

At Manito, where the grade lessened, the train slowed as we prepared to drop the helper engine. Dad touched my arm as I sat in the coach seat across the aisle from his and beckoned me to follow. We went to the front vestibule, which had already been opened by the brakeman. Dad dropped to the ground at the bottom of the steps and motioned to me to follow. We turned toward the front of the train, walking rapidly past the baggage and mail cars to where the Northern now stood alone at the head of the train, the helper engine having been shunted to a nearby sidetrack. It was an impressive sight. Two powerful steaming locomotives stood side by side, their strength magnified by the contrasting surroundings of rolling fields of wheat waving gently in the morning breeze in this isolated rural setting.

"Get on," Dad said, pointing to the ladder leading to the engine cab far above me. The first step was hard to reach because it was high off the ground, and the track ballast sloped down and away from the rails making it even a greater reach.

"Come on Junior, even you can make it," the fireman teased, looking down at my efforts but holding out his hand to help. Dad gave me a boost from behind and up I went. The inside of the cab was hot and noisy, and everything had a greasy look. There were valves and levers and gauges everywhere and a dozen different sounds foreign to my ear, each loud enough to deafen.

"Hang on here." Dad indicated a handle in the roof of the cab, demonstrating how to use it to keep one's balance. Just as I took hold, the engineer received the highball from someone on the train behind us and let out the throttle. With a hiss of steam and released brakes the engine jerked forward. The smoothness of the ride felt in the cars behind was missing here.

Slowly we built up momentum to what seemed like an incredible speed to me but what was, in actuality, probably only slightly over twenty-five miles per hour. We kept that pace to Plummer Junction. We slowed as we moved through the Y junction where our tracks from Spokane met the mainline freight tracks from south of Spokane to form a single line from this point east. From Plummer Junction we rode around twisting curves, across the high steel trestle at PeDee over a highway far beneath us, and then down the grade and out onto a long wooden-pile bridge, our progress echoing across Benewah Lake as we rattled over the wooden supports. Safely across, we swept through a short tunnel and then steamed along the shoreline and into the busy logging town of St. Maries, Idaho. We paused there just long enough for a few short minutes of loading and unloading. Then the noise and rough rhythm resumed.

For an incredible thirty-five miles more I rode that engine, watching the engineer pull the whistle lanyard for crossings, hearing the fireman call out the color of block signal lights as they flashed by. Above the noise that made yelling a necessity if one was to be heard, the great engine pitched and swerved, rocked and jumped, accentuating every little pitch or yaw of the track. My primary concern was that we were going to leave the rails at any minute. Speed picked up some as we followed the curves of the shadowy St. Joe riverbank, and it surprised me to find that the ride got smoother rather than rougher with the additional speed.

After the ride was finished I was to find out that the Northern, because of its weight and the design of its leading trucks, was considered an especially smooth-riding steam locomotive. But during the ride I felt myself jerked to and fro, up and down, mimicking the engine's every motion, testing my strength and endurance every minute of the ride. Finally we pulled into Avery, Idaho, where we were scheduled to exchange steam for electric power.

As our train came to a stop in a hiss of escaping steam and compressed air, Dad suggested we get off on the side opposite the station so no one would get excited about my being up there. Climbing down and getting off was easier than getting on because the ground here was level except for the fact that my arms felt paralyzed from nearly forty-five miles of desperately gripping any available handhold. We walked around the head baggage car, denuded of a locomotive now. The Northern moved off while the electric motor awaited its turn from a spot a few yards ahead on a siding. My legs trembled and the ground seemed to shake as my body still echoed the motion of the ride.

"Gee, what a ride," I exclaimed. Dad just grinned as we headed for the agent's office in the depot where he needed to pick up new orders. Reaching into his pocket he handed me some change.

"Here, buy yourself a soda in the beanery," he said. "It'll do wonders for your arms and legs."

The other ride I remember especially well was across the high prairie flats between Deer Lodge and Butte, Montana. This was my first ride in an electric motor. The Milwaukee Road was one of the few railroads in the United States with electric service over any extended distance. From Harlowtown, Montana, to Avery, Idaho, and from Othello to Tacoma, Washington (close to 600 miles), the major source of power was the electric engine. The Baldwin-Westinghouse units were used almost exclusively for passenger duty. They were massive locomotives: fourteen feet tall and ninety feet long, with twelve sixty-eight-inch drive wheels producing a maximum of 4,200 horsepower drawn from overhead wires carrying 3,000 or more volts of current.

These locomotives were quiet, with a distinctive high-pitched air whistle curiously mismatched to their size and strength. Their distant cousins in design, the box-cab freight electrics, came to be hallmarks of the Milwaukee Road. "The Milwaukee Road—The Electric Way" became an advertising watchword during the few decades they saw service. To the

The eastbound Columbian exchanges steam power for electric at Avery, Idaho, and heads up the grade for St. Paul Pass. My stepfather and I sometimes would climb aboard the steam engine at Manito, Washington, and ride to St. Maries, Idaho. We would do the same on the electric motor, riding from Avery to Falcon.
The Museum of Northern Idaho Collection

passenger in the train behind, these monster machines meant a quieter, smoother, and cleaner ride. Leaving Avery after being pulled by a steam locomotive, the contrast in ride for the passengers in the cars behind was obvious. The start was so smooth as to be unnoticeable unless one happened to be looking out the window. No jerk was experienced as occurred under steam power when the pistons suddenly thrust drive rods out to generate power needed to break the grasp of inertia on the train. To the Forest Service these electrics were a godsend, reducing the threat of cinder- and spark-produced trackside fires. They were a mixed blessing to the railroad, providing cheaper power because of their ability to regenerate electricity when running downgrade. But, they proved expensive in terms of needed redesign of the chassis and problems with producing sufficient steam heat for the passenger cars behind. Their length and mass were so great that special turntables and turning Y's had to be rebuilt to accommodate their size.

My first ride on an electric engine was on a Westinghouse motor like this between Deer Lodge and Butte, Montana. I was allowed to blow the whistle for every crossing (real and imagined) during that trip.
Harold Hill Photo, Warren Wing Collection

I was aware of their reputation and enjoyed watching them trade places with steam locomotives at Avery. When my stepfather told me that early the next morning we were going to have a ride on the "motor," as they were commonly called, I was thrilled and could hardly wait for the night to pass. Shortly before seven in the morning we eased eastward out of Deer Lodge, Dad and I climbed aboard (on the side away from the station again) to ride the head end into Butte 40 miles away. This section of track, mostly across flat plateaus through cattle ranch and mining slag-pile country, was known as "fast" track. This meant that the train would be operating at close to the maximum allowed speed by the track profile's running regulations. In many places this was in excess of 60 miles per hour for passenger trains and in a few it was nearly 80 MPH.

The locomotive easily built up speed, the hum of its motors startlingly quiet and smooth in comparison with a steam locomotive. We whipped by crossings with regularity, to my delight since I had been assigned the job of pulling the whistle cord. I could smell the peculiar odor of high-voltage electricity as it coursed through the transformer boards and into the truck-mounted quill-drive motors. These boards were only a few feet behind us; the odor was everywhere.

The ride was sufficiently relaxed in contrast to the steam locomotive and I could look about me and enjoy the view through the windows across the front of the motor. The fireman sat in his left-side chair, feet up against the bulkhead, calmly calling out block signals as they went by and taking time to point out various sites to me as though we were on a tour. We slowed through Silver Bow Canyon, where the walls narrowed and our tracks plus those of two other railroads and a state highway ran parallel. The large brass bell, mounted directly beneath the middle window in the front of the cab, began to ring out its regular warning that we were coming down the track.

Finally, we moved slowly into the beautiful Butte station with its long covered passenger platforms and its red brick bell tower with the Milwaukee logo emblazoned on its sides. We came to a stop on a dead-end track with the nose of the motor only a foot or two from the stanchion at the end of the track, directly in front of the station's waiting room doors. There, to my stepfather's chagrin, for all the world to see, I walked out through the open door onto the platform. I casually climbed down to platform level in front of all the disembarking passengers and the waiting railroad personnel. Making no move to slip away quietly, I wanted everyone to know that, for a while at least, I had been part of this engine's crew and had helped bring them to their destination.

It was a heady experience on a distinctive head end for a young boy and though I often rode the motor again, none of those other rides compared to this one where I detrained in full view of the public.

The last time I rode the head end was entirely different, yet a reprise almost, returning to the days of my childhood. But it wasn't with my stepfather or on the Milwaukee.

I was living in upstate New York in a small college town nestled beside Lake Champlain. The Delaware and Hudson right-of-way hugged the shoreline into town, running along the beach. It passed through an occasional apple orchard and along the edges of small basaltic cliffs with wonderful views across the wide lake to the Green Mountains of Vermont. Approaching the station, the tracks left the tangent and swung in a long five-degree S curve with the station nestled in a brief straightaway in the middle of the curve.

The D&H station was a classic: two stories high with wide sloping gray-shake roof lines and sharply edged gables. The construction was of traditional dark red brick with native granite corner pieces. The front of the second story was at street level. The bottom floor opened onto a wide brick platform complete with baggage carts and an almost always open railway express doorway stacked with interesting crates and boxes.

My youngest son and I occasionally would go down to the station during the late afternoon to watch the graceful silver-and-blue streamliner slide through on its trip between New York and Montreal. Its dome cars, refurbished from their old Santa Fe Chief days, were beautiful indeed. The long powerful diesel, perfectly matched in color to the cars behind, was a magnificent picture of power and grace. Tim, though only five, had already been introduced to the love of trains. In a small room in our basement I had built a plywood table on which rested a figure-eight of track with large holes cut into the loops of the "8" so he could stand in the middle and watch at eye level. He spent hours there with his prototype Lionel set of a Pacific locomotive and three bright orange Milwaukee passenger cars, watching it loop around as the semaphores moved up and down and crossing gates danced and blinked their red lights. The electric push-button whistle could be heard throughout the house.

One of his older brothers on a visit back home from the army had complimented Tim on his black shiny locomotive and had said to him, "That engine's a big mother!" Unfortunately, the nickname stuck and Tim always referred to that train as his big mother, a designation that sometimes required an explanation to admiring guests.

On this particular early spring afternoon, our visit to the station was a spur of the moment thing at the tail end of a shopping trip. We had missed the streamliner but I thought we might look at a few freight cars. We parked in front under the old trees that lined the quiet street and entered the station. Tim and I waved to the ticket seller, who recognized us from previous visits and then went down the wide staircase with the wrought iron banister, through the open double doors, and out onto the platform. There were three tracks directly in front of the depot: the mainline, a passing track, and a house track on which dropped-off cars would sometimes be sitting. Beyond was a narrow grassed strip and then a small railroad maintenance area including several stub tracks, a small turntable, a single-stall engine house, and a couple of supply sheds. Today the working track was empty. But we did notice that there was a small Alco diesel switcher in the engine house and that there was some sort of maintenance activity. We picked our way across the tracks and walked hand-in-hand over to the shed, where we were greeted by a man in oil-stained overalls. He was busily wiping some grease off a newly installed fitting on one of the diesel's trucks.

"Hello there, fella." He grinned at Tim. "Did you come to help me make it run?"

Tim, who was always shy around strangers, gripped my hand a little tighter and said nothing but stared wide-eyed at the engine towering above him.

"Trains are just like people," the man explained to Tim, ignoring me. "They sometimes don't feel well and then we have to fix them up with special train medicine. This one," he pointed at the switcher, "has just been fixed and now we have to give it a little test to see if the medicine worked."

Tim said nothing.

"How do you test it?" I wanted to know.

"Well, we don't want to take it far from home on a test run, but we would like to see if it can run up and down a track and maybe cross a switch or two," he answered.

"Okay if we watch?" I asked.

"Oh, I can't let you stand here while equipment is moving," he said shaking his head. "I'd really get in trouble if I did that."

"Well, it's all right if we go back to the platform and watch, isn't it?" I said. I could feel Tim's grip relax and I knew he was disappointed in not getting the closer view.

"Sure, but you can't see very good from there. Besides, a freight might come through and get in your way and then you couldn't see at all. Better let me show you where to watch," he directed.

"Come with me, young fella," he said to Tim, taking his hand. "You come along with us, too, Dad." The friendly man walked directly over to the switcher, picked Tim up under the arms, and placed him on the ladder.

"Now, you hang on tight, and Dad and I will come right up behind you holding on to you."

Up we went into the cab. Tim was excited. Dad was ecstatic. What happened next was a train buff's dream. At the engineer's direction Tim rang the bell, blew the horn, and turned running lights on and off. With the man's large hand over Tim's, the throttle was slowly moved into a running position and we slid out onto the holding track next to the mainline. For the next twenty minutes we rode slowly up and down a quarter mile of track with Tim on the engineer's lap and Dad standing close beside. We made our way back down the siding to the engine shed and came to a stop.

"I believe she's completely well," the man said to Tim. "Thanks for helping me check her out."

We were effusive in our thanks, but it was obvious that he had enjoyed it almost as much as Tim and I.

"I hope giving us a ride won't get you in trouble," I said in thanking him.

"Not likely," he said, "since I'm the superintendent."

We hurried home to tell Mom of our adventure. Tim's shyness was gone now and he poured out the story of what had happened. Mom smiled, knowing that both her boys had experienced a special afternoon.

As we left the depot I stopped at the ticket office to obtain our benefactor's name, and now Tim and I sat down at the desk to write a thank-you note for our private ride on the D&H. Trains had been an important part of my youth and the process was repeating itself in a small way with my children. It is no wonder that through the years I've often found occasion to say thank you to railroaders for some very special experiences. ⚒

13
LIGHT AT THE END OF THE TUNNEL

☞ We walked around the old depot, admiring its lines and appreciating the fact that the St. Maries Railroad had maintained it so well. In the center section of the building, the lights were on in the crew room where some men sat around a table enjoying their coffee. Out front, the mainline and several tracks of the East Yard were still in place and part of a working railroad. It was an interesting sight and full of memories for those of us who remembered when the Milwaukee was still operating.

There were seven in our group, which was preparing to trace the former Milwaukee branch line from St. Maries, Idaho, south to Elk River. Four were enthusiastic railroad buffs and their wives, all very interested in the Milwaukee. Another was a former Milwaukee railroader who had worked on trains passing through here. My wife and I completed the party.

We strolled around back of the depot and looked at the pieces of Milwaukee freight cars that had been used as riprap to support a dirt bank above the parking area. Walking past the east end of the depot, one of the buffs turned to the former railroader and said, "Once upon a time wasn't there more to the depot than this?" The grin on his face suggested that it might be a leading question.

"Sure was. Used to be a freight shed or baggage storeroom attached to this end," the ex-conductor replied.

"Where did it go?" Another grin, broader this time.

"I guess they dumped it in a trash heap somewhere." This time the reply was accompanied by a returned grin.

"How come?" I asked naively.

The ex-railroader knew now that there was no avoiding the rest of the story, so he explained.

"We sort of took care of it one day. There was a stub track backed up to that building and sometimes we would put a car back in there so its contents could be unloaded and stored in the shed. This one day the engineer sort of gave her a little bit too much throttle and the car didn't stop where the track did."

The Milwaukee Depot at St. Maries as it appears today, used by the St. Maries River Railroad. The opposite end of this depot was accidentally "removed" by a Milwaukee train in the last few years of the railroad's operation.
Photo by S. Johnson, Milwaukee, Wisc., Public Library Collection

We were all laughing now.

"Do much damage?" someone asked.

"Well, yes, sort of. You can't back a freight car through a storage shed without leaving a trail. Took off the whole side is what it did. It was easier to tear it down than repair it."

"A little bit of paperwork that day, I suppose," one of the buffs said.

"Yep, little bit—quite a bit, actually." The old railroader laughed.

As with any group who works together day after day, railroaders often enjoyed poking fun at their own profession. I remember well the rolling laughter of Mr. Persinger, a baggageman on Dad's train. Dad's laugh was quieter but was an infectious short chuckle I always enjoyed hearing. When the two of them were together there, out of view of passengers, the old baggage car was a fun place. Dad loved a joke, too, and didn't mind when it was on him, but he was not above using his sense of humor to work out a problem on the job.

Some trains serviced an area heavily spotted with small settlements that had no ticket or freight office, known as nonagency stops. The conductor would have the extra responsibility of selling tickets to passengers who boarded at these sparsely manned stops, handling the cash sale and making change when necessary. When Dad was working Nos. 7 & 8 between Spokane and Butte, this was particularly true. The train was a three-car local. Its run was designed to stop at any station along the line where freight or passengers needed to be loaded or unloaded, stops not usually made by the Olympian. It was not uncommon for local residents to board the train and ride only a handful of miles to the next small settlement, using the train as an urban dweller might a streetcar or bus. The fares for such short distances, especially in the leaner times before World War II, were small.

Dad had a six-inch-long, heavy leather purse in which to carry change. One of his uniform pockets had been double-lined to carry the weight of change, some of which was in silver dollars, popular at that time, but he preferred the purse.

At one particular stop in the middle of the night, a middle-aged woman used to board regularly. She would ride less than 10 miles to visit her sister, and then would return home the next night. Her schedule meant that if she rode Dad's train going east, he would also have her as a passenger heading west. I had often seen Dad sell her a ticket, politely and as businesslike as usual, but had also heard him complain about her to the rest of the crew when they were having their private lunch in the baggage car.

"Somehow she always gets our run!" Dad would sputter. "It's the same routine every damn time. She asks how much the fare is. I tell her it's thirty cents. She says that's fine but then tells me that she's sorry, but she hasn't anything smaller than a five-dollar bill."

At this juncture, the rest of the crew would laugh, knowing how the story would end and mildly enjoying seeing him lose his temper even a little bit.

"Do you know how much change I have carried on board this train just to be able to sell her a thirty-cent ticket?"

One morning, as our family was having breakfast welcoming Dad home from a turn, he made an announcement.

"I finally took care of the woman who always gives me a five for a thirty-cent ticket," he said. He had shared the story at home, and Mother immediately knew what he was talking about.

"What did you do?" Mother asked.

"I was ready for her this time. When she got on she went through the same old rigmarole and handed me a five-dollar bill. I reached into my pocket, pulled out my coin purse, and gave her $4.70 in nickels. 'There,' I said, 'that should help you. There's a lot of thirty-cent fares in that handful.'"

Dad's humor was neither mean nor spiteful. He used humor to make a point sometimes, and apparently this strategy was successful because after fifty years I can still remember some of the instances.

One of the things I liked about taking a turn with him was that I got a variety and quantity of food that was different from home. We ate at restaurants where just reading the menu was a special treat. Our prepacked lunches were large and very filling—far different than the sandwiches I carried in my school lunch. Sometimes I would even find something special tucked away in the brown paper bag. Perse, the baggage man, would frequently bring something fresh from his garden. I particularly remember the radishes and the cucumbers—the radishes because Perse and Dad had a running contest as to who could raise the largest radish, and the cucumbers because of an unpleasant experience I had on one trip.

On that occasion, Perse had brought in a whole bushel basket full of cukes. He knew the crew would eat several of them and planned to give away the others to his friends along the line.

"Help yourself, son," he told me.

I really don't understand why those cucumbers tasted so especially good to me that night. Cukes usually were just an okay food to me, but that night, sitting there with the train crew and a whole basket of cucumbers, I couldn't get enough. I ate one long quartered strip after another. The men were amused and I supposed this encouraged me.

An hour or so later, my stomach rebelled and I headed for the men's room. All the cucumbers I had eaten, and the rest of my midnight lunch, too, came back up. For the rest of the night my stomach growled and complained and I was dismayed to find that I didn't feel like eating the extra-good breakfast we always had in the Butte depot restaurant. I expected Dad to say something to Mother about my greedy performance, but he never mentioned it and neither did I.

Several years after, when I was in high school, Dad found a bargain on oranges and brought home a large box of them. That evening while doing my homework, I helped myself: It tasted great, so I ate another, and another, then another. Dad stuck his head through doorway to say good-night and looked at the growing pile of orange rinds.

"That's a lot of oranges," was all he said.

Before long, the oranges and my digestive system began to disagree. I ran for our bathroom, where I got rid of the oranges the same way I had the cucumbers. I knew that both Mom and Dad must have heard me, but they didn't come out to see how I was doing, and finally my stomach calmed down enough so that I could go to bed.

The next morning, when I came upstairs, they were already sitting at the breakfast table.

"Ready for breakfast?" Mother asked.

I shook my head and mumbled something about not being hungry. Dad looked up and said, "Might have been the cucumbers." He had waited for over three years to make his point.

But railroaders also make errors in judgment. Along the right-of-way there are many stories they tell about their own lapses in clear thinking while on the job. Passengers and crew members have been left behind, orders misread, and baggage lost.

Ross Snider, one of Dad's brakemen and a congenial man I liked very much, used to complain about rough rides. Most of the time such prob-lems were due to unusual roadbed conditions or bad springs or a flat spot on a wheel of a coach, but Ross used to enjoy placing the blame, mostly in jest, on the engineer.

"Who's driving this thing?" he'd regularly say to Dad if he happened to be thrown a little off balance as the train moved into a sharp curve. Dad just smiled at the rhetorical question, but the truth of the matter was, on rare occasions, no one was driving!

Railroaders in the Bitterroots tell a funny, though potentially tragic, story about a snow service crew operating near Avery. These crews ran a short four- or five-unit train of specialized equipment that kept the rails clear of snow between Haugan, Montana, and Avery, Idaho. Heading up the train would be a big rotary plow that could throw snow far to the side of the track. Behind this there was usually a two-unit electric motor, fol-lowed by a flanger car used to clear away snow close to the rails, a caboose, and then another special car called a cut-widener, which enlarged the swath the rotary had made through a drift.

This specialized work train would run up the grade from Avery, over the summit, and down into Haugan, pausing along the way to clear out sidings as well as the mainline. Then it would be turned around on the Y at Haugan and would make the return trip to Avery. During periods of heavy snowfall it sometimes went back and forth almost continually, pausing at one end only long enough to change crews.

When two engines are on the same train (unless their controls are electrically linked as with modern multiple unit diesel engines), both have an engine crew, one of which is assigned primary responsibility for such essential operations as braking.

On one trip, the train went over the summit at St. Paul Pass tunnel and started down the steep grade on the western side. Before long it would go through the big loop, changing its direction 180 degrees on the sharp curve that went through tunnel No. 26 just below Adair. From there it would continue downgrade to Falcon and eventually arrive in Avery. Shortly after starting on the downgrade, crew members noticed that the train was moving far faster than usual, making the cars sway so much that keeping one's balance became almost impossible.

For a few brief moments panic took over. But conductor and brakeman considered opening the valve that would set the emergency brakes, a maneuver seldom taken because it slammed personnel and equipment around and often did damage. Up in the two-unit electric engine, the crew worried as the indicated speed was far from safe. Frantically they waited for the controlling engineer in the rotary plow unit to apply the brakes. In the rotary, the engineer and fireman and another crew member were waiting for the same thing, assuming that the braking control was in the hands of the engineer of the electric motor behind them.

The fireman in the electric engine finally worked his way forward to the engineer, and they quickly agreed to set the brakes. The train eventually slowed and ground to a halt with the head end all the way through the tunnel and the sharp curve at Adair. Each engineer had been critical of the train's speed down the mountain but was reluctant to criticize the other whom they assumed had control.

That long curving tunnel at Adair offers an exciting passage even today when the traveler goes through on a bike or on foot. It bends sharply in a ten-degree curve and once into the tunnel it is as dark as any tunnel can be. Even with flashlights it is easy to become disoriented as to the direction the tunnel is curving and to end up walking in a series of short straight paths that veer first toward one side and then the other.

Darrel Dewald tells of walking through there with his wife when the railroad was still operating. She expressed concern about the possibility of a train coming through while they were in the middle, but he reassured her that they were safe. Shortly after exiting on the upper end where a small wooden trestle crosses Manhattan Creek near the Adair station, a freight train, running as an extra or unscheduled train, came rumbling through. Mrs. Dewald was not pleased and did not forget the experience.

"After the railroad was closed down," Darrel relates, "and the rails were gone, we were walking through that same tunnel. I made the mistake of jokingly saying something like, 'It must be about time for No. 16 to come through.' Our pace increased considerably and my wife made sure we got out of there as fast as possible. She let me know she didn't consider my joke very funny at all."

Walking through that tunnel, or any tunnel for that matter, does give a feeling of being back with the railroad. With goosepimples on my arms and the hair on my neck rising, I stood outside the mouth of St. Paul Pass tunnel at East Portal one day and listened to a dull rumbling roar, steadily growing in volume, echoing out of the tunnel's mouth. I had heard the sound of an electric motor going through a tunnel and now it seemed I was hearing it again—unbelievable because even the rails were gone, but the sounds were surely there, loud enough for anyone to hear. Then suddenly, around the curve of the snow shed at the end of the tunnel, swept four dirt bikes, the abrasive noise of their high-pitched engines no longer disguised by the echoes in the tunnel.

My wife and I laughed about that experience and then wondered if we couldn't re-create the sound of a Baldwin-Westinghouse motor hauling the Olympian through one of these tunnels. On our next trip we took two new items with us. One was a one-million-watt handheld floodlight that plugged into the truck's cigarette lighter, and the other was a cassette tape of a Milwaukee electric box-cab locomotive, complete with whining and rumbling gears, tolling bell, and the peculiarly high-pitched air whistle.

Late in the afternoon following a full day of exploring and searching for sites up Loop Creek valley, we headed for Avery, knowing we would pass through a series of tunnels. We paused at the entrance to the first one. The sign said, "Caution. Turn on lights in the tunnel." We obeyed.

One million watts of simulated train headlight pierced the dark ahead. Into the dash stereo went the cassette. Down went all the windows in the truck. Up went the stereo volume as far as it would go. Then we drove slowly through the tunnel, holding our heads as far outside as possible to capture the effect.

It was fun, but it was more than that—it was a touch of yesterday. We repeated the act at every tunnel, desperately hoping we would meet an oncoming car whose occupants could then share the thrill with us, and we laughed all the way to Avery.

No matter what the activity, when we were working around the historic sites their longtime importance was in our mind and often influenced our behavior in odd little ways. While I was setting up the photographic gear my wife would frequently wander around the area with her head down as though she were looking for something she dropped. Such a posture often resulted in finding pieces of old pottery, odd scraps of railroad-related metal, a rusted barrel hoop or an old boot, and similar relics from the past. In the presence of antiquity we tended to become reflective and even found ourselves lowering our voices sometimes, almost speaking in whispers as though humbled to be visitors in such a place.

One day I was busily involved lining up an unusual angle for a picture looking up at one of the high trestles in Loop Creek valley above Avery. It so happened that the spot I had chosen to shoot from was literally in the front yard of an old mining cabin. Its moss-covered logs, dovetailed at the ends, were canted at an angle giving it a studied casual look like a Scotsman's tam worn to one side of the head. It nestled into the landscape, the lower course of logs partly buried beneath ground level and the rear of the cabin tucked up against the slope of the hill. This was a logical place to search since evidence of early activities was obvious just by the presence of the log cabin. I was lost in my lens openings and shutter speed calculations, only minimally noticing Karen.

When I finished we took a break and she told me what she had found. "I know where he built his outside fire and where he dumped some of his trash. I also know where the mine entrance is. It's only a few yards away, across the little creek over a plank laid there for a bridge. It's not very large, I had to duck, but it's big enough to walk into. I didn't go very far because it was really dark in there and I wasn't sure how well shored up it was."

"I'd like to see it," I said.

"It's right over here," she said, starting to move away. Then she stopped and said, "I think you might be even more interested in the grave."

To move about through the old camp stimulated speculation about who had lived and worked here. Looking at the grave with its small rough, makeshift cross created one of those quiet reflective moments.

I knew that the mine had been worked quite recently by a local miner who had held grandfathered mining privileges in the national forest. The rangers had told me about him, but they had said nothing about a grave. We decided to report our find to them.

At the headquarters administration building, which incidentally sits on a former railroad site itself, we described what we had found.

The ranger said, "I believe the fellow mining it [he called him by name] died a year or so ago. But I don't know anything about a grave. We'll have to investigate it since federal law prohibits burials in the forest for environmental reasons."

"What do you do when you investigate it?" I asked.

"First we'll ask around to see any of the local folks know about it. If not, someone on our investigative unit will have to go over the site."

"And what will you be looking for there?"

"To put it bluntly, we have to find out who has been planted there," the ranger said. Then, seeing the look on my face, he added, "so we can find next of kin and get the remains moved to a better place." As it turned out, no one was "planted" in the grave. It was simply a memorial cross that friends had erected where their friend had worked and died.

While in the Bitterroot area we would often stay at a rather primitive sportsman's lodge some miles away or in our travel trailer. During one of our earliest trips we decided to sleep in the back of our pickup in a forest campsite. It was late in the summer, so when the sun set extra early because of the high mountains surrounding us, the temperature dropped with it. Our small campfire felt good but we could only stay warm on the fire side while the other side clearly demonstrated the principle of radiant cooling. We decided to go to bed, despite the early hour.

The North Fork of the St. Joe tumbled down its rocky course close enough to the truck that the pleasant sound of the cascading waters was clearly heard. Early historical records indicated that this spot had been an Indian campsite, heavily used in annual forages for berries and wild game. The railroad had built a major construction camp here in 1908. According to local lore, very early in the white man's coming to the valley, the area had been used as the burial site for one or two well-known local residents.

We lay in the back of the truck, comfortably warm now in our sleeping bags, and talked about our other camping trips. We had once spread our rolls on the ground in the Black Hills and nearly froze, so cold that we didn't even notice the numerous rocks we had failed to clear the night before. We had camped alongside a wilderness airstrip in Alaska on a fishing trip. During the day we had encountered Kodiak brown bears and had been advised to store our cache of salmon fillets and all our food at least a hundred yards from where we slept. As we recalled that frightening day and night, strange noises surrounded our truck. I was thinking about ghosts of pioneers and Indians when my wife broke the spell.

"Will this plastic truck-bed cap keep out an animal?" my wife wanted to know.

I began wondering about it myself. I had seen bears along this same area years before, and the rangers had said that the bear population was now larger than it had been then. The noises grew louder. Suddenly something brushed against the outside of the truck, inches from my head. Scurrying noises came from the front hood and scratching sounds from the nearby log table.

"What was that?" I whispered.

"How do I know? I thought you'd know," my wife replied.

"I don't know."

"I don't want to know," she said.

Finally, our fatigue became stronger than our fear and we drifted off. In the morning, no tracks or spoor gave us a clue as to whom our visitors had been, but the rangers suggested such ferocious creatures as squirrels, "camp robber" gray jays, porcupines, or maybe even a skunk.

"No bears?" I asked.

"Probably not," the ranger said with a smile.

Later, we wondered what we would have done had a bear visited our camp.

"I suppose the best thing to do would be to just stay quiet and not cause the animal any problems," my wife suggested.

"A sleeping bag doesn't make much of a weapon," I agreed. "Besides, I remember Dad saying, 'Don't ever fight unless you have to. If you have to, be sure you can get in a quick telling blow.' No one really wins a long fight. I'm sure that holds true with a bear, too."

Dad often passed along interesting little pieces of advice that I would remember for over fifty years. He once said to me, "It is easier to get help or obtain a favor from a person who has power than from someone who doesn't. Always ask the boss, not someone who works for him."

As a teenager I once put his words to good use in the Chicago office of a general manager of the Milwaukee Road. As a college student I regularly used our family pass to travel between Iowa and Washington during Christmas holidays. This was a nice privilege but it had limitations. Passes were good only on specific trains, and if you used a pass you were forced to fit your schedule to the eligible trains.

On my way back to college at the end of vacation, I arrived in Chicago many hours late due to a snowstorm in the Dakotas. As a result I missed the one train on which I could travel to Kansas City. I was stuck in Chicago overnight with very little money and the prospect of being late for the beginning of school as well. I walked around the station wondering what to do, when an idea occurred to me. I would follow Dad's advice.

I located the general offices for the Milwaukee, got the office number for the general passenger manager, and went to that office. I told the receptionist that I was the son of a longtime Milwaukee employee and that I had a very large problem. "My father has told me to see the general manager about it."

She wanted some more details, but I was persistent in my request to see the boss. I didn't want to give her the opportunity to say no. Finally, she made a quiet inquiry on the intercom and then said to me, "The general manager will see you for a few minutes."

I was ushered into a large plush office with paneled walls and deep carpet. It seemed to me that all of Chicago was spread out before me beyond the floor-to-ceiling windows. A pleasant-looking middle-aged man stood and offered me his hand.

He offered me the magic words. "How may I help you?"

I explained my predicament in detail, not omitting that my problem was due to the Milwaukee train being late, something not of my own doing, and stressing the long and meritorious career of my stepfather who worked for him.

"I think we can take care of this problem," he said, reaching for the phone.

"Get me the general passenger manager of the Santa Fe, please," he told his secretary.

When the other man got on the line, this gentleman said, "this is Johnston at the Milwaukee. I need an emergency deadhead okay for

Kansas City." It was obvious he received an immediate affirmation because he hung up promptly and gave me directions.

"You'll have to hurry, grab a cab, don't take time to walk, and go to the Santa Fe station. The cabby will know where it is. They're holding the Chief. They have a compartment reserved for you. Hurry now!"

I thanked him and rushed out. When I got to the Santa Fe I went to the gate, identified myself, and ran down to the platform. The conductor was pacing back and forth outside the only open door on the train.

"Are you Johnson?" he demanded.

"Yes sir, and thank you." I knew enough to be humble because I was aware that the Chief was a first-class luxury streamliner, one of railroad's finest all-reservation and all-Pullman and that the Santa Fe publicly prided itself on the Chief running on time. They were already 20 minutes late at the start of their run, minutes spent waiting for a Milwaukee Road deadheading college student. I was ushered to my compartment and had the best train ride from Chicago to Kansas City of my life.

When I returned home for the summer, I told my dad about it.

"They held the Chief?" he asked incredulously.

"Yes."

"And what did you tell Mr. Johnston?"

"I told him about my problem and that I needed help. He didn't seem to have any worries about calling the Santa Fe," I explained.

"Did you tell him why you were calling on him for help?"

"Yes, sir. I told him that I knew he was in a position to do something for me because he ran the Milwaukee. As far as passenger trains were concerned, he was the boss."

"Judas Priest!" Dad used his favorite exclamatory outburst.

"And is that all you told him?" he asked me.

"No. I told him you told me to do it."

"Oh God," he said, and walked away. ⚔

14
IT TAKES ALL KINDS

In most respects, the 1940s were relatively modern times for railroading. Significant steps forward in railroad technology had been made. Air-conditioning and streamlined comfort were common. Modern technology was applied to freight as well as passenger handling. Gone were the days of open-windowed coaches and the shoveling of chopped river ice into the hatches of reefer cars. Diesel power, streamliners, and dome cars were the norm. Electric lanterns and marker lights had generally replaced oil lanterns. But in contrast, some of the people who frequently used the Milwaukee for everyday transportation through parts of Idaho and Montana were clear reminders of earlier times.

Having railroaded in the area since 1908, Dad had seen it all and I remember looking at yellowed snapshots (long since lost) of him wearing the working man's black vest and coat topped off with the wide-brimmed hat of earlier years. I don't know how much Dad missed the past, when life was simpler, but I do know he wished me to know of those times and the people who lived in them because he took time to tell me about them.

"Do you see those two fellows with the big suspenders?" he asked on one of our trips together. "The ones with the plaid wool shirts and heavy pants?"

I had indeed noticed them when they had boarded at St. Joe and walked heavily down the coach's aisle.

"They're loggers. Men who go into the woods, look for timber they can cut and send to the sawmills where it will be finished into lumber," he explained. "Look at their boots," he directed.

Their boots were heavy, taller than a regular working shoe but not as tall as a surveyor's boot. The leather was dark, stained from hard use and frequent wetting which required greasing to keep the boots supple.

"They don't use just any boots, you know," he told me. "Their life often depends on good footing and they want the best in boots. The two brands they like best are Bass or White. The White boots are made in St. Maries."

"They look like pretty tough guys," I said.

"They need to be tough. They have to walk or wade miles, balance on wooden planks while they undercut a tree, be able to make the tree fall where they want it to so it can be easily cut up and hauled, floated, or skidded away. They work in all kinds of weather, put in long hours, tromp through the snow and wade in the rivers. Lots of what they do is not only hard work but dangerous, too. In the old days, before the railroad was here or before some of the small logging trails were cut through, they used to pretty much live in the woods in temporary primitive camps—cold during the winter and wet and muddy when it rained. The floors of the shack they slept in and the mess halls where they ate were often dirt. They sat on split trees to eat in some of those mess halls—good food and lots of it—but it was a tough life," he said shaking his head.

In my youth I missed the significance of his knowledge of some of the details. He had never been a working logger, that much I knew, but he had seen most of the things he told me about—flumes, donkey engines, log booms, and weekend excursions to a town for relaxation. I had observed him swing an ax and admired the skill, almost an art, with which he split wood. I wish I had asked more questions about where and how and why he had learned such things. Now, I wonder about the old rusted peavey with a split handle that stood in the corner of our garage.

He used to annoy me when he would stick his head into my bedroom in the morning and cry out, "Time to rise and shine! It's daylight in the swamp and the birds are on the wing!" I have since learned that this was a common wake-up call in early logging camps.

He pointed out some miners riding on the train one trip and told me of the many futile attempts to find pay dirt along the St. Joe and how they moved from one spot to another carrying the tools and grub bags with them, always looking for a better vein or more color. He showed me a mine or two that could be spotted from the right-of-way and took me on some unforgettable trips to Metaline Falls, Washington, riding as dead-heads in the cupola of a Milwaukee caboose. There we saw a different kind of mining, where men were digging for chemicals and materials used in manufacturing and building rather than for gold, silver, or copper.

His stories of the building of the railroad introduced me to many different kinds of labor and skills that had been utilized in constructing the railroad. He talked about the difficulties encountered in surveying a route through the Bitterroots. My older brother had worked as a "stick

This old miner's cabin still stands today, almost underneath one of the Milwaukee's high steel trestles in the Bitterroots. It may very well have been one of those pointed out to me by my father when I rode with him as a boy.
Photo by S. Johnson

man" for a railroad surveying team in one of his first jobs as a teenager. He had told me how hard it was to climb steep mountainsides or scale slippery rocks so that a proper sight could be made. Dad pointed out some of the places above Avery where the surveyors had encountered similar difficulties. Recently I studied one of the original right-of-way maps drawn by the engineering draftsmen, who worked from the data supplied by the first surveyors. The carefully noted details and precise equations on the large sheets disguised the impressive effort that went into gathering the field data for such maps.

Dad told me about the roughnecks who subcontracted by the acre or linear foot to clear brush and loose rock from the prospective right-of-way, noting that they would sandwich such work in among their regular chores of tending to their homestead, animals, and other everyday tasks.

"Lots of them were local ranchers, homesteaders who didn't have an easy way to make hard cash. Generally speaking, they were pretty hard workers and dependable. Putting in a long day's work was nothing new to a man who had to 'prove up' his claim to get full title from the government," he explained.

"Others," he said, "were roustabouts brought in by the trainload. The railroad tried to keep those fellows in camps off to themselves because they were about as hard drinking and ready-to-fight bunch as I'd ever seen." He laughed as though remembering some specific incidents. "Usually they came in on a mixed extra, riding in a coach attached to a supply train, but sometimes there would be a couple of dozen sent on a passenger local to a place that needed some clearing after the main-line work was finished. I sure hated to see them come aboard. If you could get them playing cards it was pretty good, as long as you could keep the booze away from them. But let them get a few belts of hooch in them and . . . " He shook his head.

During the course of a number of conversations over the years, he related stories involving many workers with special talents who came to help complete the line. It was then I first heard of "gandy dancers" and learned of how the railroad made use of rail layers, muckers in the tunnels, "coyote men" who handled explosives, steam shovel operators who could lay a one-yard bucket on a line as precisely as you and I might dot an *i*. Men specialized in building trestles—bridge carpenters for the wooden ones and high steel workers for the tall steel trestles—were good with their hands and eyes and nimble on their feet, walking along a high timber or beam as though oblivious to the height.

While researching the construction of the bridges, I discovered how difficult it had been for the Milwaukee to find some of these specialists. The period during the Road's construction was one of general railroad expansion throughout the country. Competition for specialized workers was keen. The line through the Bitterroots, already predicted to be the most expensive railroad construction in history, was made even more costly by the premium wages necessary to draw these men to this isolated area.

Workers came from all over, but specialized workers often became linked with different ethnic groups or geographical areas. Many of the pile drivers came from French Canada. There were more Swedish laborers in rockwork than any other ethnic group. High steel workers tended to be from St. Louis, Chicago, or some other metropolitan area and carried an urban as well as a trade-related aloofness with them. On the other hand, wooden bridge builders were drawn from either the Pacific Northwest or from the Minnesota area, and tended to think of themselves as carpenters first and bridge builders second.

"If you needed anything fashioned out of lumber you just asked one of those fellows," Dad said. "They could build anything that was made of wood, large or small."

My introduction to ethnic and geographic differences came through listening to my stepfather. "This piece of roadbed once had 50 Japanese and Chinese workers moving dirt and rocks in baskets and wheelbarrows," I remember him saying. "They worked steady and long hours. Small in stature, but very strong men."

Importing Chinese and Japanese laborers—more Chinese than Japanese—for railroad construction was common around the turn of the century. Most, if not all, of these laborers from the Far East that Dad referred to were probably Japanese, however. The Milwaukee had worked out an agreement with Japan to provide laborer employment in return for a contract to handle the freighting of raw silk imported into Pacific Northwest ports for transportation to mills on the eastern seaboard. However, Dad always referred to them as Oriental rather than designating a specific nationality.

Riding along the St. Joe below Avery, Dad pointed out the old "tote" road, a narrow and twisting gash along the hillside often high above the tracks. Early workers had called it the "goat" road because of its precarious location.

"That was the first road into this place. Wasn't much of a road but a lot better than a shotgun trail."

"What's a shotgun trail?" I asked.

"That's a trail that's so rough and narrow that it's hardly any trail at all—just a bushwhacked sort of path through the woods. I would guess some of them followed Indian trails but I don't know for sure."

I was always interested in hearing about the Indians and urged him on.

"Well, I've already told you about how the Indians used to come here for berries and to hunt. Did you know that they used to bring cattle here to be butchered for meat for the construction workers? Not only that," he went on, "a number of Indians worked as graders on the railroad bed during early construction. They were good workers, men who didn't seem to have much to say and tended to keep pretty much to themselves. Lots of different folks worked to build this railroad."

Dad wasn't much for labeling people, so I hadn't heard the slang names for different nationalities at home, but he told me of a number of them and how sometimes the groups hung the nicknames on themselves, such as Dagos, Swedes, Bohunks, Jacks, Norgys, Canucks, and probably others I've forgotten. But I never heard him use any of these terms in a derogatory way. He did point out, though, some of the differences in cultural habits of men who came with different backgrounds.

"Lots of the workers coming here from the Orient and from Europe, too, had different tastes in food than Americans. This caused the railroad all kinds of difficulties in stocking the commissaries since one group wanted spuds while another liked rice. Some wanted lots of good beef while others wanted fish or rabbit."

"How did the railroad manage it?" I asked.

"Mostly by letting the groups which were really different have their own separate camps where they could do as they pleased about food and living habits without any problems from others. Some of the local roustabouts didn't think much of this idea and complained, but the foremen didn't pay any attention to such talk. The important thing was to be sure that everyone got treated right and had plenty of food and warm clothes."

"How did it work out?"

"Pretty good. It was interesting, though, to go by one of those camps during some special holiday they celebrated and see the different clothes and their celebrations. Oh, there were problems. Lots of fights, sometimes between different groups and sometimes between members of the same group. But that wasn't anything new to railroad construction.

"Listen, Stanley," he said. I listened because I had learned that when he used my full first name he had something important to say.

"You remember this. Good men and bad men don't come from different places. They come from everywhere. Listen to what a man has to say before you decide if he's good or bad. In the long run, don't trust a bad man and always give a good man a chance to prove himself. Except a drunk. Don't ever trust a drunk, not even when he's sober." He ended his sermonette with this out-of-context exception. Frank, one of the most tolerant men I have ever known, simply had no use for a drunk and took every opportunity to make sure I felt the same way.

As you might expect of an early teenager, my initial interest mostly was about what the bad guys were like and what they had done to be called bad. Dad never gave me any list of characteristics to help me understand the bad men, but he did make sure I understood that there was a seamy and often unpleasant side to life.

While approaching East Portal one afternoon, he pointed out the former site of Taft, the rough and bawdy temporary construction town built in the valley during the boring of the long St. Paul Pass tunnel.

"Lots of bad men in a camp down there once," he commented, pointing to the narrow valley far below the railroad grade.

"Did you ever go there?"

"Just once, and then for only about an hour. I never saw such a bunch of rowdy drunken bums in my life. No place for an honest or a sober man, I told myself, and I hiked back up to the railroad grade. And that was when the town was almost dead, the construction nearly finished. It must have been hell when the place was going full blast."

Another time, at St. Joe, he pointed across the river to where the town of Ferrell had once stood.

"It was far bigger than St. Joe," he said. "A regular town with a hotel and shops and saloons—mostly saloons, I guess. People used to say, 'Ferrell? That's a town with 30 saloons and only one honest man.'" He laughed.

He also pointed out places along the right-of-way where crimes had been committed—a prospector murdered by another miner, a fight between two gandy dancers, a barroom shoot-out. One time, during our late afternoon walk before returning to the station for the run home from Butte, he took me to a small wooden bridge.

"See that support?" He pointed to a square timber sticking out horizontally at right angles to the tracks.

"One day, years ago, a mob hanged a man from a rope tied to that timber. There was trouble between the union and the management who opposed it. This man was a strong supporter of one viewpoint and some men from the other side hanged him here. There's been lots of that kind of trouble from time to time, in mining, in logging, even on the railroad. Unions are a good thing when bad things happen to workers. But good things can sometimes turn bad, too. There are some things worth fighting for, but not nearly as many worth dying for—or killing for either."

When making the trip from Spokane to Butte, the most exciting part of the trip usually was the first few hours. That was when we went through the mountains and was when special experiences such as riding in the

engine were most apt to occur. As we got near the end of the run, I struggled to stay awake as I watched daylight sweep over the broad valleys to
the west of Butte. But if I dozed off, I always woke up for Deer Lodge, the
last major stop before Butte.

It was a small town located in the heart of cattle country, and known for
its railroad background and terribly cold winters. But for me Deer Lodge
held a special kind of interest. Just beyond the depot and almost right
next to the tracks stood the tall gray stone walls of the territorial prison.
The gun towers sat at the corners of the wall like castle turrets as the train
moved by. I stared at those walls as though I might be able to penetrate
them with some sort of x-ray vision and see the bad men inside and learn
of the crimes that brought them there.

It has been replaced by a modern state correctional unit outside town.
The old prison remains as a tourist attraction and one can walk inside the
walls and view the cells. The prison's former theater had removable seats
so that the gallows could be set up for a hanging when required. But when
I saw it as a youth I was completely dependent upon either my stepfather
or my own imagination for information.

Dad enjoyed detective magazines. He was also interested in history,
particularly Western history, and it didn't take much urging for him to tell
me of some of the men who had experienced having the territorial prison
as a home address. I don't remember the details of a single one of those
stories now, but I have never forgotten some of the themes: a drunken
cowboy or miner gets into a fatal argument with a saloon owner, or two
transients bushwhack a traveling salesman and are tracked down by a
local posse, or a bank is robbed in one of the many isolated small towns in
west-central Montana. I also remember that I was disappointed that Dad
never had any stories to tell of holdups on the trains he rode. He shared
stories about train robberies, but they were always someone else's train at
a spot far away.

Despite my focus on the bad guys, there were lots of good guys and I
heard many stories about them, too. During the 1940s there was a small
sawmill alongside the track at Calder, Idaho. From the elevated view of
the coach window I could briefly watch many of the operations taking
place there while we paused to unload freight or accommodate passengers. I was particularly impressed with the tall cone-shaped sawdust
burner. It billowed clouds of white smoke through the screening, which
kept sparks from escaping into the forest.

A sawdust burner and pieces of an old sawmill still stand beside the former right-of-way at Calder, Idaho. From my train seat as a boy I could look down into the mill and watch operations while my father's train paused briefly here.
Photo by S. Johnson, Milwaukee, Wisc., Public Library Collection

"Lots of small logging and sawmill operations in this area, though not as many as there once was," Dad said. "Used to be a man who lived near here who started out with a few acres and built it into the biggest logging operation around. He even laid track up Big Creek drainage to bring logs down to this railroad, then the 1910 fire came along and pretty well put the kibosh on that. About seven or eight years later we had some pretty big winds that knocked down a lot more timber, and that finished him off. When you're in the logging business and you run out of trees, you run out of money."

"Is he still logging?" I asked.

"I don't think so. He left for somewhere else, Oregon I think, and did some logging down there but he'd be pretty old now, perhaps even 80 or 90. Maybe even dead. Too bad, he was a nice fellow—friendly and sociable to everyone that came along. Honest, too. The loggers used to say that his handshake was better than a Philadelphia lawyer's three-page contract."

It wasn't until just recently that I realized he was probably talking about Fred Herrick (who had a station stop a few miles above Calder named for him). Dad really valued honesty and he was right about Mr. Herrick. According to the history books, Herrick ran into more bad business luck in Oregon and eventually went bankrupt. He was so admired that Congress voted to return him the large performance bond required of logging companies so that he might have a little more cash to help out with his financial struggles.

Not all the good guys have good things happen to them. Fred Herrick was an example of that kind of poor luck. Another incident illustrates the same kind of good man–bad luck scenario. According to a widely told story, a man was badly burned near St. Regis. While waiting to get him to medical help in Missoula, he was wrapped in oil-soaked cotton waste, a common treatment for burn victims then and still used today in a more refined manner. The fire victim was loaded onto a freight car for the trip and one of his friends, hearing of the misfortune that had befallen his partner, hurried to see him before the train left. Entering the dark freight car holding a candle, he saw him lying on a pallet and rushed to his side. Flames from the candle ignited the poor man's bandages and before help could arrive he had burned to death.

Dad had some personal heroes—often people who were important to him for private reasons but, not necessarily heroes who would attract wider attention. A time or two when his train was delayed and I asked him why, he would say that the engine had thrown an eccentric rod. I never inquired further because I thought it was his way of being clever and using a throw-away phrase to explain a complex problem. He must have picked up my skepticism because one time when we were delayed because of mechanical problems while sitting in the yards at Avery he brought the matter up.

"You've never seen an eccentric rod, have you?" he said.

"I guess not," I said, figuring I was about to be the butt of one of his jokes.

"Well, come on. I'll show you one. I'll even do better than that. I'll introduce you to Little Jim. He can replace an eccentric rod faster than any man I've ever seen."

We walked down the tracks the half mile or so to the roundhouse area, and there he took me up to a man who couldn't have been much over five feet tall. I noticed however that he had wide shoulders and the biggest biceps I had ever seen. Dressed in greasy and stained overalls, he wiped his hands on an old rag and shook my hand.

"My wife's boy," he said, a phrase he always used, more sensitive than he needed to be of his position as a stepfather. "I want to show him an eccentric rod."

"On or off an engine?" Little Jim asked.

"Either one."

I was led to the side of a large passenger engine, the kind that would later that same day replace the electric motor on the westbound Olympia and pull it into Spokane. He stopped by a heavy steel bar, which was part of the drive rod apparatus that carried power from the cylinders to the large drive wheels. It was one of the smaller rods but big nevertheless.

"How do you lift one?" I wanted to know, awed by the size.

Little Jim laughed. "Well, first you swear at it just to let it know who's really the boss. Then you have to know how to find the balance point so you can hoist it up by a derrick or crane of some sort and then you bolt it to where it belongs. If you haven't got a derrick you need a bunch of strong men who won't let go when they realize how heavy it really is. That's a piece of steel you don't want to drop on your toe."

A railroad car-man was another of Dad's heroes. I never heard all the details, but Dad's train had been derailed a short distance outside a small station in the early days of electrification. The coach he was in was sitting at an angle, off the tracks—or "on the ground" as railroaders say—but not overturned. Dad made his way to the front vestibule where the car had been coupled to a baggage car. The couplers had opened and the engine and baggage car were a few yards farther down the right-of-way, upright but also on the ground. Dad started to open the door when he saw a broken piece of trolley wire slowly swinging back and forth, showering sparks every time it touched a metal support on one of the broken poles nearby. The wire swung like a Fourth of July sparkler, back and forth, right in front of the vestibule steps, and every third or fourth swing would touch the edge of the steps sending sparks flying.

Dad hurried back and yelled for everyone in the coach to stand in the aisle and not touch anything metal. Fortunately there were only a handful of passengers and one other crewman to worry about. In looking out the window they could all see the reason for the warning and needed no further encouragement to heed his warning.

Someone on the engine crew had already used a trackside callbox to summon help, which came quickly. Ordinarily, the first step in such an emergency is to open a cutoff switch for the overhead power. All the crew had manuals showing the location of these and were trained in how to use them. In this instance though, the closest switch was being blocked by the derailed engine.

A worker from the depot arrived and hurriedly rigged some kind of insulated pole to temporarily prop the wire in a way that changed the arc of its swing so it missed the coach. At his shouted directions, everyone piled off at the opposite end of the coach and scurried to the opposite side of the track.

"Thank God for electricians," Dad told him.

"Hell, I'm no electrician. I'm a car-man. Spend most of my days fixing stuck windows and tightening loose screws," the man replied. "I'm scared to death of electricity."

It didn't matter to Dad. The man was permanently placed on his list of heroes.

I had my favorite people, too, not necessarily heroes but people I wished I could meet. One of them was a man I call "Avery's Special Fisherman."

The St. Joe River has long been known for its trout fishing. During pioneer times Spokane restaurants would buy baskets of trout wholesale for their patrons' dinners. Steamboats on Coeur d'Alene Lake were known to heave-to shortly before lunch or dinner so that crew could catch enough trout for the passengers. It never took long. Not infrequently, Dad would bring home a few trout given him by one of his fisherman friends somewhere on the St. Joe, a treat for the whole family.

I learned of this special fisherman from one of Dad's brakemen. He came down the aisle as we left Avery one day, laughing hard as he approached us.

"What's so funny?" Dad asked.

"I was just talking to the fellow that runs the beanery."

"And?" Dad asked, quizzically.

"He's taken trout off the menu."

"I didn't know he served trout," Dad said.

"He hasn't, in the past. But the last few months he's had some kind of an arrangement with an old-timer who lives up one of the draws. Seems as though this fellow has learned the secret to catching trout as quick and easy as in the old days."

"What's the matter? Did he fish out the river?" Dad asked.

"No. No, he's still catching a lot of fish. Big fat trout, fatter than most people can remember seeing for a long time. The trouble was, he got loose-mouthed about his catching methods and that did him in."

"Too much competition?"

"No. Too few eaters."

"I don't understand."

"Seems as though this guy had tried fishing lots of places and then one day he found a spot loaded with fish and has been using that as his own private fishing hole ever since. Trouble is, the place is just downstream from where a couple of cabins have fixed up a drain they use to carry off their wastewater and sewage."

"Oh God!" Dad said.

The brakeman walked off, still laughing at what he had heard.

"Did that man ever give you any fish?" I asked Dad.

"No, certainly not. Not that I know of anyway."

"I'm glad of that," I said.

"Well, you needn't worry about it. The fish we get are okay and I don't think this fellow will be fishing there or that those folks will be dumping their raw slop into the river anymore either, once the word gets around."

"Gee," I said, wrinkling up my nose at the thought of where the man had been catching his prize fish.

"Tell you what, though," Dad said. "Just to be safe, I'll wait a while before accepting any more trout to bring home."

"Good."

"And Stanley?"

"Yes?"

"I don't think it's necessary to share this with your mother—not if we ever want to have trout in the house again." ◿

15
TOILETS, SPITTOONS, AND FORBIDDEN MAGAZINES

☞ "If you want a boy to become interested in something, tell him to stay away from it." There's a lot of truth in that old saying and I think my childhood proves it.

When I was a young child my home was a place of rules, gently administered, but more rules than encouragement to explore beyond the edge. As a consequence I grew into the teen years without having given my parents too many concerns about where I was and what I was doing.

Mother seemed to worry most, and the majority of the rules were hers. Frank had a few (and tacitly endorsed Mother's) but his were seldom as directly stated or as rigidly enforced, though I hesitated to break them every bit as much as hers. The details of everyday living were not overlooked. And, of course, there were specific rules about what one could and could not do while riding on the train.

Dad's were simple. "Don't annoy anyone. Don't get in the way of the work of the train crew. Don't get hurt."

Mother's were far more comprehensive and included a wide range of potential eventualities ". . . just in case . . ." Mother's rules covering the behavior of a young boy while traveling on the train relied heavily on restrictions. There was, for example, a categorical list of places and situations to avoid.

I was to stay away from most public restrooms except in times of genuine need. Even in such emergencies it was necessary to personally clean all the relevant equipment with a paper towel (a wet and soapy towel was even better). Such logistical demands obviously cut down on impulsive visits of whim to the men's facilities. Perhaps this was what Mother had in mind all along.

Dad dealt with the same "dangerous" situation with a succinct, "Wash your hands before and after, wait your turn, and don't talk to strangers." The last caution was redundant since I was instructed generally to keep my distance from strangers.

Strangers were broadly defined as almost anyone we had not known for a significant length of time, a period rather poorly defined, as I recall. Strangers were considered individuals likely to be engaged in a variety of suspect and possibly nefarious and evil practices if given the opportunity. However, a general amnesty was invariably granted to anyone we may have met even so briefly in church. But as it turned out, I never encountered a church-going, men's-room, do-evil-things-to-children stranger and thus was saved from an often hinted at but never thoroughly explained horrible fate.

Whether train crew members were really strangers or only semi- or quasi-strangers, depended on which parent was making the judgment. To Mom, the crew represented slightly less risk than average, but still were not to be unqualifiedly trusted. Dad gave the crews better but not totally positive ratings and, for that matter, was not so blindly unforgiving of the church-met group either. His approach was more of a middle ground while Mother's stance was quite polemic.

Also, I was generally discouraged from random exploration of the unknown (event, place, situation, idea) no matter what its nature. This careful approach to new experience may best be understood by some elaboration of my experience with the evils versus the opportunities of public restrooms on or related to trains.

For a young child, three days on a train is a long time. The monotony of semiconfinement can be broken by looking at scenery and occasional visits to the water cooler only so long. Other opportunities for boredom fighting must be sought. Every train car had two restrooms, one for men and one for women. As a little child I always used the women's room, accompanied by my mother. With elation I discovered that when I became old enough to go the men's room I was then too old to go with Mother to the women's room. The result of this distinction was that a journey into the specially designated "men's place" offered me the opportunity for visiting a type of promised land where I was at least temporarily unobservable and beyond the reach of my mother's long arm of parenting. This was a new type of freedom indeed and societal conventions were irrevocably on my side.

In those days the men's room on a train car was actually a semisuite of three small rooms separated from the outside hallway by a full wall with access via an open doorway blocked by a heavy fabric curtain. That doorway opened into the middle and largest of the three rooms. This area housed washbowls, mirrors, and a single small bowl with a pencil-thin spigot shaped like the curved neck of a drinking swan. It was intended to be used for brushing one's teeth.

To the right of the washroom was a small door with a brass handle and a sliding sign above the handle that announced "Free" or "In use" depending on whether the lock inside was on or off. This door offered entry to a space scarcely larger than the toilet inside. It definitely was not a room designed for group activities or even a single person of very large stature. In the opposite direction was a third space partitioned off by a wall the height of the back of the two facing coach seats inside. On the side next to the hallway wall a long bench ran the width of this room at right angles to a pair of coach seats, which were next to the window. This area was used for sitting, smoking, and spitting—mostly spitting, it seemed to me.

These restroom facilities encompassed a whole list of things both exciting and eye-opening to a young boy. I found toilets that when flushed allowed the participant to peer right down on the gravel railbed and ties flashing past below the open sewage outlet. This brief view was made even more exciting because it was accompanied by an increased firsthand roar of train and track noises bouncing back through the open pipe. I learned, too, that there were rules about when to flush. The posted sign's warning was clear.

PASSENGERS WILL PLEASE REFRAIN FROM ALL
FLUSHING WHILE TRAIN IS IN STATION

I learned, too, that the stainless steel oval washbowls enclosed in the smooth-topped commode (an arrangement new to me since I was used to washbowls that stood on legs) had several fascinating characteristics. Upon turning the faucet the water mysteriously appeared from some orifice hidden beneath a small overhang on the back edge of the bowl and then coursed flatly down the side of the bowl at a slight angle. This angle, coupled with the motion of the train and the natural circular forces somehow imposed by the spinning of the earth, caused the water to swirl around in an elliptical arch, higher on the back and front and lower on the sides as though a circle had been bent, depressed at each side but somehow suspended elsewhere. With experimental varying of the strength of the flow, one could magically control the height of this unexplained swirl until the highest edges flirted with flowing over the edge and onto the top of the commode.

I subsequently found that the water, which was held in the bowl by a plunger controlled by a lever next to the faucet handle, could also be controlled. By manipulating this plunger, I could make washing my hands a scientifically significant experience. I also discovered soap dispensers, shaped like upside-down pears and hung from dispensers that allowed them to rock to and fro with the motion of the train. A press upward on the bottom left a globule of distinctively smelling liquid soap in the palm of your hand, far more fun to use than the orange bars of Lifebuoy at home. My hands went through a new and unfamiliar period of cleanliness because of this device.

In the sitting room part of the suite (Dad used to laughingly call it the spit and sit and tell lies area) I encountered a seemingly unending number of interesting storytellers; great swirls of cigar smoke; and encountered a brand-new artifact in my young life as an explorer, brass spittoons, which clanged like Oriental gongs when squarely hit with a properly shaped and aimed brown chunk of Red Man chewing tobacco.

Each of these facets of the men's room contributed to a wondrously eye-opening set of experiences for a young boy. Unfortunately I was not yet wise enough to keep my discoveries to myself but made a very large tactical error as I innocently shared them with my mother.

She was not overjoyed, and her reaction was immediate and thorough. To sum it up, my free parole was revoked and I was placed on a rigidly codified probation. I now also carried with me a new set of subregulations: Disallowed strangers, places, and activities and contraband objects were now more or less categorically defined with the added safeguard of, "and anything like that, too!"

I began to realize that risk taking, for either of my parents at this stage of their life, consisted of such daring venturings as ordering a new item on a restaurant menu or perhaps the deliberate flouting of the city ordinances by shooting off a one-inch Lady Finger in the backyard on the Fourth of July. Even such escapades as these seemed doomed to failure, when Mother glanced over her shoulder on one particular Independence Day (an obviously misnamed holiday) to find a state trooper, hands on hips, watching a middle-aged woman lighting and tossing illegal firecrackers into the barbecue grill. She received only a tongue-in-cheek warning followed by the trooper's suggestion that she place the Lady Fingers in the grill and touch them off all at once to lessen her chagrin and feelings of guilt.

When younger, Mom and Dad actually had been involved in a number of exciting new experiences including being with the railroad as it was being constructed through Indian country and across unknown mountain passes, helping to explore and settle a new frontier in the Northwest. But at this point I was not yet a teenager and was continually reminded of the improbability of finding anything particularly useful, fun, or exciting in the unknown.

However, my memory for what I had seen and experienced was good and patience paid off as restrictions were gradually eased. During my teenage years I returned to the men's room both literally and figuratively, and in retrospect I am surprised when I reflect on all the interesting and positive things I learned there. Playing with the washbowls and staring down the open toilet soon lost their appeal but person-to-person experience with older patrons more than replaced them.

One of the more interesting experiences on my cross-country trips in the sleeping car was to note the ways in which various men handled their morning ablutions. I had never seen any other man except Frank in such a situation and he never offered much in the way of instruction. Just by watching on the train I learned about electric razors, the use of cologne and deodorant, and the care with which some men looked after their manicures and the details of trimming their eyebrows, beards, and sideburns.

Of course I picked up some other information that wasn't all that positive but perhaps was socially useful in an entirely different way. I learned, for example, that there is a great variety in content, method, and tone of profanity. I had not heard much swearing in my home and when I did it was always in connection with some traumatic incident such as the smashing of a finger. The resulting oaths in such instances were explosive, but brief and to the point, and were always negatively directed at the specific object in question. I discovered in the men's room that profanity sometimes is used in entirely different circumstances and manner than those to which I was accustomed.

The lesson learned was not how to swear. It was to weigh the social context before responding and to realize that better judgments are made by considering the situation and circumstances rather than basing your response on some a priori absolute.

I also acquired some opinions and made some value judgments about smoking and spittoons. I decided that quite apart from any moral stance, smoking involved a definite social context. It looked like fun but involved many negatives including watery eyes, mixing of both good and bad odors, a lot of coughing, ashes on one's clothes, and expense. Long-term health concerns were not yet commonly recognized.

Watching chewers use a spittoon involved some real ambiguous feelings. I found the sight of brown spittle seeping from the corner of someone's mouth repulsive. But it was fun to watch the varying accuracy of different chewers' aim for the spittoon. A missed shot was gross, the error in aim often resulting in widespread splashing of dirty brown spittle, but a bull's-eye with its immediately resulting metallic clang of success was occasion for my silent equivalent of whatever that day and age's high-five might have been. If there could have been any way I might have achieved the necessary specific gravity and density of expectorant without using chewing tobacco I would have been severely tempted. Alas I remained a distant observer appreciating only the quasi-athletic aspects of this generally unappealing activity.

Perhaps the most important lesson learned was one of increasing self-confidence and independence. Sometimes this came through deliberate attempts to spread my wings, efforts that would at times be blessed with pure success. Other times resulted in unexpected consequences, which may have taught the lessons just as well.

On one occasion when Dad was working on the Olympian, I decided it would be an entertaining act of defiance to stay in the toilet while the train was in the station and to flush clean water down on the tracks. I knew that the trainmen came through just before pulling into a station and checked the lavatories by knocking on the door and asking if anyone was inside before locking the door with a key. I figured that if I timed it just right and said nothing I could stay inside and no one would know the difference. Then after enjoying my flushing experience I could sneak out, unlocking the door from the inside, and no one would be the wiser as to the identity of the platform flushing culprit.

I saw Ross Snider, Dad's brakeman, head for the women's room at the front of the car, and knew he was checking that area. While he was busy I slipped into the little room at the other end of the car.

Sure enough, he knocked and called as expected. I kept quiet. He locked the door. The train pulled into the station and after waiting a few minutes to be sure that Mr. Snider and Dad had left the train I flushed as planned. Then I quickly moved to leave the scene. Alas, I discovered that the door could not be opened from the inside when it had been locked

Electric power connected, a 1947 Columbian stands ready to leave the busy Avery, Idaho, platform behind as it continues east. It was at this location that I unwisely chose to experiment with forbidden toilet flushing.
Photo by Wilbur Whittaker

with a key. I was trapped. My only hope was to sit tight, so to speak, until we left the station and the door was unlocked and then to slip out unnoticed, which I did, listening carefully for movement outside my door of escape. I heard nothing, so I slipped quietly out into the adjoining washroom only to find both Dad and Mr. Snider sitting on the bench seat watching me. I didn't explain and neither man said a word as I hastily exited the room. It wasn't mentioned during the rest of the trip either. In fact, I was never reprimanded. I guess Dad figured I had learned my lesson and that was sufficient.

It was years later before I learned from Dad that one of his friends who was traveling that night had seen me enter and noticed I was locked inside the toilet when Ross Snider came through. Knowing I was trapped he tried to help me by quickly finding Dad and telling him where I was. Both Dad and Mr. Snider had been standing outside the door when I flushed and had heard my pleased giggling as I did so. They decided to leave me there and have some fun at my expense.

Much social maturing occurred in those gender-restricted rooms—a maturation which was not easily shared with parents. I listened carefully as a parade of travelers with interesting stories occupied my attention. I allowed myself to vicariously explore the locales of others' experiences. The scenes and events thus imagined were often far less bucolic and protected than those to which my parents had sought to have me exposed.

For the first time I learned of some of the sordid realities of life as our train rolled through the literal backyards of the small communities scattered along our right-of-way. It seemed as though these storytellers recognized each tavern and barroom along the way and knew stories about their patrons. I acquired the names of the places that served the largest or least generous drinks. Bitterroot House and Indian Joe's Bar & Grill and Little Mary's Place may now be gone but they are not forgotten.

Equally well noted and carefully but secretly filed away in my new-found awareness were tales of establishments that served far more than liquor. These narrations, sometimes only offering titillating hints and in other cases related with embarrassing though perhaps mythical hyperbole and detail, caused a humorous yet worrisome mind-set in my largely unwounded psyche. It was years before I could be socially introduced to women with certain names without automatically encountering an inwardly raised hypothesis. During the teen years, a period always rife with fantasy anyway, this sometimes created conflict between my church-oriented rearing and my libido: Should this person be shunned or welcomed even in my imagination? Obviously I could not seek my parents' advice in this respect.

My actual early exploration of the realms of forbidden fruit were much less daring. In truth these initial forays were both precipitated and defined by my parents. It was all their fault. Magazines were the problem—the detective magazines in the suitcase on the crew's seat in the front of the coach. I might have had some curiosity about them, but hearing my mother say to Frank, "Do not bring any more of those pulp magazines home, they are nothing but trash and their pictures are outrageous," stimulated a far stronger interest than I had before.

Looking over Dad's shoulder, I frequently sneaked a look at whatever page was open while he read in the pre-train-time hours in the station. Subsequently I elevated my daring by borrowing an issue when it was left unguarded and then hiding it inside a newspaper or larger magazine so I could read it later when Dad was busy with his work. Sometimes I would sneak a copy into the little room inside the men's room. This offered an opportunity for examination where discovery was no worry, but the rewards of privacy were tempered by the fact that if I were to read too long I was apt to anger others who needed the facilities.

I eventually graduated to an age where I could pick up one without timidity and leaf through its pages in front of Dad without his comment. He sometimes would subtly seek to divert my interest by offering me something more uplifting such as *Life* or *Look* but he never stopped me. Of course when I reached the point that this literature was accessible to me without restriction I found that the content was both less bizarre than I had been told and less interesting than I had imagined.

I never did share with Mother or Dad my men's room maturational transition from childhood to adulthood. There were times I was tempted to tell them, but I never did. I am still unsure whether the timidity I felt stemmed from my concern for them or for myself.

I can remember years later Mother looking at me and asking, "Where did you ever learn a word like that?"

I could have told her. ☙

16
BITTERROOT WINTERS

God apparently created winter for children. I can remember the enthusiasm with which I ran to the window to check the color of the sky early
on winter weekend mornings. If the sky had that peculiar saturated tone
of gray that every child of the northern latitudes quickly learns to recognize, there were squeals of delight.

"It looks like it's going to snow," I would announce to my parents.
Then, throwing open the back door I would take two or three deep
breaths and proclaim, "It feels like snow—it even smells like snow!"

I don't remember my parents' reaction. Perhaps they were happy to
entertain the idea of my being paroled from the boredom of a house
shrinking under the confinement of winter. I do remember, however, that
Mother worried about snow in the mountains because of the threat it
brought to my father's safety. Dad didn't seem to worry about it, but he
disliked the extra work it caused him. Bad weather meant different
clothes, slippery car steps, station platforms not yet shoveled clear, but
through which he had to wade to bring copies of running orders to the
engineer, and temperatures so cold that the railings froze to anything that
touched them. In cold and snowy weather, running schedules could
become meaningless, and different spots for meeting other trains had to
be found, further complicating and changing familiar routines. The
severe winters always carried with them the threat of frozen switches, broken air lines, or steam boilers that always chose the worst of times to stop
working, leaving cars cold, passengers grumpy, and train crew frustrated.

I was allowed to ride with Dad on his turn during the winter months
only a handful of times. Other times of year, tagging along with him was
simply a matter of asking. In the summertime, if there were any objections
at all they were most apt to come from Mother. But in the winter, requests
were met with the combined reluctance of both parents. A carefully
planned presentation and appeal had to be coupled with fortuitous timing
in making my pitch if I was to have any chance of having my request
granted.

The snow in the Bitterroots threatened to bury the railroad at times. This 1910 scene at Roland shows the magnitude of the problem. The west portal of St. Paul Pass tunnel is in the background, the peaked roof of its snow shed still above the snow. Darrel Dewald Collection

Riding the train with Dad in the winter presented pros and cons, too. When I traveled with him I relished being able to do things alongside him: to walk with him beside the train in the dark, watch him perform various duties with other train crew and station agents. But in the winter the weather, schedule changes, and the pressure of added tasks made it more difficult for him to share his time with me. He didn't tell me to stay out of the way, but I had learned to recognize when my presence was more of a problem than a pleasure to him.

As a consequence, I learned to be creative in finding things to do. While it was still light outside I was aware of the bad weather rolling by outside my window. I would watch the snow blow in swirls as the train rushed by and see the whiffs of steam float away from the train into the winter air. I luxuriated in being inside, warm, comfortable, and cozy in the steam-heated railroad car. When I grew tired of watching the weather outside, it was fun to curl up on a coach seat with a good book, secure from the unpleasantness of winter.

Sometimes though, I was allowed to experience just a touch of winter in the mountains, enough to make me feel like a pioneer resisting the tantrums of a seasonally ill-tempered Mother Nature. The baggagemen were a bit more relaxed about my wandering than was Dad and were more apt to let me explore on my own. So, when I became bored with the more passive roles of reading or of experiencing the outside blizzard vicariously through the coach window, I would often head up to the baggage car. I had traveled the run often enough to be able to match certain activities with different locations, so I knew when to best make my move and increase my chances of becoming involved in something interesting.

There were always little things to do there. Freight manifests had to be checked and I helped with matching items on the list to cartons piled in heaps in different sections of the car. If an already separated batch of luggage and freight was due to be unloaded at the next stop I helped drag things to the doorway. But it was when the big heavy sliding door was opened that the excitement really began to build.

Working around any piece of railroad equipment carried its own form of danger. I had learned very early (and suffered a badly bruised shoulder in the process) that heavy baggage car doors, if open or unlatched, might suddenly slide with a change in the train's movement. After having one learning experience I knew enough to stand back as the door was opened and to wait until it was securely latched before going near it. But the thrill of being close-by in the eye of danger, remote as it might be, was like walking past the lion's cage at the circus.

The one standard rule, enforced by the baggagemen and Dad alike, was to not go near the open door while the train was moving. I was allowed to bend this rule the tiniest bit as the train's momentum slowed but was always told to "hang on" as the final jerk of inertia accompanied our stop. I didn't expect to fall out, and didn't really think I would do much more than scrape a knee or elbow if I did as the train slowed to a crawl, but just the same, I religiously followed that advice.

The real fun was in helping the baggagemen unload. There were many items I could easily and safely handle and they gave me free hand with those. Plummer Junction, though only just a few miles out of Spokane, usually meant cord-tied bundles of the next morning's paper to be shoved out the door onto a waiting baggage cart. St. Maries frequently involved hexagonal metal boxes the size of small suitcases, carrying cases of movie film being shipped to local theaters. These had to be handled with more care than newspapers and it was fun to fantasize about what adventures were leaving the train to find a new home in St. Maries. I always carefully studied the labels on these cases hoping there would be a hint of their content. All I ever found were the names or initials of movie companies and the addresses of distributors. St. Joe often had an interesting variety of baggage to be sorted and unloaded. Sometimes it was produce or gunnysacks of unidentifiable machine parts. Once it was a case of live rabbits whose long white ears stuck up through the cracks where I could scratch them. And on one memorable trip it was a large elk's head, spread antlers carefully wrapped in excelsior and brown paper, coming back to a St. Joe hunter from a Spokane taxidermy shop.

I liked unloading, because it made me feel that I had something special to do, a responsibility that made me important to the train and part of its crew. This coupled with a few moments' exposure to the breath-robbing snap of winter midnight cold, the sight of everyone's breath steaming out into the open air, and the feel of snowflakes as they sometimes blew in through the open door while we worked, added up to an exciting time for me.

But it was the stops at the tiny isolated settlements in the middle of the dark St. Joe Valley and along the dark slopes of the Bitterroots that I really enjoyed. At these places no houses or depots warmed by potbelly stoves were to be seen, no baggage carts or station platform lights or agency workers greeted us as we slowed to a stop. When the baggage car's door was opened usually only a faint glow of light shining from inside the baggage car interrupted the dense blackness of the mountain winter night. Much of the freight could be pushed out the door onto a waiting cart or simply dropped to the ground alongside the track. Sometimes though, it would be necessary to climb down to the ground to help unload a particular piece. Freight and baggage was a baggageman's responsibility, and though they weren't always happy about being out in the cold they knew this was part of the job and accepted it stoically for the most part. But sometimes a brakeman or my father would help with the outside chores, though I never understood then why a conductor should ever handle baggage. It seemed to me the same as asking the captain of a ship to serve as a dockhand, but Dad obviously viewed it differently and more democratically.

Sometimes the freight needed to be placed in a locked storage building alongside the station platform. This meant finding the proper key for the brass locks the railroad used for such purposes. It was typically the train-men who carried the keys to such locks: brakemen, flagmen, and of course the conductor. When Dad did this, some of the demotion I felt he had received in handling baggage was removed by that ring of heavy brass keys he carried. I was sure that the keyring had keys to very special and important locks. When the temperature dropped, the trainmen would sometimes fumble with the lock on a trackside storage building, letting loose a string of profanity over frost-nipped fingers as mittens were removed to turn a stubborn key. Dad did the same, though his oaths were usually pretty mild and apt to be muttered rather than said aloud.

Such occasions never arose at the bigger stations, which had freight handlers assigned to such duties. But at the smaller isolated outposts, the trainmen and baggage crew were on their own. Since these small places were allotted only the brief stops in the train's schedule, the work was always done quickly.

At such stops the baggage door was quickly opened and shut again as we paused for only a few minutes, sometimes only a few seconds. But while it was open I would stand by the side of the door, still hanging on to the handle, and thrust my head out into the darkness. All I could see to the front was the glare of the locomotive's headlight on the track ahead, shining through a haze of steam and cooling air drifting up and away from under the cars. To the rear everything was an inky black.

Inside the train, which I had come to know so well in the protective company of my stepfather and his friends, was safety and warmth and companionship. Outside was danger, cold, and loneliness. The contrast between the inside and the outside of the train was frightening at first, unsettling, but exciting and fulfilling, too. Standing in those open door-ways, if even only for a few moments, I experienced enough of a different outside world to appreciate its challenge, yet was given the opportunity to safely stay where I was until I was ready to venture out on my own terms.

At my young age I didn't reflect on the experience of standing in those open doorways with any degree of sophistication. Essentially, it was fun, a bit daring. Looking back, it seems to me that this was healthy risk-taking for a young boy, a growing experience I comprehend only in retrospect. I never discussed this whole business with Dad, and I'm not sure why. I wish now I had, but I expect he was more aware of what I was doing than I realized.

The cold that hunkered down in these mountain valleys was no imaginary fantasy and truly nothing to be taken lightly. When a high-pressure cell stalled over the area in the winter, bringing high blue skies during the day and brilliant starlight at night, the plunging temperatures, which left little red to be seen in the thermometer, would sometimes split giant trees far quicker than a logger's ax. Though I never heard it myself, residents would talk about the trees being split, the sharp report of their death echoing like a rifle shot. Dad told me stories of temperatures so low during the building of the right-of-way that construction workers would stay awake all night to be sure that a fire was kept in the cast-iron potbelly stoves in their tents and slab-board huts. Even so, buckets of water a few feet away would still freeze solid.

It was partly the cold that caused the Milwaukee to first explore the virtues of electrification very early after its arrival in the Bitterroots. The railroad discovered that the low temperatures could drain off the heat from even the largest steam engine's boiler despite the best of well-laid fires in their grates. This could reduce even the most powerful engines to overweight pieces of too-rapidly-cooling steel with insufficient power left to get the job done. Low temperatures presented no challenge to the electrics, however. When the box-cab motors arrived they climbed the steepest grades on the coldest days and nights, ignoring the temperature. The steady hum of their gears boasted that they were undaunted and unaffected by what the thermometer said.

The men who worked the trains were aware of the dangerous strength residing in the cold and shared that warning with those who rode their trains. Invariably when I went with Dad during the winter he would remind me several times to keep my hands off the metal handrails by the cars' steps. The moisture in the palm of the hand was enough to make the skin freeze tight to the steel, a bond almost instantly formed and broken only by tearing the skin or by quickly finding enough warm water to break the grasp of the cold metal.

Railroaders dressed appropriately for the cold. I remember seeing Frank's outside winter clothes carefully laid out on the seat next to the brown leather suitcase on the coach seat he used as a sort of office. Coming to a stop he would stand and carefully put on the successive layers of clothing that protected him from the cold. Even his conductor's hat was replaced by a heavy fur cap with a turned-down visor. I would watch him ready himself like a knight sliding into his armor in preparation for the joust.

Passengers received special attention. Those disembarking received special warnings, not only about cold grab irons but about slippery steps and icy platforms. A broom and a small coal scoop were kept nearby to clean off the steps when the doors were first opened. Two train crewmen (instead of the usual one) assisted passengers on icy and snowy steps. Dad and Perse, the baggageman, kept two wooden boxes full of old blankets in the baggage car. "To wrap the young kids in should the heat fail," Dad explained to me.

Mechanical things needed extra attention as well. Frozen switch gears and handles would be regularly baptized with salt. Dad would routinely stick a small lunch sack full of salt in his mackinaw pocket before leaving the train and sprinkle it on the places typically causing problems. The train crews knew where the problem sites were, but the deer and elk just as quickly learned where train crews were using salt. Dad would often point out the numerous tracks in the ground where animals came to lick at the soil where the salt had spilled.

Certain localities seemed to attract the worst weather conditions winter could offer. Probably the place I remember most when I think of winter and trains and the Bitterroots is East Portal, Montana. There, at the east end of the long tunnel, was a small cluster of railroad buildings. Alongside the lonely tracks were several houses for the section gangs and substation operators and their families, along with a few small storage sheds for track equipment and supplies. Across the tracks, opposite the houses, was a tank for fuel oil and a bin for coal. The large brick substation sat up against the hillside, huddling in the deep snow, like a medieval castle, only dim lights showing through its tall windows. No other signs of civilization were to be seen at this hour.

In the friendlier seasons of the year, East Portal gave no clue as to why winter considered this place one of its own. Originally the site of construction camps for workers digging the tunnel, the small flat space carved out of the mountainside sits at the head of a relatively small and unimpressive draw, several hundred feet above the valley below where the interstate sweeps by oblivious to the history overhead. During reasonable seasons, a dirt road gives access to the site. But during the isolation of winter, the cold flows down the mountainside and into the draw like an arm of a glacier, moving as though drawn to this place by some hidden force. And when the cold air carries snow, it seems as if all the snow of all the peaks and valleys surrounding East Portal roar into this place like a

Trackside building occupants at East Portal, Montana, depended upon long narrow pathways to get from their houses to trackside. Snow was a constant winter problem in this area. We measured more than a foot of snowfall in an hour one cold night in the 1940s.
Darrel Dewald Collection

giant maelstrom, riding on the river of frigid air that cascades down the draws and gullies, penetrating and filling every crevice with its unforgiving cold. Trainmen used to say that East Portal and Haugan (just a few miles east) were the coldest places on the railroad.

Deep snow is common throughout the Bitterroots, and railroaders came to expect it. But one place that they could almost be sure would get a lion's share of any snowstorm was East Portal. When the snow fell, it stayed until spring, piling up in countable layers, marking each storm as a tree's rings note the passing years.

By the time winter was becoming long in the tooth the snow would often be twelve and fifteen feet deep. The tracks ran within a long straight channel cut though the snow by the rotary plows. Looking out a train window all you could see was white. Then, in the middle of this white canyonlike wall, a narrow slit would reach out to the side at a right angle. Only three or four feet wide, sometimes tunneled through the drift with snow for a ceiling, it would end in the doorway of a house, shed, or station. It was common for the snow to be higher than the eaves of the buildings, and extended tin chimney pipes could be seen sticking out of the snow, providing an outlet for the stoves inside. These nearly buried structures were where those living at East Portal spent the winter months like animals in a burrow.

For all the snow and cold weather, East Portal was a busy place. Section crews housed here worked the tracks. Rotary steam and electrically powered snow plows were often there and the substation was vital for providing power to keep the railroad running. The long siding track made the location useful for train meets outside the tunnel. Dad's local train always stopped at East Portal and I looked forward to it. I felt a certain romance in the place because of its isolation from civilization and its proximity to the long black tunnel, which hung with icicles during the winter.

One night we sat there on the siding for over an hour, held up by some problem down the line that required us to wait and meet another train here instead of further along the right-of-way. It was snowing the largest flakes I had ever seen, so big that the geometric pattern of a flake was momentarily visible in your palm.

It was not especially cold this particular night and there was no wind, but it was snowing very hard. Thousands and thousands of these huge flakes were coming straight down, falling like confetti in some never-ending celebration. We sat in the baggage car, the door open, eating our midnight lunch and watching it snow. One of the baggagemen decided to measure how fast the snow was coming down.

He took a bamboo order loop off a peg on the wall. These were four-foot-long pieces of bamboo, shaped like an elongated *p* with a split in the loop end where orders could be stuck or tied. The idea was that the giver would hold the stick out by its handle, and the receiver would pick up the stick by allowing his arm to go through the loop, jerking the staff away from the holder. This way orders could be passed to and from moving trains without the train having to stop. There were always several of these available on pegs in the baggage car.

Leaning out the open baggage car door the baggageman softly laid the stick flat on top of the trackside snow bank, the handle pointing toward us in the car. We sat there watching the snow level climb higher and higher, until only the handle of the stick sticking out of the bank could be seen.

Finally the train we were waiting for came through. The baggageman stood on a chair in the doorway, leaning out with someone holding on to the back of his overalls. He used a yardstick to measure the height of the snow above the handle sticking out of the snow. It was agreed by the rest of the train crew, who by now were all involved in the important measurement, that in just a little over an hour it had snowed over a foot!

Fifty years later I sat in a meeting of ex-Milwaukee employees and railroad buffs and looked at photographs belonging to a man who had operated the substation there during those same years. He talked about building a homemade skidoo so he could take his family down the snowed-in dirt road, and showed pictures of the frozen cascade that stretched up the mountainside where in warmer weather a tumbling mountain stream rushed.

I asked the speaker about the snow and my memory of the measured amount. Apparently the crew's measurements had been shared up and down the line, because he remembered being told about the thirteen-inches-in-an-hour snow.

"Was that amount correct, do you think?" I asked. "Or has my memory elaborated on that night's snowfall over the years?"

"I'm sure it could have been pretty close to right," he quickly affirmed. "We used to measure snowfall all the time, and when we got one of those silver-dollar snows, it would pile up faster than you could believe. Those snows were light and fluffy though and didn't cause many problems. However, the wet spring snows were heavy and caused derailments and slides and all kinds of problems," he pointed out.

"It was some experience for me," I said.

"It was an unusual place," he said with a small smile, which quickly faded. "I hated to leave. Now I can't stand to go back and see it sitting there stripped of the rails. Buildings just sit like piles of trash where they have been bulldozed in or are collapsed from old age and poor maintenance. I don't go back. I just look at my pictures."

"I enjoyed seeing the pictures," I said lamely. I didn't know what else to say.

All in all, there was beauty and majesty in the way winter painted the Bitterroots with different colors and shapes. But it was necessary to realize that these scenes were not painted for the benefit of human observers. They were the portrait of natural forces at work, forces that ignored those who rode the rails through the area. The large flakes resting on the palm of a hand were beautiful. The tons of packed snow, ice, and rocks that frequently slid down the mountainside across the tracks were ugly and dangerous. I carry memories of both sides of winter.

The first time I ever rode the electric motor during the winter there were only a couple of feet of snow on the ground. It was enough to make the mountains look like scenes from a Christmas card with snow-laden boughs of cedar drooping gracefully and icicles hanging from the walls of tunnels.

The engineer had alerted me to the possibility of seeing deer along the track, a fairly common experience at any time, but more so during the winter. The roadbed proved an easy thoroughfare for them and their brown coats stood out against the snow, making them easier to spot. Occasionally one would stand and stare at us from the trackbed ahead, its eyes reflecting the headlight of our motor. Often they would stand until we were right on top of them, apparently mesmerized by that light. The engineer would give a little toot of the motor's whistle (a shrill air whistle). This would startle the deer, and it would bound over the small snowbank to the side, its white tail upright and flashing in defiance as it disappeared into the woods.

Dad pointed out some "elk flats," sheltered, flattened places, usually beside a stream, where the animals would gather in small herds in winter, pawing at the icy covering over the grass in search of food. He told me of cooks in the dining car throwing apples and carrots into these areas to feed the elk and how some freight crews would carry bales of hay on the caboose platform for the same reason. In 1994 Darrel Dewald, one of the last of the Milwaukee's conductors in the area, told me he did the same thing. I realized that my experiences covered fifty years of railroad crewmen showing the same compassion for the animals alongside the railbed despite the changes in my world and in their railroading.

One winter experience with the deer of this valley remains firmly in my memory, a bitter recollection I would rather forget. On this occasion, I was riding on the Westinghouse motor as we made our way up the grade near Kyle. We seemed to be running in a deep white ditch. The rotary plow and the flanger car had cleared the track but to each side was a high bank of snow, almost at eye level from our vantage point well above the rails. In some places it was piled and tumbled into irregular drifts. In others the sides were straight up and down with layers of snow showing on the channeled walls where the plow had cut through the season's snowfalls. We went into a short, curving tunnel and there surprised a small herd of deer. Six or eight of the graceful creatures had crept into the tunnel to escape the cold and the wind.

They paused, panicking only for a second or two before they rushed to escape out the far portal of the tunnel. We followed them, close upon their heels. Once outside they found themselves in one of those stretches that were straight up and down on each side. They tried to flee, graceful even as they stumbled over the uneven ties, trying to outrun us.

I was only about ten years old, too young to be instantly aware of what was happening. The sight of the deer, the sound of the whistle, and the yelling of the engineer and the fireman and Dad all at once only conveyed excitement, not tragedy, to me. I can still hear the confusion of cries and shouts—Dad's awareness that the deer might not escape, the fireman's hope that there would be a break in the snow, the engineer's proclamation of their doom.

"I don't think they're going to make it!" the engineer yelled, hanging on the whistle lanyard.

Dad turned to me and started to say something, taking me by the shoulder to turn me away from the window. But he was too late. No matter how much you might want to, you can't stop a moving railroad train in a few feet. One deer stumbled and fell, disappearing from sight below the front of the locomotive, quickly followed by a dull thud. Then another did the same, and then two together, side by side. One of these was flipped up onto the front platform outside our vantage point, flecks of blood and wet hair plastering against the windshield.

"Judas Priest!" Dad swore softly under his breath, putting his arm around my shoulders.

The fireman rushed by, heading for the long hallway that ran alongside the compartments full of electric relays and switches behind us. I could hear him gagging as he went. Then it was all over. We were running smoothly down a clear, white pathway with no obstacles in front of us. The deer were gone. Only the red specks on the windshield remained. A few miles up the grade, as we met another train, Dad and I left the locomotive to return to the baggage car behind.

Once there I said to him, "It doesn't seem fair."

"No," he agreed softly. "It doesn't. But it's no one's fault really. Sometimes life is like that. Everyone does what they have to do, wanting to take care of themselves but not wanting to hurt others. Sometimes it works out well. Sometimes it doesn't. Tonight it didn't . . . but it's no one's fault, there's no one to blame." He looked at me and I saw sadness in his eyes. "Try to forget it," he said kindly.

I tried, but I couldn't. Now I am older than he was then, and it still doesn't seem right that life isn't fair and that sometimes people get hurt not because of error or sin or someone's mistakes, but simply because that seems to be the way things work out. In my heart I know he was right. It is a waste of time trying to find someone or something to blame. Sometimes life is like that. Sometimes it's white like the snow. Sometimes it's black like the night. Perhaps, as he told me, it really is no one's fault. ᴥ

17
LOST AND FOUND

☞ One of the best things that happened to us on our odyssey was becoming sensitive to the many facets and layers of Milwaukee history in the Bitterroots. I was quite comfortable in dealing with the station stops along the Milwaukee mainline, and photographing these was our initial objective. I had traveled these so many times as a boy that I remembered most of them by name.

I could geographically locate in the right order most of the timetable-listed places along the right-of-way from memory. Many of them had distinctive features—Plummer Junction's triple Y of tracks, Avery's roundhouse and the fish pond next to the depot, Roland's trackside cataract beside the tunnel mouth, Deer Lodge's prison with the stone walls right beside the tracks, and Butte's classic station that sat at the terminus of a dead-end stub track.

But there were some parts of the search I could never have predicted before we began. What started out to be a search for remnants of major Milwaukee railroad operations in contemporary scenes soon broadened. I began to perceive of the railroad in terms of historical layers, different segments of time, and the correlating metamorphosis of the railroad itself as it moved through these distinct periods. I learned of new places along the right-of-way, and obscure operations by the railroad.

I studied the railroad's changing functions over the years and found myself drawn to libraries and museums and private collections where I could pore over old photographs, books, and articles. There I learned of the Milwaukee's firm bonding with the history of the West. Time periods took on their own distinct characteristics, and I began to think of them as distinctive eras I could identify by name: the pioneers' development of the St. Joe Valley; railroad route planning and the beginning days of construction; victories and defeats in the railroad's struggle to traverse the wilderness; natural disasters (including floods, slides, fires, particularly the 1910 conflagration, and even earthquakes); developing problems for the financially distressed railroad; and finally, the ugly demise that followed the Milwaukee's remarkable struggle to survive.

In most instances it was relatively easy to trace the role of the railroad through such periods. But in others, the search became a fascinating game of hide-and-seek, incorporating searches for elusive pieces of history, missing names, and unfamiliar places. We combed through historical sources as a child might look through a box of lost and found items for a lost mitten, always alert for something the right shape or color or size, casting aside those items which did not meet our criteria. We searched for missing roads and town sites, information about obscure residents of lonesome grave sites, and the significance of a uncovered old boot and barrel hoop. To top it off, an entire concrete arch bridge and two whole railroad tunnels were lost, or at least misplaced. Who would think things like that could ever be missing?

One of our most interesting quests resulted from a misunderstanding about a bridge. On a privately prepared map of Milwaukee routes we saw a note about a concrete arch bridge near Plummer, Idaho. Every railroad develops its own way of constructing such things as bridges. The Milwaukee used several designs, girder and truss and pile bridges abounded, and over deep gorges steel viaducts with long supporting girders were common. The Road used concrete arches in the approach abutments to its trestles, tall graceful arches, but quite narrow to ensure strength on steep mountainsides. So when we read of a concrete arch bridge over 400 feet long we were amazed.

Such a bridge was a major departure from the usual Milwaukee design style—in conception and size. This was something we had to see. We checked the railroad's track profile to make sure that the description wasn't an error. Sure enough, there it was, "concrete arch, 417 feet long." Now to photograph it, which proved to be anything but easy. We asked local residents, checked county maps with a town clerk, and questioned ex-railroaders who had ridden through the area. The replies were confusing.

"There are a couple of streams through there which the railroad might of crossed that way . . . no way to get there that I know of except cross-country through the bush on foot," was the town clerk's response.

"What bridge?" was the most common reply to our questions.

We finally located an early settler who had arrived in the area with her homesteading parents before the railroad was built. Following a hand-drawn map with written instructions, we turned off a small back road into a driveway next to the farmhouse where she lived.

She graciously admitted us after some careful questioning about who we were and why we were there, and took us into her front room. The walls were covered with mementos of her family and the past. Many of the photographs were decades old.

"I'm a widow," she explained as though by way of an apology of some sort. "My husband would have been interested in your project. He loved this place and knew it well."

"Could you tell us something about the early days in this area? Perhaps about settling here and the coming of the railroad, and things like that?" we asked.

Alert and full of rich memories, surprisingly full and complete for someone her age, we were treated to a panorama of frontier life as she talked. She depicted the scenes as aptly as though using brushes and a full palette of rich and glowing colors.

"There was no road then, you know," she answered when we asked about the route from there to Benewah Lake. The lake lay at the head of Lake Coeur d'Alene some miles away and several hundred feet lower than where we sat, a route they had initially traveled to reach their homestead site. "We rode on horses mostly, or walked, until we cut enough brush to begin thinking about a road. All the nearby homesteaders got together and built the road. It wasn't much," she said, staring into the distance. "But it was a big improvement, let me tell you." She chuckled as she spoke.

"What about the railroad?"

"It came after my father and mother had built our cabin, a year or two later as I recall—maybe even a little bit before. I'm not sure now, but early . . . very early . . . I was quite young then. My, but we were glad to see it come," she asserted strongly.

"Do you remember any big railroad bridges?"

"Oh my, yes. Really big ones, two of them very close together. Here, let me read something to you."

She walked slowly into an adjoining hallway and searched through papers piled on a table. Choosing several she came back and started to read.

> We rode down to the lake, going by the way of the big trestle. My, the sight was grand. The trail follows the brim of the big

canyon for a mile and it is so steep at the side of the trail that it made me dizzy to look down.

"That's from a series of letters my mother wrote to her mother—not actually sent, you see, because her mother was dead by then, but she wrote them as a record of what she might have said had Grandma been living still—a whole series of letters. I have them now. She gave them to me a long time ago. Over the years I've typed most of them as they're hard to read otherwise."

"When was she writing this?" we asked.

She sorted through the papers, and smiled when she found the date.

"Goodness. A long time ago. June 11, 1911, it says."

"Is there more . . . about the bridge?"

She read to us of two steel trestles being constructed and about the children observing the construction from a distance during the day. The letter told of how the pioneers and the railroad construction crews interacted.

> Our road to the lake (from the cabin) will be built down this canyon and under the bridge. There is a large bridge crew stationed at the larger bridge doing some work, and Tom goes every day to get scraps from the cook house for our little pigs.

We visited with her for some time. My wife remained behind at the farmhouse, looking through old pictures while I drove to the nearest town to photocopy the letters she let me borrow. When I returned we talked some more, and we compiled pages of notes about their early living conditions including some more information about the railroad. Before we left she read some more.

> They finally put in a station near the big trestle. Made it a lot easier for us to catch the train to St. Maries that way. We only had to walk a mile to get there.

"Only part of the walk was uphill," she said as though she had just remembered what it had been like.

"And what about a bridge made of concrete, on the railroad, perhaps beyond where the station was?" we asked before we left.

"A railroad bridge of concrete?"

"Yes."

"I don't believe I ever heard of any such thing. Not around here, anyway." We had run into another dead end despite our good fortune to have visited with this remarkable woman. It was a delightfully pleasant dead end and even productive in some ways, but the bridge was still missing. Later, after a seven-mile hike down the roadbed on a warm fall day, we found that there wasn't any concrete arch bridge at all. No wonder people had said "What bridge?" The concrete arch was simply an unusually large culvert, built in an elongated arching style to provide a drainage course for a small creek as the Milwaukee had done in many other places. We had misread the track profile and taken the mapmaker literally. In this case the lost was never found because it had never existed. It was disappointing that we hadn't located the "one-of-its-kind" bridge, but the insight we gained into early pioneer life around the railroad and our too-short visit with a true living pioneer more than made up for the disappointment.

Reading the letters given to us by the helpful woman who as a girl had seen the railroad arrive led us to other sites. The letters spoke of going to the landing on the river to catch the steamboat to St. Maries or Coeur d'Alene. We had read of similar activities in other biographical and transcribed oral history works as well. Playing detective, we traced through old Milwaukee track profiles and plans and noted that there was a siding near Ramsdell, Idaho, which had been built to service the old Rutledge and Winton Timber Company.

Hiking out onto a peninsula that stretched between the St. Joe River and Benewah Lake, we came to the tunnel, which lies at the east end of the long wooden trestle that stretches across the lake. We went through the short tunnel and just on the other side found an old siding heading off toward the end of the peninsula. Tracing it on the map we recognized many of the landmarks the letter writer had noted. The peculiar tree-lined channel of the river in the middle of the lake was at our right, and the curving finger of land that ended near where an early pioneer entrepreneur had built a camp and store to service his boat landing, known widely among the pioneers as Silvertips Landing, lay ahead of us near the end of the siding. By walking the old siding it was easy to see how the coming of the railroad had affected this valley and become a part of its history, substituting rails for water and changing the lives of those in the region forever.

We weren't finished hunting for missing bridges, however. There were numerous pictures of wooden trestles along the early Milwaukee right-of-way bridges that could not be found. Some were accounted for by the steel trestles that in a few cases had been replacements for wooden constructions. Our search was made more difficult because many years earlier the railroad had changed its original bridge numbering scheme so that contemporary bridge sites had numbers that did not fit with the original scheme.

The answer to what had taken place was not hard to find. The railroad had built long wooden flumes for mountain spring and stream water to carry soil to lower sites, where it was used to fill in ravines initially bridged by these wooden trestles. Families of early railroad construction personnel even have photographs of such operations. Our real search involved identifying just which ravine fills were wooden bridge replacements and which had always been fills. Using old photographs to match the topography of the surrounding hills and the information stored in various railroad, government, and private records we began to piece together the numbering system and to locate the old wooden trestle sites.

With the help of the Forest Service we located and recorded small sump holes, which appear rather regularly on the present right-of-way. We were surprised to find that the railroad had not bothered to demolish the original wooden structures but had simply covered them with fill dirt and rocks. Now, nearly a century later, some of those old beams are decomposing and the earth is settling into holes caused by rotting timbers.

Recently an unexpected rainy winter caused runoff water to dam up behind one of these fills when the drainage flow routes became clogged with debris. The fill, upgrade from Adair, wasn't built to sustain this kind of pressure and suddenly gave way, pushing an estimated 10,000 cubic yards of debris down the mountainside, wiping out about 150 feet of old right-of-way and a segment of the Loop Creek road in the valley below.

It was a tragedy to see yet another piece of the right-of-way gone, but there was a silver lining to the disaster. Those knowledgeable about the railroad's construction habits were eager for the slide to settle so they might clamber over it looking for pieces of the old trestle, timbers unseen since about 1910. Once in hand, such pieces could provide much information about the nature of the bridges and the rate of decomposition in the buried timbers.

Despite our efforts to do thorough research before going on a hunt for some missing piece of history, some of our findings were purely serendipitous.

During construction in the Bitterroots, the railroad had to blast and drill away thousands of yards of rock as it bored 17 tunnels in the East Portal–Avery stretch. Constructing a tunnel was dangerous, sometimes slow, and almost always expensive. As a consequence, the railroad tried to avoid having to drill a tunnel, preferring to cut through blocking hillsides wherever possible and economically feasible.

In 1908, the right-of-way construction, just upgrade from the long Kelly Creek trestle, came to a halt where a shoulder of the mountain blocked the way. Test bores indicated several hundred feet of dense, solid rock. The depth and height of the rock face was intimidating, and a tunnel seemed the only answer. This part of the grade had been subcontracted to a man named Johnson (no relative, as far as I know). The foreman met with his engineers to study the problem. The meeting probably went something like this.

"Well, what do you think?" the foreman asked the group assembled in his tent.

"It looks like another tunnel to me," one said.

"A tough one, too; that's solid rock all the way through and hard and dense," suggested another.

"That's going to slow us way down. Can't afford to be so far behind schedule," the foreman protested.

"Hell," one of the coyote men drawled. "We can blast the bigeminies out of that mountain. I never saw a rock yet that a good blast couldn't shake up a bit."

Construction workers who handled the blasting operations had long been called coyote men and wore the label with obvious pride. The speaker was no exception. The foreman was listening with a different attitude, however.

"How much powder would it take?" he asked.

The coyote man said he'd get back to him shortly with an amount needed as soon as they took a few more measurements. When he returned later in the day, his answer took everyone by surprise.

"Twenty-five thousand pounds of explosives? Good God, man, you'll blow away Missoula with that amount," said one skeptical engineer.

"Wouldn't expect someone not used to handling the stuff to understand," the coyote man grinned condescendingly. "But if you know what you're doing, you can handle any amount of powder needed for a job. The secret is in knowing how."

The bicycles clearly show the size of the boulders thrown over 700 feet in the Johnson's Cut blast during railroad construction. Large as they are, for decades these boulders had been overlooked as blast evidence.
Photo by Tim Johnson

Over the objections and skepticism of others the foreman gave the blasting approach his okay and the charges were prepared and placed. When the time came, the fuses were laid and everyone cleared out of the area, retreating a long way both up and down the grade. Then the fuses were touched off.

"There's fire in the hole!" The traditional cry echoed up and down the right-of-way.

The warning was an understatement. Truth was that there was fire in the hole, up the mountain, down in the valley, across Loop Creek some 700 feet below, and all over the construction camp nestled on the banks of the river about a half mile away as the crow flies (though one would suspect that there were few crows left in the area to fly that route following the gigantic blast).

Pieces of rock flew in every direction. Some of the debris was gravel as small as birdshot and it peppered the hillside, ripping leaves off trees and bushes. Larger chunks soared out over the valley, and some very large pieces rolled and bounced down the steep mountainside toward the valley and the unsuspecting camp below.

The devastation was widespread. The shoulder had been removed just as the coyote man had promised.

The problem was that pieces of that shoulder had been thrown for hundred of yards. Trees were downed along the stream below. Tents and a mess hall were flattened in a construction camp on the valley floor, but apparently no one was killed or seriously injured.

But, when all was said and done, the shoulder was gone and the boring of still another tunnel had been avoided. The site of the blast, now called Johnson's Cut, is easy to find, and the wide, flat space on the outside of the former right-of-way gives a good idea of how much rock was loosened and blasted away by the prodigious amount of blasting powder used. However, time has largely obliterated most of the other signs of the blast. New trees and bushes have long since grown up to cover the scarring of the greenery. The hillside is full of rock, much of it pushed there in daily construction activities. Down below, the rocks in the river now all look pretty much alike, and all of the construction camp buildings have been gone for decades. Hard evidence of the unusual results of the blast are not easily seen. Still, U. S. Forest Service archeologists feel that there should be more evidence remaining.

Then one day, only a short time ago while we were actively engaged in our project, one of those archeologists was driving slowly up the narrow Loop Creek road he had traversed dozens of times. As he went around a small curve he noticed for the first time, a large gray boulder off to the right. It was partly hidden with bushes and trees and was covered with moss and lichens.

"I don't know why I never noticed it before," he reported. "It was bigger than a Buick!"

Later, as he and others looked around, the area was found to be covered with boulders from the cut far up the mountainside. One looked familiar to the archeologist and he searched through old photographs, finally finding one that showed three construction men posing in front of this same boulder, shortly after the blast.

In 1995, my son and I photographed the rock with three U. S. Forest Service employees in front, posed the same as the construction workers. The young men, unfamiliar with the area and its history, were intrigued with the story and the rock and their role in the scenario.

"At least this is one artifact no one will steal," was one's comment.

Our search for lost tunnels met with mixed results. Sometimes we found what we were looking for, other times we didn't. But one search in particular was very successful.

We already knew which of the existing tunnels on the right-of-way had sheltered over 600 refugees from the big 1910 fire and we had visited each of these. One day we met a knowledgeable local worker who directed us to a small drainage tunnel a few yards off to the side of where the tracks had run, well down the steep embankment beside the railroad grade. It was well hidden by bushes and a rocky ravine, and we probably would have missed it without his directions.

"A railroad employee missed the rescue train and crawled in there to get away from the big fire," he told us. "He probably spent a bad afternoon and night, but the water trickling through the tunnel kept him from burning up and the draft from the fire caused enough airflow to give him oxygen."

This tunnel was small, nothing like the ones on the grade through which trains had run. It was large enough to stand up in at one end but dwindled to a size that required crawling on hands and knees at the other. It curved in the middle resulting in total darkness. One of my sons ventured through the tunnel (something I wasn't about to do). In the middle he found a peg pounded into the wall, which looked as though it might have held a lantern. The experience impressed him.

"The light of my flashlight was almost like a lantern, and I could imagine someone driving the peg into the wall to hold the lantern high to provide more light. It might even have been the man who was running from the fire. It was hard to believe that I was standing there looking at that same peg. Going through that tunnel was like crawling into the past," he told us later.

We searched in vain, for a couple of mine adits, which were related to railroad history, but managed to visit nearly every thorn-covered blackberry bush on that mountainside.

One major search consumed a considerable amount of time both in research and fieldwork, but all of our efforts were unsuccessful. The Milwaukee numbered its tunnels consecutively, east to west. This was a useful locating strategy but caused some problems when tunnels added later required some sort of a decimal or fraction number be assigned to the afterthought tunnels (such as "10 1/2") in order not to upset the whole line of designated numbers. Visiting the tunnels in their numerical order presented us with a mystery when we discovered that after leaving tunnel No. 37, the next tunnel we encountered was No. 40.

In the gap between the two a branch line left the mainline for Elk River, Idaho, and it had two tunnels listed. We thought perhaps that was the answer until we found that those two had different numbers related solely to the branch line. To make things even more confusing, and a bit spooky at first, we found one of those two missing as well, but later determined it had been daylighted (blasted open into a cut rather than a tunnel) due to later railroad and highway rerouting.

Still looking for the missing tunnels, we read many pages of railroad literature dealing with construction, inquired of local historical museum archivists, studied old photographs, and queried exrailroaders who had worked the line in that area. The response was uniformly the same.

"What tunnels?"

Most of those we asked had not even noticed the gap in numbering, or if they had, thought nothing of it.

"Who knows why the railroad did anything?" one oldtimer suggested. "They named towns that didn't exist, and misnamed or misspelled some that did. Wouldn't have bothered them a bit to hide a tunnel or two just to be ornery," he added.

One of our friends who lived in the area and had been very helpful ferreting out some other pieces of missing information even went as far as to walk and drive the old roadbed through the gap between the two numbered tunnels, looking for large cuts and sheared-off cliffs that once might have been tunnels later daylighted. He found some possibilities but no firm evidence. I hold to the philosophy that it is very difficult to hide a railroad tunnel, so I made plans to keep on looking. Then, just before going to press with this book we received a letter from Darrel Dewald.

His curiosity had been stirred by our search, and he finally found the answer. The two tunnels had never been built. The Milwaukee made plans during the 1920s to change the routing of the mainline east of St. Maries, near a place called Omega, in order to eliminate some sharp reverse curves. The new route would have required two more tunnels. The numbers were set aside, "just in case." Somehow, the railroad never got around to making the change and left few records about the extra tunnel numbers. Another mystery was solved, but I'm rather sorry to see that one disappear. While it remained unsolved it was a good excuse to go back still another time to various parts of the old right-of-way.

While unsuccessfully searching for the missing tunnels we did find some very interesting people. We talked with a railroad man who remembered having his lantern go dead as he walked beside a long freight stopped in a tunnel high in the mountains.

"Do you have any idea how long it takes to walk the length of 20 freight cars when you are in total darkness and have to use your hands on the side of the cars to feel your way clear to the end of the tunnel?" he asked us. "It's funny to talk about it but no damn good when it actually happens to you."

In St. Maries we were directed by one local businessman to another a couple of blocks down the street. We found the second man just entering his shop and he invited us inside to talk. Once there, he pulled out a photograph album from below the counter. Flipping through the pages he showed us pictures of construction workers putting a concrete lining in one of the largest of the tunnels, original pictures like I had never seen.

"That's my father." He pointed to a figure in one of the photos. "He was in charge of the job."

Coincidental meetings such as this one happened quite frequently. In still another instance two men who were showing us some of the lesser well-known sites along the right-of-way took us into the edge of a tunnel and called us over to look at the wall. There we found dates roughly carved into the concrete. One was 1910, the year of the biggest forest fire in the area. The other commemorated the year (not long after the fire) that the railroad was electrified and trolley lines were first hung from the tunnel ceilings.

We found such experiences humbling. It is too easy to overlook the amount of personal effort and dedication that went into the construction and operation of the railroad. Every place we visited seemed as though we could see faces of pioneers watching us, men and women who had literally given their lives to what we were now seeing.

Most of these shadowy faces remained nameless. A few we might have recognized from my father's stories, and a handful of others became legitimate local folk heroes, familiar to many. But one man's persona persistently stayed with us. His presence gave us energy and lent purpose to our searches.

Oscar Blake had come from Oregon to homestead up a gulch above Lake Benewah before the railroad arrived. He had often visited Silvertips Landing, and indeed had carried his stove on his back from that landing clear to his homestead cabin several miles away. He had walked to Worley,

The turnout and tracks of an old lumber company spur still remain near Ramsdell, Idaho. The tracks follow the route of a trail used by early homesteaders to reach Silvertips Landing on the shores of the St. Joe River, where they boarded boats or picked up incoming freight.
Photo by S. Johnson, Milwaukee, Wisc., Public Library Collection

Idaho, even a longer distance, to buy horses and mules—first his own and then others to resell to neighboring homesteaders.

When the railroad arrived, he accepted its intrusion into his wilderness in good spirit and wrote of riding it to St. Maries. A restless man, he followed the logging activity to the Marble Creek drainage and had helped winch a donkey engine far up that creek near the Hobo Pass area. As we read and reread his memoirs, he seemed to personify the spirit of those pioneering souls who helped the area grow and the railroad be successful.

One summer we drove and hiked to the recorded location of his homestead. It was a spot as close to 1900 as you could find. Although there were no timbers or rock chimneys or empty wells to tell us he had been there, we knew that he had. By visiting the site of his old homestead we had made firm contact with someone who was very important in our quest for rediscovering the past.

Standing there in the quiet woods, surrounded by second- or even third-growth forest, I wondered if he had ever ridden with my dad. There is no way to know, of course. But I suspect Dad knew about him because Dad was interested in those who stood at trackside and waved as the train went by. And if they did know each other, I am sure they got along well. Both were pioneers.

18
FALCON IS A SPECIAL PLACE

☞ I couldn't see my own feet in the blackness of the mountain night but I could feel the Frenchtown Quarry gravel even through the leather soles of my shoes. Hard and knife-edged, it was sharp as flint with thousands of points pounded into ballast to hold the rail-bearing ties firm and solid. Moving slowly and gingerly I followed the faint outline of my father's figure and the sound of his voice. A few feet down the track, away from the darkened sleeper and below the gleam of the twin, red rear-end markers shining above our heads, we stopped. Cupping a hand around his ear he turned and leaned his head toward the front of the silently standing train.

"Do you hear that?" he asked in a hushed voice. "Listen! It's the wind from up around Adair blowing down the valley and through the tunnel. You can almost always hear it here, particularly in the summer. Some say it sounds like a dying man's cry for help, a ghost from the big fire. Hard to say."

Feeling the hair rise on my head I held my breath and listened. I could hear it, a soft, expressive wavering sound, a sighing sound as low and melancholy as a dirge sung by a monastery choir. It made me uncomfortable.

"That's spooky," I said.

"Well, it's really only nature's automatic block system of course," he chuckled, referring to the tall electrically controlled signals that signaled directions to the engineer in flashes of yellow, green, and red. "That's all it is," he said.

"But listen—don't make a sound," he whispered. "You'll see what happens. It will stop all of a sudden, telling us a train is coming just like a block signal does. Then a few seconds later you'll see an engine come out of the tunnel."

"Now that really is scary," I said.

"No it isn't. You're just making it so with your imagination. The train entering the tunnel blocks the airflow is all. That stops the sound. You'll see. We'll wait till the ghost tells us No. 7 is coming and then we'll climb aboard our train and get out of the way," he said.

The site of Falcon can be clearly seen from the higher right-of-way across the valley. The "moaning" tunnel was to the left of the picture, the station site a little to the right of center, and the west switch to the far right. The distinctive rock cliffs of Shefoot Mountain rise in the south behind the right-of-way.
Photo by S. Johnson, Milwaukee, Wisc., Public Library Collection

Falcon became indelibly marked in my memory because of what I experienced there with my father. Without these experiences it would have been like any one of a dozen wayside stations along a mountainside track in Idaho, unremarkable and unremembered. Like Dad used to say, "Falcon's not much of a place, but it's a special place." In the last days of the railroad it could very well have been described as "a wide spot in the road," if there had been a road, which there wasn't; anyway not one accessible to anyone residing in the few trackside buildings there.

Falcon lies almost 300 feet above a narrow, rough, dirt Forest Service road on the valley floor, a stagecoach road hewed out of the forest just after the turn of the century. The road wanders casually, almost aimlessly like a narrow footpath through the tall firs along the twisting bottom of Loop Creek Valley. It runs about ten miles from Adair on the east to where the creek merges with the North Fork of the St. Joe River on the west. There it joins another Forest Service road and becomes a slightly more respectable and businesslike thoroughfare as it continues westward to Avery.

From the road next to the creek, Falcon is reachable only via a leg-tiring and lung-searing climb. It starts with a traverse of that fast-flowing sometimes thigh-deep, ice-cold stream and then continues with an ascent through brush alders, beargrass, and thorn-laden blackberry and huckleberry bushes. It follows a faint packtrain trail in a climb so steep that these same prickly vines have to be used as handholds. Three to four feet of snow make it even more difficult in the winter.

The trip down to the road from the track is no picnic either. A slip can mean a good working over by the thorns or even a more serious fall. Climbing down is as tiring and as hard on the legs as ascending.

During Falcon's railroading days, supplies usually were dropped off by passing trains. But sometimes schedules and shipping dates didn't match or sudden needs arose, so residents were forced to make a journey to the "outside" for necessities. The trail had such a bad reputation that section gang members would ride on the open scooters in wind and cold for three-quarters of an hour to get supplies. Anything was preferable to scrambling and sliding down to the road to get supplies from a truck from Avery only to have to climb back up the steep mountainside with a full backpack.

By the railroad's own admission, Falcon was a long way from anywhere significant. Milwaukee Road literature of the 1940s described it as 1,761 miles from Chicago and 428 miles from Seattle. The Employee Timetable in the 1950s tells it all: "Falcon—No office." Of pertinent interest to the railroaders who worked there, it was, by rail, about 17 miles west to Avery, Idaho, and eleven and one-half miles east to East Portal, across the Bitterroots in Montana.

In either direction the roadbed skirted a number of precipitous rock cliffs and twisted through the mountains via dark and sometimes wet tunnels and across some of the highest railroad steel trestles in the United States. This all provided breathtaking scenery for the traveler. But because Falcon lay almost 1,000 feet above Avery and over 700 feet below East Portal, a trip by foot to either meant a long uphill walk. One of the old section-hand jokes was to ask if you had found a way to walk to Avery that was downhill both ways.

Across the valley to the north and 600 feet higher, in a stunning panorama, the railbed eventually ended up on the other side of the Adair

Loop. It ran from east to west along the side of a mountain equally as steep as Falcon's. Then it turned sharply northward and disappeared from view as it wound its way up the last two miles to the long St. Paul Pass tunnel.

When I first saw it, Falcon was lush and green with a still young second growth arising from the total devastation of the 1910 fire. The station and sidings were nestled among the young fir and pine forest on a 3,420-foot-high shoulder carved out of a Bitterroot crest. In early days it was romantically designated by someone as Long Liz Point in memory of a young lady of apparent charm but dubious character who plied her trade in the area. In the warmth of summer and early fall it was a beautiful spot carpeted with wildflowers and the new growth of the pines.

The site was used primarily as a place for trains to meet and pass since the mainline was only a single track. Off and on through the years it also served as a place to house section gang workers and their families in semi-permanent railroad housing. In the Milwaukee's early years in the valley the place was much busier and incongruously even boasted having a jewelry store at one point. But subsequently its small station house was purely utilitarian and housed neither a regular waiting room nor an agent. Lovely in the summer except for the mosquitoes, Falcon was widely recognized by railroad people as one of the coldest spots in the Bitterroots in the middle of winter and well noted for its snow. Automatically operating spring switches there were routinely exchanged for manual switches in the winter because of the snow and ice.

There were three separate tracks there: the mainline, a primary siding used for train meets and capable of handling 118 typical railroad cars, and a short working stub siding of only 12 cars. But Falcon was easily approached and passed by rail without much notice from train passengers. Only a few feet from the west switch of the siding the mainline track disappeared around a rocky headland. At the opposite end the track similarly vanished from view a short distance beyond the east switch, in this instance by snaking through a lazy figure-S curve and then plunging into Clear Creek No. 2 tunnel.

Because of the isolation and hardships, the railroad wrestled with the decision of whether to have people assigned to Falcon on a regular basis. As a result of this indecision there were long periods when no one lived there. Only a locked frame building off to the side of the tracks, filled with some tools and emergency equipment, offered any sign of civilization.

Still, because of the heavy freight and passenger traffic on the line, Falcon was often a busy place as trains were regularly scheduled for a meet at this convenient passing track.

Both the east and west turnouts leading from the mainline onto the long siding were what the railroad designated as spring switches. Spring switches must be manually moved so that a train can be shunted to the siding from the mainline, but once the holding train is on the siding and the switch has been returned to the mainline-clear position, the holding train may move back onto the mainline without further moving the switchpoints by hand. The pressure of the trains' wheel flanges moves the switch rails so that the wheels may safely roll from the siding onto the mainline without derailing. When the switch is cleared by the last car, the pressure disappears and strong tension springs cause the switch to move back once more to the mainline-clear position.

These switches are designed this way so that they automatically favor the mainline, saving crew members time and effort by not having to manually change the switch when a train moves from one track to another. This is particularly helpful in bad weather. Every time a switch must be thrown a crew member must get off the train, unlock the switch with a large key, throw the switch, wait for the train to move through the switch, re-throw the switch, relock it, and then get back on the train.

I acquired all this trivia about spring switches because I actually helped my father perform each of these steps. Through these experiences, usually occurring in the dark of night, which can be especially frightening to a young boy, I began to gain self-confidence. At the same time I experienced the deepening of a bond of personal understanding for a strong but kind and gentle man who was guiding me. His quiet and unassuming strength became a catalyst for my own development, the bond persisting throughout my life. All of this happened in the rather plain, unremarkable surroundings of this isolated railroad siding called Falcon.

Although I accompanied Frank to new places as he worked, in most instances I was essentially a viewer, a nonparticipant. It was at Falcon that I was first invited to be actively involved. The change in my role came to me the first time as a total surprise.

It was past midnight as we stood together on the station platform at Avery, Idaho. It was August but a chill was in the air, typical for this hour of the night at this elevation where autumn hints of its arrival before summer departs the lower valleys. Though there were people about working on the

The east switch at Falcon was near the "moaning" tunnel. This is the way the westbound right-of-way looks today near that spot.
Photo by S. Johnson, Milwaukee, Wisc., Public Library Collection

train and loading freight, the platform was largely deserted. As had often happened before, Dad touched my arm and quietly told me to come with him as he headed toward the electric motor. It had just been coupled to our train at Avery and was now waiting to pull us up over the curving steep grade to St. Paul Pass. I knew I was in for a ride of nearly twenty miles in the electric engine, a ride I enjoyed because I would probably see deer in the headlight of the locomotive. It was fun winding around the rocky precipices and through the tunnels, where I would be treated to an inside view of blasted rock and curved slabs of concrete that could not be seen from the windows of the train behind.

Our usual ride went to the west switch at Falcon, where Dad and I would climb down to throw the switch, which would allow us to take the siding for a meet with a westbound train. Often we met No. 7, the westbound version of our own train. But sometimes we would wait for a special or occasionally a long freight with special running rights due to some quirk in the schedule.

Once our train was past the switch, Dad would release it so the spring could move the switch points to once more give the mainline train clearance to roll safely past. Dad would then signal the engineer with his lantern as we boarded at the rear vestibule of the darkened sleeper of our train. Our train would then slowly move up to the east switch, where we stopped to wait for the oncoming traffic.

Dad would swing down the hinged vestibule floor that covered the open steps and lock it into place, then close and latch the bottom half of the split door so we could safely lean out and watch ahead for the first glimmer of a headlight. Once the other train had cleared the west switch our train would move out without a pause since there was no need to manually throw the spring switch. We always stood there a few moments watching the red markers of the other train disappear in the darkness. Then Dad and I would move through the two passenger cars between us and the baggage car, where we would eat our lunch.

By the time I was a teenager I realized that this little exercise was done solely for my benefit. When I wasn't being given the head-end ride, the brakeman took the responsibility for getting off and opening and closing the west switch while Dad stayed inside in the warmth of the coach. One of the perks of being a conductor was relief from much of this type of work, though Dad was disinclined to shirk any share of the labor involved in making things run smoothly.

This particular night at Falcon was no different than any other until we got off the engine at that west switch. As we moved to the switch stand, Dad handed me his chain of heavy railroad keys. "This one's for the switch," he said indicating a short heavy brass key. "Undo the lock. The motor's headlight will give you plenty of light to see what you're doing."

I moved quickly to the task, thrilled to be awarded this honor right in front of the engine crew. The lock opened easily and I saw that it was fastened with a chain to the stand so it wouldn't be lost or forgotten.

"Let's turn the switch," Dad said, moving to my side. "First we lift the handle, which is on a hinge—here, put your hands right next to mine. Then we move it a quarter turn. Watch the indicator above turn with it so the engineer on the train can tell which way the points are set."

I pushed as hard as I could, and with his help the switch smoothly moved into place.

"Should I lock it?" I asked.

"No, not until we're through with it. But be sure the handle is hinged down. That will keep it in place." I carefully followed his directions.

"Stand back from the track," he cautioned. Then he raised his lantern in a signal to the engineer and our train slowly moved through the switch and onto the siding, stopping once the turnout was cleared.

Following his step-by-step directions, I reversed the switch position and put the lock back in place as he held the lantern so I could see.

"Now let's get aboard," he directed as he moved with me close behind to the sleeper steps.

"Wait!" he said. I stopped, wondering what was the matter.

"Here, take this," he said handing me his lantern. "Now walk out away from the train a half dozen steps or so. When you're ready, raise the lantern up over your head and down again and he'll know it's okay to move to the east switch."

"Me?" I asked.

"Of course," he laughed. "You're the one who has the lantern. Go ahead. Give him the highball."

"He'll leave," I said.

"That's the general idea."

"He'll leave me."

"Not unless you stop to enjoy the view. This train isn't a hotrod you know. You'll have time to climb aboard. Go ahead. We've got a schedule to meet."

The east portal of tunnel No. 22 at Falcon. The beams holding up the snow shed are over 12 inches square and remain in fine condition. Wind blowing through this tunnel made a moaning sound we could hear clear down at the west switch, over a mile away. Photo by S. Johnson, Milwaukee, Wisc., Public Library Collection

With some trepidation I gave the signal and ran stumbling to the train. I was urged on by the two quick toots of the engine's whistle acknowledging my signal and dragged myself aboard as quickly as I could. I was up into the vestibule and the floor was down and the bottom door half closed before the train moved.

"That was scary," I admitted to Dad.

"You did fine, though you probably shouldn't have run to the train. You might have fallen on the rough gravel," he responded.

"I wanted to do it right," I said, "but I was afraid I'd get left behind."

"Nothing to be ashamed of. Lots of responsibilities are a little frightening," Dad said. "And there are often things to worry about, such as being left behind or in some cases being so far ahead of others that you're just as much alone. Good workers manage to do both—fulfill their assigned responsibilities and take care of their fears. You did fine," he said for the second time.

I leaned out the doorway to watch for the oncoming train. As it passed I had goosepimples on my arms, but now I was viewing the scene from a new perspective. I had played an integral part in making an important railroad operation work. It was perhaps my earliest clear awareness of the good feeling that comes with a challenging job well done. I performed these same tasks several times again on later trips, but that first time was the most important and a remarkable experience for a teenager.

There were a number of other good experiences at Falcon. Dad was very safety conscious and had warned me against such dangerous habits as walking on the rails. But one night as we were throwing that same switch, he broke character and said to me, "Do you have a penny in your pocket?"

"I think so," I said, handing him one. He walked over to the rail and placed the penny on it.

"Watch," he said as he signaled to the engineer to enter the siding.

"Will it do any damage?" I asked.

"To the train? Not likely," he laughed. "Anyway a penny doesn't do much of anything these days."

After the train moved by, he retrieved the penny and handed it to me. When we were back on board in the light I marveled at the flattened piece of copper in my hand, touching its polished smoothness with my fingertip.

"That's neat," I said. "Let's do it with a nickel or a dime."

"Humph," he said, already regretting what he had done. Then he added a moral, just to redeem himself. "See what a train can do to a piece of metal? Best to keep hands and feet away from there unless you want to collect hamburger. Damn foolishness to even mess around with pennies," he added with a sheepish look on his face.

"Yes, sir," I said. But he had introduced me to new possibilities, and in the years since I have arranged to have trains flatten dozens of pennies, nickels, and dimes, which I have given to friends and my own children. Bad habits are just as easily learned as good ones—you just need to learn to recognize which is which.

Sometimes Dad and I would have long, deep discussions as we stood in the coolness waiting for another train. The air in those mountains was always crystal clear and you could see a million stars hidden to the eye in the glare and smog of the city. We talked about a lot of things, how far away the stars were, why the sky was so black at night and blue in the day. As I grew older we sometimes discussed more sophisticated topics such as the size of eternity or the reason that some evil things were perpetuated while the good too often seemed transient. He encouraged me to ask questions and challenge ideas though he never had a lot of absolute answers. He was not well educated, but I felt he was very wise. And his humility taught me not to be afraid to say "I don't know."

19
IT WAS LIKE A FAMILY

As a young child I was unaware that I had a different last name from my stepfather—there are other things far more important to a youngster. But as I became a teenager, my stepfather's name was confusing to my friends and often embarrassing to me. My friends didn't understand why I should have a different last name than my father—second families weren't as common in those days, nor as easily discussed. When I would try to explain, the sound of Dad's name would sometimes cause fits of laughter and unkind jokes among my peers. I must admit that Fiebelkorn is not a name one hears every day. I once whiled away time at the phone directory desk at O'Hare airport looking for that name in cities across the country. Only a very few times did I find it listed. In the late 1880s it was more common in Wisconsin, where Dad was raised among other German-American families.

But his name was no problem for the early Milwaukee railroaders with whom he worked. They were used to names with ethnic roots. Swedish and Finnish and middle European names abounded among the workers. Irish names were common as were Italian and Slavic. Railroaders, and the pioneers among whom they worked shortly after the turn of the century, called people by names that seemed to fit them for one reason or another, or were easy to say and remember: 49 Williams, Brown Gravy Sam, Long Liz, Hurry-up Harry, Few Clothes Johnny, Dimmer Whipple, Honey Jones, and Ptomaine Dick, to name a few. Offense was seldom intended or taken. But Dad's name was cumbersome and almost impossible to spell, so railroaders up and down the line called him Feebee. As I grew older and more comfortable with his given name I would sometimes playfully call him Feebee and he would just grin in acknowledgment.

In my search for those who might have known or heard of him I would ask, "Perhaps you might have known my dad? He worked this division all his life as a conductor."

"What was his name?"

"Fiebelkorn. Frank Fiebelkorn."

On those too few occasions when I was fortunate enough to find some-one who did recall him, the response was almost uniformly the same.

"Fiebelkorn? Oh, you mean Feebee!" It was said in a friendly and familiar way.

There seemed to be no pattern as to whom he chose as friends or close acquaintances. Several were former train-crew members, some of whom worked directly with him—an engineer and a brakeman and a conductor who had started out as a car-man. One was a station agent who remem-bered mostly his distinctive F. F. F. initials signed to the bottom of a 31 Order, which always required the recipient's signature. Others remem-bered him from contacts made along the right-of-way.

"He used to bring my dad newspapers from Spokane when he was on Nos. 7 and 8. He'd toss them off from the baggage car as the train went through. They were always rolled up, held together with a big red rubber band," one said. "I rode with him as a boy," another offered. These friendly but brief memories were enticing but sometimes more discour-aging than satisfying. I would have liked to find even one person who remembered him in small detail and could share these images with me. Such hopes may have been unrealistic considering the passage of so many years.

Since he lived to be almost ninety, many of his friends had passed on before him. He seemed to recall them personally and spoke of them fre-quently when an event or place jogged his memory. The past was impor-tant to him, but he held no merit for simply living a long time. He would see a newspaper story about someone reaching their 90th birthday and would snort and say, "He didn't do anything but grow old, and he took longer to do it than I did at that." But, even while saying this, he was espe-cially saddened by those who were taken away too soon.

He always tried to attend the funeral of any railroading peer, especially when it was a friend. Mother worried about it being a morbid habit but he insisted it was out of respect.

"They will come to my funeral," he said.

"Never," Mother replied.

"Why do you say that?" he asked.

"Because you're going to outlive them all. You're too stubborn to die first."

She was almost right. He lived a long time, but the man who preached his funeral sermon, 2,000 miles away from the Bitterroots, remembered him from many years before. Upon Dad's retirement he had sent a short note, which I found among Dad's keepsakes. He had written:

> I remember with fondness a "Rail" who was always thoughtful and kind to us as we traveled from Alberton to Missoula to take our music lessons. At that awful hour of four in the morning on cold winter Saturdays it was comforting to know we could finish our sleep on the coach seats, knowing you would waken us in time to get off at our destination.

Forty years later I was introduced in Alberton, Montana, to the brother of the man who wrote that note. He was now a white-haired, elderly gentleman, gracefully aged and still full of energy though less active now. Darrel Dewald brought him to see us in the old Montana Hotel where we were staying. When he arrived, I asked my usual question, "Did you know my dad?"

"Feebee? Of course."

"Did you work with him?"

"Worked with him for a short while before he retired. I was just getting started. He was a good railroad man. But that's not why I remember him."

That had been over fifty years ago, I realized. But he remembered Dad from even earlier. "Long before that, when I was just a youngster, I hurt my leg really bad and it didn't heal right. The doctors decided I should go to the Shriner's Children's Hospital in Spokane to get it taken care of. I rode there on his train."

"Can you remember the trip in any detail?"

"Oh sure. He was very interested in why I was going. After we left Alberton he came and sat down beside me and talked to me about it. The part I remember most though was the return trip."

While we sat there in the cozy front room of the old hotel, a place where many railroaders had relaxed between runs over the decades, nursing their coffee as we were doing, he related his story. I listened carefully, seeing my stepfather as he had, in his dark blue uniform, a crisply white shirt matching his closely shaven face. He had a smile on his face and genuine interest in his voice as he spoke with the man who was then only a small boy.

"They did some serious surgery at the hospital. I was in a big long cast and couldn't walk. Frank carried me onto the train in Spokane and then he brought me a pillow. When we got to Alberton, he carried me off again. I remember that like it was yesterday. I'll never forget it."

I thanked him for telling us about his memories of my dad. Three Milwaukee locomotive engineers were involved in memories of those early days of railroading. One I learned about from a scrap of paper, another I met, and the third was introduced to me by Dad himself. Each helped fill in another piece of the image of my father.

After Dad's death, I found in his belongings a yellowed clipping of a train wreck at Spokane Bridge, a trestle spanning the Spokane River at the Washington-Idaho state line. The sad story relates how a construction train rolled over, pinning the veteran engineer beneath it, where he died from the scalding steam. The clipping is undated, but Milwaukee construction of the Coeur d'Alene line began in 1910, so that date is probably close to accurate. Dad would have been a young man then, but he was apparently already showing his deep commitment to the "Milwaukee family." The story the clipping told was far larger than that of a single isolated train wreck.

In 1993, over 80 years after the construction of the Milwaukee's Coeur d'Alene line, I was introduced to a stately and distinguished gentleman at a Milwaukee old-timers meeting. He carried himself erect, moving slowly but with great dignity. He was wearing a suit with a white shirt and a neatly knotted four-in-hand tie, dressed as my father might have been.

"That's Fred Coombs. He's over 90," someone told me. "He worked the same division as your stepfather. Maybe he knew him."

"That name is familiar," Fred said in response to my usual query. "Let me think about it a minute. What was his first name?"

"Frank. A lot of the railroaders called him Feebee," I added.

"Feebee? I remember Feebee. I guess his name was Fiebelkorn, now that I think on it. I'd forgotten that. I always called him Feebee."

"Then you knew him?"

"Oh, yes, sure, of course. I hauled his train from Butte or Deer Lodge lots of times."

I started to ask for details but the postluncheon meeting was called to order. After the usual listing of the sick and departed and the almost always unanswered call for new business, the chairman said, "Mr. Coombs has asked to speak."

Everyone's attention turned to the gentleman with whom I had been speaking. He stood slowly, his wife unobtrusively helping him rise to his feet.

"I just want to say something about this young man's father," he announced pointing to me.

Young? I was over 60, but who was I to correct him.

A Railroader's Prayer*

Dear Lord:
We're about to start on another turn along a track which can be dangerous and threatening as well as beautiful and satisfying. We feel so much more secure when we know your hand is upon the throttle and your eyes upon the rails lying ahead of us, calling our attention to the important signals of life, helping us avoid harm, and encouraging us to perform our tasks well.

Please be with us this day once again, protecting us along your right of-way of life, pointing out the beauties and wonders of our route, and encouraging us to satisfactorily finish our assigned tasks. Stay with us until our names are written on the great last call-board of life and we log-in at last at our home yard, standing among friends, companions, and fellow workers in peace and gratitude.

Amen.

* This prayer is used as an invocation at the meetings of the Tacoma, Washington, Milwaukee Employee's Old-timer Meetings.

"He asked me if I remember his father. I do indeed. Mr. Fiebelkorn, Feebee, worked the Idaho/Rocky Mountain division as a conductor and I hauled his train. I remember Feebee well. He was a small man, in stature that is, but a good worker, a railroad man, and friendly. He was probably the friendliest conductor on the division. I remember that very well. He always said please and thank you."

He sat down without further words, but all I could remember for the moment was his pronouncement, "I remember Feebee." Fred Combs, the second of the three engineers, was gone a year later. I had found him just in time.

I heard about the third engineer directly from my stepfather. I used to like to hear Dad talk about train wrecks and disasters as he had seen many and been involved in a few. Most of the time the discussion centered around inanimate phenomena: torn tracks, derailed train cars, washed-out bridges and similar items. But one night at Falcon, when we had a particularly long wait for the train we were to meet, he shared his personal memories of the great fire of 1910.

In late summer of that year a gigantic forest fire swept through the Bitterroots pouring out columns of smoke so high that they could be seen for over 500 miles. Thousands and thousands of acres of virgin timber were destroyed and many lives lost. The Milwaukee Road, including the St. Maries–East Portal area and especially Falcon, was right in the middle of the conflagration.

Avery was saved only because Milwaukee workers and other townspeople lit backfires on the edge of town and the main blaze passed them by. Elsewhere the line was encompassed by disaster. Many of the trestles were wood and quickly caught fire. People up and down the line were quickly evacuated by rail, sometimes only minutes ahead of the flames.

On the night of August 20, 1910, engineer John Mackedon and his fireman were alone in an engine running downgrade toward Avery. Fire was all around them, and they were worried about getting out alive.

"At Kyle he found out that there was an SOS at Falcon. People there, gathering to escape the fire, were about to be overrun by the flames, which were racing across the mountains, pushed by a hurricane-like wind. John backed upgrade into Falcon and found the buildings and a string of flatcars already on fire," Dad related.

"What was far worse, a large number of people including women and children—people who had gathered there from up and down the line

In 1910, a Milwaukee rescue train carried forty-seven people to safety in this tunnel from the approaching forest fire. This is the same view they had looking out the westbound portal of Moss Creek tunnel.
Photo by Tim Johnson

and from homesteading cabins and logging camps in the woods—were standing on the platform begging for help. John didn't hesitate. He backed into this very same siding where we're standing and sorted out the boxcars until he found one that wasn't burning too much, coupled up, and told the people to douse the flames on the car and climb aboard. They swarmed all over it and on his engine, too, and were packed inside the boxcar, but he got them aboard and hauled them to safety though he had to stop twice and put out fires on bridges so they could get through. Two whole trainloads of people were transported west from Avery to stations as far away as Washington to safety."

"Did you know him?"

"John Mackedon? Of course. I worked with him from time to time though at the time of the fire I wasn't in the fire zone myself."

"He was a hero," I said.

"Yes, he was a brave man, but he wasn't alone," Dad said. "I used to know a conductor named Vandercook, Harry B. Vandercook. We used to call him Harry B., though I don't remember why. He was some hero, too, I can tell you—he and his engineer, a fellow by the name of Blundell, I believe. It happened near here, in the same fire, but a short time after John Mackedon had rescued all those people."

"Tell me," I urged.

"Well Harry and his crew had brought a number of people from Falcon on up the line to St. Paul Pass tunnel where they would be safe. Someone got to counting noses and realized that a superintendent by the name of Marshall was missing. They realized that somehow he'd been left in Falcon. Harry and his fireman didn't hesitate a minute. They backed that engine and caboose down the grade, through fire, across smoking trestles. But they had to stop at Adair. The fire was just too bad. By then the trestles were actually on fire and they had to stop to put out fires on their old wooden caboose after they came across one. It was so hot that the engineer just opened the throttle and everyone lay down on the floor to get away from the heat coming in the windows.

"The fire was getting worse but he took time to load up a bunch of folks in Adair and started off uphill from Adair, heading for the tunnel or even into Montana if they could get that far, or as far as necessary to escape the fire. By this time the whole mountainside was pretty well burning up or just about to anyway. They only went for a short distance when they decided they'd had enough and they stopped the train in the middle of

Moss Creek tunnel. Almost 50 people waited out the fire there. That tunnel's just about opposite us across the valley.

"Strange thing, Harry B. wasn't a very spectacular kind of fellow, pretty much kept to himself and unassuming. You wouldn't have guessed him for the hero type. Just proves you can't judge a person by the way he looks."

Dad went on to tell me about some other men who had lost their lives in railroad accidents. Due to the long time he had been working in the area he had known most of them personally.

"Was Harry B. your friend?" I asked.

"Yes, he was a friend. But he's gone now," he sighed, "like a lot of good men. You don't know what it is to really lose something important until you've lost a friend."

There were tears in his eyes. They glistened even in the dim light of the vestibule. Dad didn't cry often but he wasn't ashamed to show his emotions. I well remember how distraught he was when an early-morning phone call told him of the stroke that had disabled Perse, his old baggage-man friend, and the tears when Mr. Persinger died. It seems to me that he always cried about people, not things. People had real value for him.

His love and concern for those with whom he worked was amply returned. When we all decided we had had enough gold mining and gave up on the abortive diggings above Superior, Dad was taken aback when a suit was filed against him in Superior by a man who claimed he had not been paid for supplies. Dad rushed to his lawyer with a box full of "paid-in-full" invoices and was told not to worry.

"It will be over in an hour," the attorney reassured him.

But he did worry, not because he thought he would lose in court but because his honesty had been questioned. His personal values were far more important to him than money. He rode the train to Superior, as a passenger this time, and went to court. Sitting next to his lawyer, waiting for the judge to enter, he felt a tap on his shoulder. Turning around he saw both his brakemen. They had come to lend support and show him their confidence in his integrity. He talked about that gesture for years.

One of those two men, Ross Snider, was particularly close to Dad. Their relationship was almost like father and son even though Ross was in his thirties. He probably knew Dad more personally than anyone along the right-of-way, and stayed in touch after Dad retired and moved to Missouri. One of my nicest memories concerns Dad, his small flat rocks, and Ross Snider.

Chicago, Milwaukee & St. Paul Railway
H. E. Byram, Mark W. Potter and Edward J. Brundage, Receivers.
TO PUGET SOUND—ELECTRIFIED

FORM 31 FORM 31

TRAIN ORDER NO.

This train order was initialed by my stepfather on January 18, 1927, at Haugan, Montana. The order reads, "No. 18 Meet Work Extra 935018 at Henderson."
Courtesy Darrel Dewald, S. Johnson Collection

Dad always carried a small pocketknife with him. He used it for eating apples, cutting fingernails, and casual whittling. Most often though he used it as something to be sharpened.

Whenever he was standing around by the trackside, as at Falcon, he would pick up a small flat rock, take out his pocketknife, and using the rock as a whetstone he would slide the knife back and forth across the smooth surface of the stone, honing the edge to a razor sharpness. I never knew him to have a dull knife. Sometimes he would find a particularly well-shaped stone for honing and he would save it.

When Dad retired I compiled, with the help of family and friends, a book of keepsakes and memories of his railroading. It included snapshots, maps, timetables, notes from friends, and similar items. One friend sent a bag of dirt from the roadbed by a station. Another a sliver of a depot platform. Ross Snider, his longtime brakeman, sent me a small flat stone. Ross had arranged to have the train stop at a place where he knew Dad had a cache of these stones. I gave it to Dad with the book; he cried that time, too.

One might think it unusual to remember a man sharpening his knife on a rock. I had thought that my memory of this little intimate habit of Dad's, standing there talking while he moved his knife back and forth across a stone, was just part of my own personal book of memories. But I discovered I was selfishly wrong. He was special to others as well. I realized that when Ross Snider remembered, too.

My stepfather worked as an active conductor until he was seventy-three. The railroad was good about keeping aging employees in their positions, realizing the value of their experience and judgment. He decided to retire almost on impulse, giving no warning to even the family.

"I was sitting in the coach watching the St. Joe flow by just above St. Joe," he told us later, "and I decided it was time for someone else to take over the job." He asked my sister to type a retirement note to the division superintendent, and that was it.

A year later, with my mother a near invalid from a serious illness, the two of them decided to move to Missouri where most of the family was living. I was in New York so they were alone in Spokane. I flew West to drive their car back, loaded to the ceiling with jars of home-canned fruit.

"You know, they don't have Bing cherries like this in Missouri," he confided in me.

Arrangements were made for them to travel by Pullman on the Olympian. I took them to Union Station, and we watched the beautiful orange and maroon cars glide toward us across the high trestle over Spokane Falls, then come alongside the platform where we stood waiting.

The conductor stopped to chat. He, like virtually everyone else on the western half of the railroad, knew my stepfather and wanted to wish him well. I took that opportunity to go see the Pullman porter assigned to their car. I wanted to explain to him the circumstances and ask for his help with Mother's limitations and Dad's last ride on the Olympian. My effort was unneeded.

"We know Feebee's traveling with us, and we're ready for him. He and I go back a long ways together—a long, long ways," he said.

He explained how the berth would be left made-down for Mother, but that the railroad had arranged to leave the seat across the aisle unsold so Dad would have a place to sit while he watched his favorite scenery. He also told me that the dining car steward would bring their meals to them in the Pullman. A brakeman on the crew, taking the Olympian east from Spokane stopped by to reassure me about the same things. The railroad was taking care of one of its own.

Far too soon Mother and Dad were in their reserved seats and the distinctive cry of the conductor's "board!" echoed down the now nearly deserted platform. Two sharp blasts accompanied by bursts of steam from the Northern's whistle, acknowledged the highball and the train moved away, car after car leaving me behind. I stood and watched the observation car as it disappeared into the tunnel east of the station. It was the last time I would see the Olympian. It was the last time I would see my Dad on his train. In more ways than I could imagine, my family was leaving me alone beside an empty track. It was the loneliest sight in the world.

20
LAST TRAIN WESTBOUND

☞ Dad's life was centered about the railroad as his half-century of service to the Milwaukee Road amply testifies. He talked from time to time about men who had lost their lives in accidents or died natural deaths while working on the railroad. He felt that would be a good way for a railroad man to go. A number of railroad old-timers have expressed similar feelings to me. For him, it wasn't to be. He died in the flatlands of the Midwest, close to his birthplace but far away from his beloved railroad and cherished Bitterroots. However, I remembered his wish. This story about a railroad man's funeral, though fictional, follows a scenario Dad would have liked for himself.

"Fifty years isn't such a long time," thought the old man. "Not when you have seen seventy, almost seventy-one all together."

"But," he reflected, "it is a long, long time to work for the same railroad."

Long before, in those early days that far preceded this last run, he had occasionally speculated about what his final turn might be like. He had thought he might approach it like any other run—signing in at the dispatcher's desk, checking equipment and supplies, joking with the rest of the crew, the brakeman, the engineer and fireman, even with the flagman who was almost a teenager, the youngest one of the crew. Then going about his business, he'd follow the regular routine with no changes, doing and saying nothing special right up to the last minute when he would finally turn in his trip-card for the last time.

He had considered other possibilities. He'd mused about making it a gala occasion, a good time full of jokes and laughing recollections and funny stories, friendly wishes and hearty good-byes from friends along the right-of-way, perhaps even some gifts for the crew. But now the time was here and it had rushed upon him with surprising speed toward the last. He was aware that neither of his supposed scenarios had been accurate. Instead he found himself now feeling contemplative, thoughtful, strangely subdued, and remote from the responsibilities and activities that usually drew his attention. He was absorbed with trying to store away each tiny detail, concentrating on the companionable scenes and sounds and smells that would for him never be the same again.

He savored the comforting motion as the train slowly picked up speed, luxuriating in the sway of the car. Once under way, the regular clickety-clack of rail joints marked the final passing miles as though being carefully counted aloud by each set of wheels, their public accounting becoming fixed in his private memory like a childhood lullaby.

"I never thought I'd be lucky enough to enjoy this last turn without having to work," he said to himself, temporarily breaking his reverie. It seemed pleasant but unfamiliar and somewhat strange to him, not having to worry about collecting tickets, counting fare money, or reading orders—just enjoying the ride, uninterrupted and alone with his thoughts.

The company had arranged for all this. "It's the least we can do," they'd said, and he appreciated that. The crew was equally kind, respectful, almost deferential. In their own way they were sharing something special with him. And, in the midst of work, each man found time to stop by, alone and individually, without fuss, pausing to share a quiet reminiscence with him. In those moments words had not seemed necessary. Now at full speed, familiar landmarks rushed past in brief blurs, each presenting him with some particular memory, helping him recall moments from the past. Most of the landmarks were those that passengers and crew most likely might never notice. But he did.

Swinging crossing lights and the cry of warning bells slipping by, reminding him of that warm fall morning years ago when he had first driven his own automobile to work. For an instant he felt again the thrill of leaving the horse-drawn streetcar behind as he passed by, only the admiring gaze of sidewalk observers being able to keep pace with him. The remembered scene evoked a smile even now.

As though resonating his memories, the train wheels reminded him again of where he was as they thundered across a girder bridge, proudly pronouncing their confidence in the hollow strength spanning the deep ravine beneath them.

He recalled another bridge with a rail split by the force of forty cars too heavily laden, carrying him and his crew to near disaster before the slowing train stopped inches away from what would have been a much earlier and premature final run. He remembered as well that not all of his friends of yesterday had been as fortunate in times of peril and was at once saddened and thankful at his own good fortune.

At a small station comfortably nestled in a friendly valley, the laughter of children echoed as the train slowed and then crept carefully past the platform. Standing on a baggage cart, the children, accompanied by their parents, called and waved to him as his car rolled by. For the briefest of moments they became his own children, small lads enjoying a once-a-summer thrill, taking a turn with their father, wearing his conductor's hat with glee, proudly carrying his ticket punch and clutching at his hands in delicious fear as they dared stride past the hissing, throbbing locomotive held at bay by the grasp of strong steel rails.

As the train swept by an isolated siding, a roaring blur of empty box-cars suddenly filled his vision and then just as quickly disappeared, left behind in a swirl of homeless dust to stand alone once more on their silent siding. Their brief passing projected momentary images of old friends from years long past. Young men with strong futures and stronger hopes walked confidently, even laughingly, along the unsteady catwalk atop a local freight, helping him cut out cars for a small village along the line. They called out to each other in their joy of being fit and able and young.

He knew this final trip was a fleeting leisure briefly stretched across too few hours until the run would be finished for the final time. He had but a few precious moments to consider each of the apparitions the passing wayside presented before they were whisked away by the progress of the train, will-o-the-wisps passing into memory before finally vanishing without a trace like time itself.

"Fifty years isn't long," he thought again, a bit more sadly this time. "Not long enough." Yet he felt they had been good years, profitably spent and he was glad to have been able to revisit them a last time on this final trip home. He paused before each one, viewing them like scenes hung in a row, a gallery of precious images of a personal retrospective reflected in the mirror of his memory.

At the edge of the city the train slowed its rush and in a determined workmanlike manner picked its way along the yard tracks moving carefully across busy intersections with the ease that comes from old tasks easily performed in familiar surroundings.

Edging toward a place where it could rest, the train hesitated as though considering its goal, then finally stopped beside the platform at the end of its run. Only a specter of steam drifting upward from between two cars and the irregular throb of an air pump hidden inside some unseen tank offered any sign of recognition of the group waiting there to meet it.

"They're all waiting for me," the old man thought, recognizing familiar faces. "They're out there waiting for me. They didn't forget."

The train crew, responding with familiarity to the old man's ways, did not embarrass him with public fanfare or open acclamation. Instead, they waited until all the passengers had left, until the old man was alone among friends. Then they moved along the nearly deserted platform to the car next to the engine. They paused there, accompanied by the old man's family.

His three sons, long since grown men themselves, moved forward and as though by signal the baggage car door slid open. They moved quietly, pensively, but with more respect than sadness as they helped the crew slide the burnished casket onto a waiting baggage cart. Silently they pulled the cart away, along the platform, through the now gentle wisps of steam, past the muted car wheels, taking the old man home.

On the platform the train crew stood, hats in hand, and watched him leave. Only the slow, persistent tolling of the engine's bell broke the silence to say good-bye. ⌁

21
FALCON REVISITED

The odyssey is over. I have seen and walked or ridden nearly every foot of old railbed that I longed to see. My storehouse of memories has been enriched. People, places, and events have been woven into a tapestry far richer than I had anticipated.

Still, and I have indeed been asked, how could the memory of an old railroad stimulate such drive and energy and sense of purpose? How could the experiences of youth be so strong as to impact on the life of an aging man and his family?

I have no ready answer. The past is far too ethereal for me to be able to describe. I am not sure I even adequately understand what has happened to me during this quest. I left home for my first long-term employment, trading the Northeast for my Western home, my eyes then more on the future than the past. Though I did not know it then, I was never to experience those scenes again. My mother became ill, my stepfather retired, and they moved to the Midwest to be nearer family. Even our family home in Spokane disappeared, wiped away by a noisy and crowded interstate. I had left without even looking back. Now I would give much of what I have for one more glance over my shoulder.

One day I lived in the West; the next I lived in the East, immediately surrounded with people who were philosophical strangers. I went to another world, naively believing that the heritage I carried was universal. I blithely and unsuspectingly offered myself and my culture to those I met and worked with, expecting acceptance or at least understanding. I experienced only curiosity and rejection. My ways were as strange to them as theirs were to me, and I felt true loneliness for the first time. This culture, home, and hearth to those raised there, but alien to all I had experienced, devoured me like a wild beast, tumbling my ideas and heritage, my ways of the west, in its mouth as though testing their taste and texture, then spat them out in open rejection.

I was disillusioned—more than disillusioned, I was shocked. I had not anticipated the culture shock I suddenly experienced. But I was determined to be adaptable. I knew I could change if necessary, and I did. I learned the ways of Roman and Goth and I walked their highways, but as I did so, it was difficult to remember the earlier kindly paths I had known. Normally, with the passage of time, old ideas are replaced with new like a tree loses its leaves in the fall and puts forth new growth in the spring, fulfilling a promise inherent in the metamorphosis. Looking at the changes in myself, I felt instead that the old had merely starved and died, leaving behind an ugliness that was uncomfortable to the new.

Still, it did not seem a particularly difficult transition in most ways, subtly deceiving in its easiness. The new pathways I followed during the intervening years generally were good to me. They were, at one time or another, exciting with adventure, rich with experience, rewarding in accomplishment, fulfilling in achievement. But the transformation was incomplete, leaving me with a yearning for fulfillment, a dissatisfaction with accomplishments that were substituted for relationships.

Now the ease and free time of retirement has helped me recognize the source of this nagging irritation and dissatisfaction. I longed to once more hear my cherished values expressed in familiar tones and accents spoken in friendly environs. As I became aware of this, I realized, with a satisfaction that seemed incongruent with the finding of an incompleteness in my life, that I missed my home. My odyssey was really a search for my own personal grail. My journey was becoming a crusade to recover, restore, and protect and maintain whatever memories were left in the land that had created me.

It is impossible for me to separate the pieces that comprise this longed-for scene: Father, Mother, the railroad, locations, activities, sites, situations. I don't even try. They fit together in a balanced harmony that is so pleasing to my ear that I have no desire to hear them separately. This is why Falcon had become so important to me. It contained each of the elements I was seeking. Not merely a place or scene, it is a melodic blending of a pleasant past.

To understand what I mean it is necessary to relive some of the events and processes of our earliest visits to the railroad's route through the Bitterroots.

On our first return, using topographic maps and an old track profile we managed to locate specific trestles and identify tunnels by their railroad designated numbers (often by counting the consecutive places where the railroad route far above us suddenly disappeared into a mountain only to reappear a few hundred yards later on). Sometimes we could see the tunnel's concrete or hewed rock mouth. More often we could not. The search for identifiable landmarks was difficult at best and frequently unrewarding. But at last, peering through field glasses from a distant mountainside, we identified a stretch of roadbed that we felt must be Falcon, distinguished by pinpointing the tunnel that lay to the east end of it and the contour of the mountains above and behind it. We could see neither the railbed route itself nor any other direct indications of the railroad—no roadbed fills, buildings, signals, or telegraph wires. We were too far away and too many feet below the level of the old route.

My wife knew a little of Falcon, not as a site but as a place where I had had some rich experiences with my stepfather. I had told her of some of these as anecdotes from my past, sometimes shared with our children or our friends, more often just between the two of us. Because of this, it was not difficult for her to see and understand my excitement at being back. As we drove on to Avery that first late afternoon, I was too excited to discuss the day's events logically. Time slipped by in a rushing reverie, and we arrived in Avery far sooner than I had expected.

Standing by the old Avery depot in the afternoon sun, tired, sweaty, and hungry but elated by what the day had given us, we talked more about what we had seen. The trip had been very gratifying, an overwhelming success, even more than expected. Alberton had been a fun experience. I had once more seen East Portal, a place I thought was lost to me forever. I had at last returned to Loop Creek Valley to see many familiar sites. But throughout our conversation, there was an awareness of the one thing missing—I had not yet really returned to Falcon, the place I most wanted to visit and see again. Knowing that it was "somewhere approximately above us," at a given spot above our road, on the valley floor, was not enough.

I wanted to actually be there, to pick up a handful of dirt and let it trickle through my fingers, to touch the cracked side of an old telegraph pole near where it had kept the west switch company, to again feel the rock beneath my feet, to stand and try and re-create the feel and spell and spirit of the place. I wanted to do more than return to a site. I wished to go back to a landmark in my life.

I ran my hands along the weathered boards as I stood on the old cracked concrete stoop by the agent's office door opening onto the Avery depot platform. I expressed my mixed feelings of contentment and disappointment.

"I haven't seen Falcon yet," I said quietly.

"Don't worry," Karen said. "You will. We'll come back and we'll make it to Falcon." As usual she was more patient and optimistic than I, and as is so often so, she was right. We came back the next year, the summer of 1993.

As we planned for the second visit, one aspect of our trip to Loop Creek Valley became clear. In the rush of seeing so many old sights again we had been in too big a hurry, trying visit them all in one day as though they might disappear with the sunset. Some places were worth more than a passing look. They called out to me, pleading for an investment of more time and extra effort to thoroughly experience everything they had to offer, something to carry home which would be far more than a simple image. If I could make it to Falcon, I wanted to reexperience as much of the remembered ambiance of the place as possible so that my sensations and feelings during this revisitation would be part of the memories I would carry.

The planning this time was easier. We knew where we wanted to go and how to get there. Oh, there were maps and old timetables to study and landmarks to list, but all of that was fun, an enticing preview of the trip to follow. The physical logistics were handled even easier when at almost the last minute it became possible for Dennis, my oldest son and the only one of my children who ever rode on a train with his grandfather, to come with us on the trip, flying from Indiana to meet us in Spokane on our way to Avery. Having him along made the experience richer still. Since then my other two sons have visited there with us as well and the memories expand and become more complex each time we return. Sometime, I would like to take my two daughters there, too.

As we prepared to return, we talked about and listed the places we wanted to see. The list would become long and disorganized, full of changes and substitutions. But no matter how many lists or changes were made, the top priority was Falcon. Karen and my son wished to see Falcon, too. But their sensitivity discerned my needs and we decided that since it was such a special place for me, we would separate and make our way there from two different directions with me arriving there first, ahead of them by an hour or so. They wanted me to have my return there a private experience.

I was to be dropped off where the new road leaves the railroad roadbed and returns to the valley floor, just beyond a former siding called Kyle. I would then continue along the roadbed alone, with a trek of about five and one-half miles upgrade to Falcon. Dennis and Karen would drive to where the road climbs steeply up and out of the valley. At that point it once more crosses the old track route at a small grassy spot where there is a short stretch of railroad roadbed accessible between two tunnels. Adair was once just beyond this crossing, upgrade in the opposite direction of Falcon, literally at the other end of the tunnel on the east. After parking the truck to the side of the road they planned to wait awhile before starting in order to give me time to travel the longer distance to Falcon and have some time alone there. Their journey from where the truck was parked to Falcon would be about two and one-half miles downgrade.

Each of us had a bike because we thought we would be able to pedal part of the way. Cameras, topographic maps, and binoculars completed our gear. Food and water would be waiting for us in the truck parked beside the road at the upper end of the valley. The plan was to meet at the west mouth of tunnel No. 28, which lay just to the east of the east switch at Falcon. Then we would all return to the truck parked near Adair.

It was shortly after 9:00 A.M. when we stopped to unload my bike. I pushed it up a steep embankment and around the pile of rocks and gravel, which had been dumped to block the roadbed to larger vehicles. With only a brief pause to wave good-bye I started off. The first 100 yards were very difficult as I had a great deal of trouble with my camera gear bag swinging and hitting me or the bike no matter where or how I hung it. Loaded with two camera bodies, four lenses, two dozen rolls of film and miscellaneous gear it was heavy and awkward. I was already wishing I had not brought the bike but it was too late now because Dennis and Karen had left. The road was out of view behind me, I was about to enter my first tunnel alone, and I had to make do with the arrangements as they were. It was not a propitious beginning and my spirits drooped.

My initial feelings were that I had done something foolish in trying to make this journey through uninhabited wilderness at about 4,000 feet elevation by myself at my age. I had been working for several months to physically prepare myself but even then it was more demanding and tiring than I had imagined. I worried about having overestimated my own physical capabilities. My fear grew as I stumbled through that first tunnel at Deer Creek. It was dark and damp, the roadbed was rocky and uneven and my camera bag fell off in the semidarkness. I couldn't see it without my glasses, and their lenses darkened by the bright sunlight. I had to wait for my glasses to adapt to the dark so I could find the camera bag and reload it on the bike.

Resorting to profanity directed at the bike, the camera bag, old age, and myself, I stumbled into the light again. I decided that the bike was going to have to be used to carry my camera gear but it probably wasn't going to carry me as well. I'd do it on foot. I figured out a way to hang the camera bag across the handlebars without it causing problems. As I calmed down and became adjusted to the new arrangements I began to take more notice of my surroundings and to enjoy where I was.

It was foggy and overcast when I started, but now the sun was out and everything glistened in the sparkle of a myriad of tiny prisms. I was surrounded, immersed in a carpeted panoply of different shades of greens—grasses, bushes, vines, and trees. Rising out of this sea of green, which was just beginning to softly move like waves born in the first hint of a freshening summer breeze, were thousands, probably tens of thousands of wildflowers in pinks and purples and whites. They stretched in every direction as far as the eye could see. There was beauty here I had never seen from the train and certainly had been unaware of when I stood by the train in the dark of night.

I became aware of a growing feeling of inward calmness, a vibrant serenity, a sense of being full of life in a place I felt I belonged. It was so strong, so imperative, that I paused and leaned my bike against a tree and simply stopped to absorb the tone, the flavor, the color, the spirit of this special place to which I had returned.

There was an enigma in my feelings, a mystery demanding to be solved. Here I was, probably more physically isolated and alone than I had ever been in my life, yet there was no loneliness. I felt a sense of togetherness, belonging, and involvement; a participation in an unseen communion that was undeniable.

I moved on a hundred yards or so, somewhat more slowly than before, when I was startled by a sudden sharp sound just in front of me, coming from the undergrowth to my left and down the bank a few yards from the railbed. I froze. My fear flooded over the composure I had begun to develop. There was no further sound, but from the dense background of dark green vegetation silently stepped a single white-tailed deer. It walked slowly, clear to the edge of the trackbed, stopped, and turned to look at me.

Strangely out of character for me, I said to the deer, "I'm only passing through to revisit special places. I will do you no harm and will leave your home as I find it. You need not be afraid of me. I come to this place because I have love in my heart for it and I welcome your company because I am alone."

The deer watched me for several seconds, perhaps even half a minute, looking directly at me with no movement of any kind, not even the familiar twitch of the ear that signals alertness. It stood there, calmly, interested but relaxed. Then, with no haste or sudden movement of fear, it started to slowly walk along the side of the roadbed in the same direction I had been traveling. I respected its acceptance of my confession and followed behind, moving at its pace rather than mine.

For several miles, almost to Falcon itself, we continued in this manner. The deer led and I followed. Sometimes the deer would move ahead for a short distance at a pace faster than I could maintain on foot. But it always stopped as though acknowledging my inability and waited for me to catch up.

About a half mile immediately west of Falcon, the roadbed is fairly straight for a quarter mile or so before curving around a rock face just beyond which is the west switch at Falcon. Having carefully studied the maps, I knew where we were when this piece of roadbed stretched out before me. My excitement mounted appreciably as I thought of revisiting Falcon, an experience that now lay just beyond those rocks a few hundred yards ahead. I stopped again, this time to enjoy the anticipation, a brief pause of expectancy like holding a gift-wrapped package in your lap before opening it.

"We're almost there," I said.

The deer stopped, too, looked over its shoulder, then turned around to face me. I remained still, matching its patience. It took a single step toward me, stopped again, lowered its head and nibbled for a moment at a piece of grass alongside the roadbed, then walked slowly and easily, unfrightened, down the bank and into the woods where it disappeared. I felt as though I had been escorted to this place.

I continued on to the rock face and as I followed the roadbed to where the sharp curve beyond had led the rails into Falcon I slowed my pace and came to a halt. I was back again after such a long time. I recognized it at once and it required little imagination to put the rails and the switch standard and the train itself back into the scene.

I did not dare add more.

Very slowly now, a step at a time and with frequent pauses, I walked to the site of the west switch I remembered so well. Standing there I looked

Only the roadbed gravel, an occasional tie spike, and some telegraph poles remain near the west switch at Falcon, but it has lost none of its beauty or romance for me. Photo by S. Johnson, Milwaukee, Wisc., Public Library Collection

up at the mountains and swung my gaze around to take in the full panorama—the soft curve of the roadbed towards the east, the tunnel mouth with its supporting timbers of long darkened wood far away at the other end of the sweeping curve. The wildflowers were breathtaking and the forest was lush. Tall green-black firs spiked toward the sky on the mountainside and opposite was the silver-white soft lace of alder leaves with delicate green threads of pine needles interwoven.

It was a quiet and peaceful place, as special as I remembered it and far more beautiful. What a marvel, a blessing, that some places such as this remain. In every sense and in every way it was good to be back.

I wanted to have a time of solitary introspection before the others arrived, not in a selfish sense but in harmony with my feelings of private communion with this place. I left my bike and walked to the tunnel where the tracks had once disappeared to the east. I listened for the sound of the wind as I had heard it as a boy, but only the rustle of leaves and bird songs could be heard. I walked a few steps into the dark coolness and then turned and gazed out from the darkness at the landscape framed in the tunnel's hard-edged frame. It all seemed so familiar—the same trackbed I had ridden over as a boy, the same tunnels, the same bridges, the same vistas, the same horizons. I ventured back a few feet along the right-of-way, experiencing old sensations that up to now had been relived only in fragmentary memories, pleasant and warming but unfulfilling in their incompleteness. In my mind I touched the cold concrete of a tunnel wall and traced my fingers along the handrail of a mountain trestle and walked the length of a siding where once as a boy I had watched my stepfather throw a switch in the blackness of the mountain night. I felt his presence again.

I sat on a trackside rock and talked aloud to him. I explained to him how much I had longed to come back and how I felt, having fulfilled that dream. I apologized for taking so long to return to him and his railroad, a railroad now without rails. I explained to him that I was growing old, too, and how I yearned to someday join him and perhaps in some mysterious way manage to stand by his side at Falcon once more. I explained how I had arranged with Karen for my ashes to be brought to this beautiful spot when the time comes and how that would at least move us a step closer to recommunion. And then I wept.

He didn't answer—not out loud. But I felt at ease, peaceful, and content. I was ready to leave. I had come back and knew I would return again to this special place called Falcon.

> *'Tis the gift to be simple,*
> *'Tis the gift to be free,*
> *'Tis the gift to come down where you ought to be.*
>
> *And when we find ourselves*
> *In the place just right,*
> *'twill be in the valley of love and delight.*
>
> —*Old Quaker Hymn*